Transfer of Japanese Technology and Management to the ASEAN Countries

edited by
Shoichi Yamashita

UNIVERSITY OF TOKYO PRESS

Publication of this volume was assisted by the Toyota Foundation.

Contents

Preface

The increasingly high profile of Japanese enterprises in Southeast Asia, while it has contributed to the economic growth of the region, is also a source of unease and friction in the countries involved. The desire and ability to adapt and blend into the host economies is an important problem for Japanese-affiliated companies. There has been a sharp increase in foreign direct investment by private Japanese enterprises since the Plaza Agreement of September 1985. In the first half of the 1980s foreign direct investment by Japanese firms amounted to no more than $10 billion annually, but since the Plaza Agreement the amount has increased every year, reaching $65 billion in 1989.

The major causes of this sudden increase were the appreciation of the yen and the need to find new strategies to deal with international trade conflict. A higher-valued yen, which made Japanese products less competitive internationally, and disagreements with other countries over trade practices forced Japan's companies to look for production sites abroad. Investment by Japanese firms was made primarily in the United States and the EC, but is now increasingly directed to Southeast Asia. Current Japanese investment in the ASEAN countries is motivated also by the desire to establish export bases abroad, taking advantage of low-cost labor and local government incentives.

Governments of the ASEAN nations are changing their policies to more actively attract foreign investment, offering export-oriented for-eign-capital businesses such incentives as exemption from corporate taxes and import duties as well as other privileges. The export-oriented industrialization policies of the ASEAN countries coincides with the global strategies of Japanese corporations, and thus we have seen a continuing increase in Japanese firms' investment in Southeast Asia over the past few years. It should also be noted that the change of focus of Japanese ASEAN investment, from being local-market-oriented to export-oriented, has brought with it major changes in methods of management and production control.

What kind of reception is this sudden increase in the number of

Japanese firms meeting? What is the reaction to Japanese methods of management and technology transfer? These questions provided the starting point for our research.

Japanese enterprises were latecomers in foreign investment, and they expanded overseas only in response to changes in the business climate. They replicated in the new enterprises the same business methods used at home, with no modifications to allow for adjustment to local management styles. Necessity had, in effect, forced them to operate according to the only methods they knew before they had time to study the approaches used by corporations from Europe and the United States in establishing local businesses.

Japan has adopted Western styles of modern business management, and through a continuous process of assimilation has developed its own unique tradition of business operation.

The major features of Japanese-style management are conventionally considered to be lifelong employment and the seniority system. But neither of these is a Japanese invention. Longstanding examples of both can be found in Western enterprises, and some Asian enterprises are now adopting similar methods. Neither lifelong employment nor the seniority system provides a blueprint for the establishment of a Japanese enterprise; they are simply personnel management methods found in firms with a long history of growth, particularly those which date back to the Meiji period. The best proof of this is that in the current stage of economic adjustment after the long period of rapid economic growth both lifelong employment and the seniority systems have begun to collapse in Japan, calling into doubt the extent to which they were ever essential components of Japanese-style management. To judge whether any management technique is specifically "Japanese," its place in the overall management system needs to be assessed. Consideration should also be given to the fact that this will change with the times and the business environment.

The matters of transfer and adjustment in Japanese-style management are not so simple either. Japanese-owned companies established in ASEAN countries have the status within an overall corporate structure of either an overseas factory or overseas branch, and as such are not equipped with a full set of operational resources. Operations are controlled by the parent company, with a consequent lack of consideration for local conditions, which often arouses resentment among local workers and communities. Under such circumstances, studying the operations of Japanese-owned companies in ASEAN countries is, at least in the initial stages, an appraisal of the operations of the Japanese-owned companies themselves.

Discussion of methods and acceptability of the transfer of management methods to local industry will come later, but it is useful to point out here that there are substantial differences between the management methods of Japanese-owned overseas companies and those of European and American overseas subsidiaries or local industries. These differences are found in the operational approach of Japanese managers compared to their Western counterparts. It is also worth noting that overseas assignments in Japanese companies are usually at the middle-management level, and the staff members who are assigned overseas are not necessarily top performers at home in the parent company.

During our research into Japanese-affiliated companies operating in the ASEAN countries we learned that while they have made substantial contributions in the form of the creation of employment opportunities, foreign exchange earnings, technology transfer, and promotion of industries in related fields, these companies have also been responsible for new friction. The cause of this friction may lie with the inexperience and incomplete knowledge of international business operations in Japanese companies, as well as the insensitivity and what is sometimes seen as arrogance of their staff; these can create dissatisfaction and distrust among local employees in the face of the companies' headlong drive to develop their business. These are problems which will require much more effort on the part of Japanese firms before they are solved.

Our studies also revealed that the efforts made by Japanese firms are not always fully understood by the local communities. In the matter of technology transfer, for example, local governments, economists, and journalists are under the firm impression that the withdrawal of foreign staff from a foreign-owned subsidiary signals accomplishment of the technology transfer process. For this reason European and American firms have a good reputation in this area, because their staff is called back home quite soon after operations commence, and technicians are then only sent in when mechanical problems arise. A high rate of promotion of local staff is also highly valued. Compared with this, Japanese technicians stay on in the new firms, creating the impression that Japanese-owned firms are neither interested in nor serious about technology transfer.

In reality, all that Western firms do is to train local employees in operational techniques and then go away, leaving behind a set of manuals. Japanese firms, however, establish a system of on-the-job training for local staff that includes not only operational techniques but also detailed instruction in machine maintenance and repair, quality control, technological improvement techniques, and even total factory management. Japanese technicians need to stay longer to transmit their techniques and expertise to local employees. Japanese firms need to make more of an effort to explain their approach to the local people.

Lately, an increasing number of new Japanese ventures setting up in Southeast Asia are showing less enthusiasm for staff training and greater interest in scouting for administrative and advanced technical staff from established firms. The number of managers impatient to launch into export projects immediately is also increasing. Once Japanese-owned firms abandon their in-house training, the Japanese nature of those firms is lost. The recent tendency towards a drastic increase in the number of export-oriented firms, not only large-scale ventures but also small- and medium-scale ones, moving to establish operations in the ASEAN countries is, in a sense, causing a change in their management methods from Japanese-style to Western-style.

Japanese-owned overseas companies have also come to doubt the wisdom of on-the-job training programs because of the strong tendency toward job-hopping among Southeast Asian industrial workers. If too many middle-management and technical employees who have received in-house training in Japan are lured away to other enterprises by higher pay, firms naturally begin to consider it more profitable to hire personnel who have already acquired training and experience rather than to try to cultivate them within their own company. We are now seeing a tendency for local subsidiaries of major Japanese corporations, which were once keen on staff training, to turn to head-hunting services for their manpower needs. With the decline of the lifelong employment and seniority systems, which allowed firms to take their time in training staff effectively, it seems that in-house training is no longer feasible. It will be interesting to see how Japanese-owned companies moving into ASEAN countries in the future deal with their manpower training needs.

There is no scarcity of research into the overseas operations of Japanese firms, and the amount of information on the topic is increasing as research results are published by various institutions and organizations. A review of this literature is given in Chapter 5 of this volume.

The unique aspect of the research reported in this volume is that it approaches the problems of Japanese-affiliated overseas companies not only from the Japanese point of view but also from the local standpoint. To obtain a clear indication of how widely the views of the two sides vary, our research team included researchers from various ASEAN countries who participated in our many discussions. Their contribution to our work is acknowledged with gratitude.

The research project team, which was established in Japan in 1984, consisted mainly of researchers from Hiroshima University and specialists in economics and management from the ASEAN countries. Financial support from the Toyota Foundation enabled the team to conduct a pilot project, beginning its activities with visits to Thailand and the Philippines to study the ways in which Japan was viewed in Southeast Asia.

The full project got under way in 1986. The research plan called for attention to be focused on Japanese-affiliated enterprises in Southeast Asian countries in order to discover how, as the point of contact between the two worlds under examination, they actually functioned and what problems were associated with them. The motivation for our research was to identify directions for Japanese companies to take in order to cooperate in the development of relevant countries and foster favorable relationships in the region.

We began our research in two countries with which we were already familiar — Thailand and Indonesia. Questionnaires were mailed to firms which were members of the local Japanese Chamber of Commerce and Industry, and then interviews were conducted at the firms. Later we extended our research to Malaysia and Singapore, and thus examined the situation in four of the ASEAN member nations. The research program included three field visits and workshops conducted every year with our local research partners.

The results of our research were published in Japanese and English in our report to the Toyota Foundation, *ASEAN shokoku no kaihatsu katei to Nihon no kakawarikata ni kansuru kenkyu* (A study on the Japanese involvement in the development process of ASEAN countries), December 1988, 708 pages; and in Yamashita, Takeuchi, Kawabe and Takehana (also in Japanese), "Japanese managers' consciousness on the Japanese-type management and technology transfer in ASEAN countries," *Hiroshima Economic Studies*, March 1989.

As a follow-up to our research, in October 1989 in Hiroshima we held an international conference, "Beyond Japanese-Style Management in ASEAN Countries: Assessments and Adaptations," which was attended by our seven ASEAN research partners and 50 Japanese participants, including both researchers and corporate managers with experience in the ASEAN region. The current volume is based on the papers presented and discussed at that conference. It is, however, more than a simple volume of proceedings. We have spent a year in selecting and editing materials presented at the conference to make this book. Each chapter is followed by a "Comments" section to help readers follow the directions pursued by the conference participants in our discussion sessions.

Nevertheless, this volume is not a comprehensive report on our research and discussions, and there are still some matters concerning the approach and contents which we feel have not been totally resolved. We have attempted to organize the book to cover the range from macro-analysis of Japan's foreign direct investment to a micro-analysis of individual business operations. In doing so, we fear that some unity of description may have been lost.

The major aim of our research was to identify a management style appropriate to local conditions—the creation of a "third culture" among Japanese-owned companies overseas. This is still a challenge for us for the future.

Following the above-mentioned international conference, the Faculty of Economics at Hiroshima University sponsored an international symposium to discuss new directions in business management. The symposium was attended by Japanese business administrators and our ASEAN research partners. The discussion revealed that there was an immense gap between the conceptions held by the two parties. The details of these discussions are included in "Is Japanese-style Management Applicable?" (Faculty of Economics, Hiroshima University; in Japanese, March 1990), and we hope that readers of this volume will also examine this report, because it does discuss future directions for the management of overseas companies.

Considering the extent of the influence of Japanese-owned companies on ASEAN societies today and what it may be in the future, we would have liked to have included in this volume an appeal to Japanese managers who are sent to serve overseas, and to the senior administrators of their parent companies, to consider such matters as how their companies might integrate with local communities and how they can return to those communities what is taken out in profits, but we were not able to address these topics here. The book may also be deficient in other ways, and we welcome comments from our readers on the results of our research as we have presented them.

Publication of this book would not have been possible without the assistance of many individuals and organizations. Our foremost gratitude goes to the Toyota Foundation, which funded the entire project. Without the Foundation's support we could not have conducted the research, or held the international conference which led to the publication of this book.

Thanks are also due to the Japanese Chambers of Commerce and Industry in Thailand, Malaysia, Singapore, and Indonesia, and to their members, for their generous assistance. We especially thank the managers of the Japanese-owned companies and other individuals who so readily cooperated in answering our questionnaires and interviews. We would also like to thank JETRO, the Institute of Developing Economies, and a number of other organizations and corporations in Japan for providing us with information and assisting us in other ways.

Mr. Seiji Takehana, who is no longer with Hiroshima University, played a major role in our research group. He handled the painstaking tasks of analyzing the questionnaire results and compiling materials for the international conference, and his contributions are gratefully acknowledged.

Fifteen students from overseas studying at Hiroshima University gave us invaluable help during the international conference. In particular, Miss Pannee Suwantupinton from Thailand and Mr. Ong Hong Peng from Malaysia played a large part in the compilation of the Discussion section of this book.

We would like to express our deep thanks to Miss Miki Fukumoto, who skillfully handled all the word processing throughout the long process of editing the materials for this volume.

The editing was essentially a cooperative endeavor undertaken by Dr. Nobuo Kawabe, Prof. Tatsuo Kimbara, Prof. Jozen Takeuchi, and myself, and responsibility for the contents of the book rests with us.

Finally, I would like to express my special thanks to the faculty members of the Economics Faculty at Hiroshima University and to the staff of the University of Tokyo Press who undertook the publication of this book.

December 1990   SHOICHI YAMASHITA

Part **I**

JAPANESE DIRECT INVESTMENT IN ASEAN

1

Economic Development of the ASEAN Countries and the Role of Japanese Direct Investment

Shoichi Yamashita

Recent Economic Growth in NIEs and the ASEAN Countries

As we review recent economic trends, the newly industrializing economies (NIEs) and Association of Southeast Asian Nations (ASEAN) countries are notable for having continuously achieved higher economic growth. Asian NIEs experienced double-digit growth rates during 1986–1987, and NIEs' real growth rate jumped to 12–13% from 5% or less in the previous year (Fig. 1). NIEs have not, however, been able to keep up the high pace of economic growth, which slowed in 1988–1989. The ASEAN countries, rather, accelerated their growth rate during that period. Thailand's growth rate, for example, was 4–5% in 1985–1986, but it reached 11.2% in 1988 and 12% in 1989. Thailand will maintain this rapid economic growth during the coming few years at least.

In its midterm economic planning for the 1990s the Malaysian government is examining an "Income Doubling Plan" as a follow-up to the New Economic Policy (NEP) of the 1971–1990 period (Salih and Yusof 1989). An Income Doubling Plan was implemented in Japan by the Ikeda Cabinet during the 1960s, and later in Korea in the 1970s. It is likely to become Malaysia's most strategic target in the coming decade.

Indonesia has just started its fifth Five Year Plan, which is considered to be the precondition for the subsequent "Take-Off" phase. The Indonesian economy in the 1980s was severely affected by the sharp drop in the price of oil. Indonesia has since tried to foster the export-oriented industries that are expected to replace the export of oil and gas in the future. Thus the government has been inviting foreign capital and giving incentives to export-oriented firms, as well as promoting various deregulation policies. Such open policies have stimulated the economy's recent upswing in activity.

As was first suggested by Professor Kaname Akamatsu in his theory of the "wild geese flying pattern" of economic development (Akamatsu

3

1956), the wave of dynamic economic growth has spread from Japan to the NIEs and then to the ASEAN countries. Although this hypothesis is based on the long-term observation of Japanese industrial development, it seems also to be a valid model for the economic development taking place in the East and Southeast Asian countries.

The recent economic growth in the NIEs and ASEAN countries has taken place since the G-5 Plaza Agreement of September 1985. It was led mainly by the export of manufactured goods. In Korea and Taiwan, the growth rate of exports was 30% or more in 1986–1987. Hong Kong and Singapore experienced similar increases in 1987. Thailand, Malaysia, and even Indonesia rushed to develop exports, which resulted in a 30% increase in exports (see Fig. 1). Thus a double-digit growth rate was realized in these countries.

The expansion of NIEs and ASEAN exports is related to the reduction of Japan's exports due to the yen appreciation after 1985. The mechanism and the repercussions of the yen appreciation are shown in Fig. 2. Thanks to advantageous exchange rates, exports from the NIEs increased substantially, especially to the United States and the European Community, in markets previously held mostly by the Japanese.

The expansion has, however, brought about conflict with the United States and European countries; NIEs now face the threat of foreign protectionism and the adjustment of their exchange rates. Rapid growth has additionally led to wage increases and a rise in domestic production costs, followed by a decline in competitive power—which has provided a favorable climate for ASEAN export development. Exports of industrial products from Thailand, Malaysia, Indonesia, and the Philippines have increased substantially and enabled ASEAN countries to enjoy high levels of economic growth.

The yen appreciation that expanded the growth area from Japan to NIEs and ASEAN countries is but one of many growth-promoting factors in the region. We also must pay attention to domestic factors. Five main factors in the economic expansion of ASEAN countries follow:

1) Government policies and efforts for promoting industrialization.
2) Increase of foreign investment, particularly from Japan and the NIEs.
3) Increase of export and intraregional trade in ASEAN countries.
4) Decline in competitiveness of the NIEs.
5) Increased regional political stability.

Recent development should be understood as in part the result of the intensive efforts of each government (especially the promotion of industrialization policy since the 1960s) and private sector, the diligence

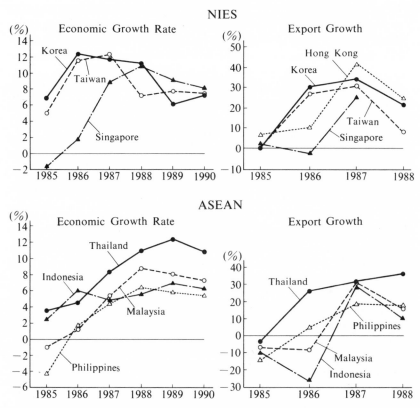

Fig. 1.   Economic Growth Rate of the NIEs and the ASEAN Countries.
Source: Institute of Developing Economies (1989), "Short Term Fore-
casting."

of workers, technological improvement, and the development of economic and social infrastructure.

It is true, however, that economic development in the ASEAN
countries has mostly depended on external factors. In Thailand, for
example, rapid growth was led mainly by the increase of foreign
investment, export of manufactured goods, and foreign exchange
earnings from tourism. Special note should be made of Thai success in
providing policy guidance for export-oriented industrialization. Without
such a policy, a high growth rate might be difficult to achieve. Japanese-
affiliated companies have played an important role in expanding
production facilities and export possibilities. The new leading export
commodities include textiles and garments, electrical appliances, ma-

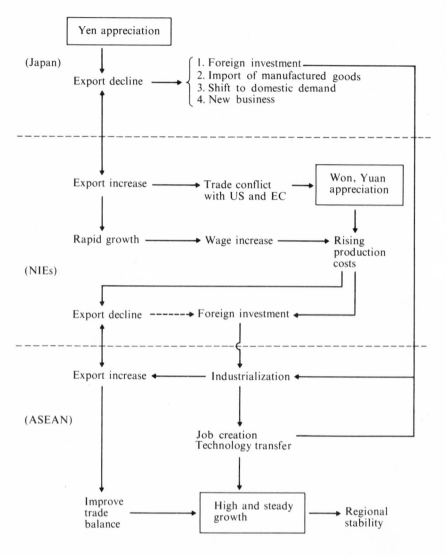

Fig. 2. Yen Appreciation and Its Effect on the NIEs and ASEAN
Economies.

chine parts, and electronics. Substantial amounts of such commodities
are produced and handled by Japanese joint ventures that have operated
in the ASEAN countries for more than twenty years.

Two notable developments in the ASEAN countries have occurred since the yen appreciation. One is Japanese companies' plans to establish complete production and distribution systems in Southeast Asia. In the electrical machines industry, for example, most of the electrical appliance parts that have been imported from Japan so far are now going to be produced in Southeast Asia, and such parts will be exchanged among ASEAN countries (Ishii 1988). Thus most home electric appliance and electronic components will be produced regionally.

The other development is the increase in foreign investment from the NIEs in the ASEAN countries. The four NIEs (Korea, Taiwan, Hong Kong, and Singapore) are now aggressively investing and settling production bases in ASEAN locations. Direct investment from NIEs in 1987 amounted to US$806 million, compared with $1,578 million from Japan; in 1988, the NIEs investment rose to $3,901 million, exceeding Japan's $3,761 million.

These changes show that the technological level of the ASEAN countries has become high and that investment circumstances are also good. Foreign investment inflows should continue to increase in the future. The ASEAN countries are expected to become strong economically and to become good partners of NIEs and Japan.

Japan's Private Direct Investment and Its Role

Trends in Japanese Foreign Investment

Private foreign investment by Japan began after World War II, in 1951. By the end of fiscal 1988 the total amount of Japanese foreign investment had reached US$186 billion. Foreign investment peaked in 1973, then slowed under the influence of the oil shocks, and became active again in the 1980s; the annual average for the 1980s was about 2,500 cases of investment for a total of roughly US$8 billion.

Investment abruptly increased just after the yen appreciation, beginning with the Plaza Agreement in 1985: total Japanese direct investment was 2,613 cases and US$12.2 billion in FY1985. In the next year it was 3,196 cases and US$22.3 billion, an increase of 83% over the previous year.

In the succeeding years, Japanese direct investment continued to increase drastically, with yearly growth rates of 50% in 1987 and 41% in 1988. Direct investment in FY1988 was 6,072 cases and US$47 billion. It must be mentioned here that the total investment for 1986–1988 amounted to US$103 billion, which exceeded the total for the previous

34 years (1951–1985) by US$17 billion. It is, moreover, estimated that FY1989 investment will exceed US$67 billion, more than Japan's yearly trade surplus.

The sudden increase in Japanese private direct investment has been driven by the yen appreciation, which, along with land price increases, have caused production costs in Japan to become the highest in the world. Because the competitiveness of many Japanese commodities has weakened, private companies look for production sites in foreign countries. Trade conflicts have also accelerated Japanese direct investment in foreign markets—particularly in the United States and the EC.

Investment Boom in ASEAN Countries

Although the leading recipients of Japanese investment are still the United States and the European countries, the central gravity of

Table 1. Japanese Direct Investment in Asia.   (units: cases, $ million)

Country	1988		1951 – 1988		Japanese Share in Foreign Investment, 1988 (%)
	Cases	Amount	Cases	Amount	
NIEs					
Korea	153	483	1,712	3,248	54.3[1]
Taiwan	234	372	2,133	1,791	30.4
Hong Kong	335	1,662	3,164	6,167	26.6[2]
Singapore	197	747	2,239	3,812	24.0[2]
ASEAN					
Thailand	382	859	1,685	1,992	26.6[1]
Malaysia	108	387	1,181	1,834	27.9[1]
Philippines	54	134	705	1,120	13.6[2]
Indonesia	84	586	1,578	9,804	28.9[1]
Subtotal	1,547	5,232	14,397	29,768	
China	170	296	567	2,036	16.1[2]
Others	19	41	463	423	—
Asia Total	1,736	5,569	15,427	32,227	

Sources: 1. The Export-Import Bank of Japan, *Monthly Report of Research Institute of Overseas Investment*, 1989.

2. JETRO, *Overseas Direct Investment*, White Paper on Investment, 1990, pp. 431–441 (in Japanese).

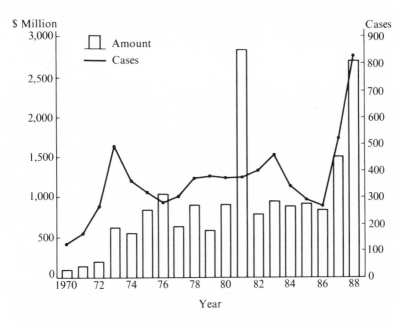

Fig. 3.   Japanese Direct Investment in ASEAN.
Source: The Export-Import Bank of Japan, *Report of the Foreign Investment Research Institute*, annually (in Japanese).
Note: The figures for 1981 include two major LNG projects which amount to US$1.8 billion in total.

investment is gradually shifting to the NIEs and ASEAN nations. Japanese investment in Asia amounted to U.S.$32.2 billion for the period 1951 to 1988, 17.3% of total Japanese investment (see Table 1). Investment in the United States and Europe is Japan's countermove in the trade conflicts among the industrialized countries, but its investment in Asia is aimed at constructing a world base for production and export, taking advantage of the low production costs and government incentives in this region.

As mentioned, Japanese investment in ASEAN countries drastically increased after the Plaza Agreement: in 1985 it measured just 292 cases and US$9.3 billion, but in 1988 it had tripled to 825 cases and $27.1 billion (see Fig. 3). According to the Toyo Keizai Shinposha's survey, the number of Japanese-affiliated companies operating in the Asian countries at the end of 1988 was 3,770, with ASEAN countries accounting for 1,805. The number of employees directly employed by the Japanese companies for the same period was 797,000 for all of Asia, and 345,000

Table 2.   Japanese Affiliate Companies and Number of Employees
(at the end of 1988).

	Number of Companies	Number of Employees (manufacturing)
Singapore	573	67 (54) thousand
Thailand	512	110 (96)
Malaysia	356	70 (57)
Indonesia	222	62 (52)
Philippines	142	36 (24)
Subtotals	1,805	345 (283)
NIEs (except Singapore)	1,685	389 (346)
Others	280	63 (56)
Total Asia	3,770	797 (685)
World	9,859	1,672 (1,171)

Sources: Toyo Keizai Shinposha, *Kaigai-Shinshutsu-Kigyo Soran 1989* (Summary of Firms Operating Overseas, 1989).

for ASEAN countries (see Table 2). The Toyo Keizai's survey is not, however, complete, and the figures may be underestimated. I estimate the total number of Asian employees to be roughly one million. Counting indirect employment—that is, subcontracted and related workers—the total rises to three million. Japanese-affiliated companies have contributed to the creation of new employment in Asia.

A summary of the reasons for Japanese companies' extensive new investment and expansion of production facilities in ASEAN countries follows.

First, the yen appreciation caused the price competitiveness of Japanese commodities to decline in the world market. Japanese companies sought to operate production out of countries with low wage and production costs. Second, it became much easier to invest abroad because the value of the yen was doubled by the dollar depreciation of the past two or three years.

Third, Japanese investment receives incentives from local governments when the direction of the investments meets the requirements of local export-oriented policies. In Asian countries government policy has drastically changed from one emphasizing import substitution industrialization to one of export orientation. ASEAN governments have also accompanied the deregulation policy with invitations for more foreign capital and with the promotion of exports. Fourth, in order to cope with trade friction with the United States and European countries, Japanese manufacturing companies needed to diversify their production and distribution systems; one effective measure has been to construct factories in the ASEAN countries and to distribute their products to the United States, the EC member nations, and other countries, including Japan.

Last, the general environment for investment in ASEAN countries is fairly good: foreign investors value not only cheap labor and government incentives but also political stability, diligence of the labor force, and the overall future market as well.

Japanese companies have now taken new steps toward the globalization of their business: production, distribution, and control. Their production bases in Asia play an important role as suppliers to the world market. Following in the footsteps of automobile and electric appliance parts producers, electronics assembly-related parts and material makers have accelerated the construction of their factories in Asia, and especially in the ASEAN countries. The presence of Japanese-affiliated companies is thus becoming bigger and bigger in the ASEAN sphere.

The Role of Japanese Investment in ASEAN Countries

Although Japanese-affiliated companies have played an important role in the process of industrialization of ASEAN countries, their contribution is limited. The share of Japanese capital compared to the total domestic capital formation in each ASEAN country is not so large.[1] Compared to other countries, however, the Japanese share in foreign investment has become the biggest in the ASEAN region. In Korea it is over 50% (Table 1). The impact of Japanese-affiliated companies has gradually strengthened since their activities began in the 1950s.

Aspects of the contribution of Japanese-affiliated companies to the process of industrial development in the ASEAN region will now be evaluated. Japanese companies have helped raise not only the production levels but also the productivity of many industries. In addition, employee training at Japanese joint ventures has considerably promoted technology transfer through on-the-job training (OJT), quality control (QC), and production management.

---

1. The ratio of Japanese investment to the domestic capital formation in each ASEAN country is about 1–2%. In Korea and Thailand, for example, it was between 0.5% and 2% for 1975–1987.

Local governments expect foreign companies to contribute to export-oriented industrialization strategy in the following ways: to create employment; to earn foreign exchange through export; to foster technology transfer and personnel development; and to develop related industries.

Governments have thus welcomed the foreign capital that produces exportable manufactured goods, creates job opportunities, and transfers production technologies and management knowhow. Japanese-affiliated companies have worked to comply with the requirements of local government.

A Toyota factory in Thailand (in operation since 1963) and National Gobel in Indonesia (established in 1970) are good examples. These car and electric appliance assemblers, respectively, have trained personnel since the very beginning of their operations. Their system for training local employees has been highly praised. Their personnel training methods and philosophy include such typical features of Japanese-style

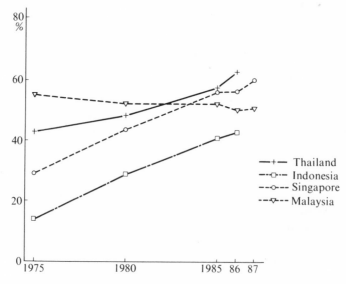

Fig. 4.   Rate of Localization.
Source: Yamashita et al. (1989: 31).
Note: Rate of localization is the ratio of local costs to total production
cost. Figures are based on responses to a questionnaire survey
of managers of Japanese-affiliated companies.

management as OJT, QC circles, job rotation, and temporary transfer of local staff to Japan for training.

Most of the Japanese-affiliated companies have promoted the localization of their parts production, which fosters the growth of local related industries. The results of our questionnaire survey show that the localization rate of Japanese-affiliated companies has risen year by year in this region. In 1975, for example, the rate of use of local parts in the production cost was about 40%, but this rose to around 55–60% in 1986 (Fig. 4).

Many local people now are proud of producing modern cars and electrical machines in their own countries, which has given them confidence in their abilities and the hope for further development.

Japanese-affiliated companies have also played a very important role in the transition from import-substitution industrialization to export-oriented industrialization. In order to produce exportable goods, ASEAN countries have to acquire higher-level technologies, knowhow in various types of management, qualified personnel, and knowledge of international business. The governments of this region have provided incentives to those foreign companies with high-level technologies and export know-how. Japanese companies have responded quickly to such government demands and changes in local industrialization policies.

Japanese-affiliated companies are thus expected to play a dominant role as promoters of the region's export-oriented industrialization. Japanese investors, however, still face many controversial issues and obstacles. One is the anti-Japanese sentiment widespread among Southeast Asian people, who fear that Japanese capital will become a dominant power in Asia again. Japan should thus be cautious about the over-presence and over-influence of Japanese capital.

Japanese shareholding has tended to increase since the ASEAN governments removed the domestic shareholding majority criteria for foreign investment, especially for export-oriented firms. Projects with 100% foreign capital shareholding have been approved when most of the products are scheduled for export. Some scholars have criticized the high levels of Japanese shareholding, pointing out that recent Japanese investment has became capital-intensive, so that the level of employment is decreasing when compared with the level of investment.

It is widely recognized, in addition, that foreign capital has distorted income distribution in the nations under discussion. It is true that the partners of Japanese joint ventures in the ASEAN countries, most of them rich overseas Chinese and higher ranking corporate officers, have acquired concessions and considerable profit when the Japanese joint ventures have done well. There is, however, a limit to how far foreign investors should intervene in the domestic problems of host countries, and investors should be cautious in this regard.

Evaluation of Japanese-style Management

Acceptability of Japanese-style Management

Southeast Asian nations have invited Japanese manufacturing enterprises in order to promote local industrialization. Because of the success and strong competitiveness of Japanese products in the world market, such nations have also examined Japanese-style management. All methods of Japanese-style management have not, however, worked out well in the recipient country. Many Japanese managers have recognized that they cannot apply their own ways as they do in Japan, a view confirmed by the results of our questionnaire survey and interviews with Japanese managers in four ASEAN countries (Yamashita et al. 1989, 1–89). The questionnaire survey and interviews were conducted during March 1987 and February 1988 in Thailand, Malaysia, Singapore, and Indonesia. Questionnaires were sent to all member companies of the Japanese Chamber of Commerce in each country. The follow-up survey concentrated on the automobile, electrical machine, and textile industries because Japanese companies were concentrated in these three sectors in ASEAN countries.

We received 132 responses to the questionnaire survey, of which 119 were from the manufacturing sector. A detailed evaluation of Japanese-style management will be given in the following chapters, but some features of the results of our survey are briefly explained here.

Japanese managers who have worked at Japanese joint ventures in the ASEAN countries gave very low evaluations of the lifetime employment, seniority, and *ringi* systems, which were considered typical practices of Japanese management (Fig. 5). The lifetime employment and seniority systems got especially negative evaluations; they were considered not to be applicable in ASEAN countries. One of the reasons for Japanese managers' criticism of these systems is that the cost burden of these practices will increase year by year. Even in Japan many companies have been modifying these systems.

Japanese managers, however, did approve of three Japanese-style management practices: career development, on-the-job training (OJT), and cooperation of management and workers. It can be concluded that they have confidence in the production management practices of

Japanese companies. Small group activities (QC circle) are also considered applicable in ASEAN countries now and in the future.

It is interesting that the managers give high evaluations to the custom of working in uniforms and the sharing of recreation and canteen facilities by managers and workers. These customary practices of Japanese companies took root during the days when Japanese society was not so rich, and are also evidence of the careful attention that Japanese managers and owners have paid to labor relations. The surveyed managers do not, however, give high marks to job rotation, the priority

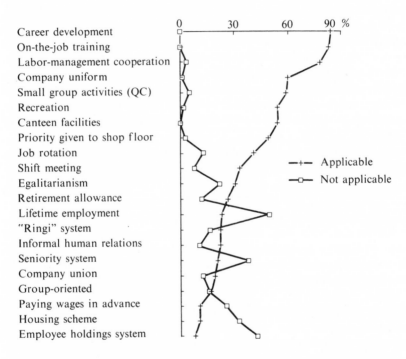

Fig. 5.   Applicability of Japanese-Style Management Techniques, as Assessed by Japanese Managers (average for four ASEAN countries).

Source: Yamashita et al. (1989: 16–26).

Note: Based on responses to a survey of Japanese managers of Japanese-affiliated companies in the ASEAN countries. The percentages represent the fraction of respondents who answered that the technique in question was "applicable" or "not applicable" in their enterprise.

given to the shop floor, and informal human relations. The applicability of these Japanese practices in ASEAN countries is doubted by the managers, who consider that written manuals and clear job descriptions are necessary and preferable.

The survey results cannot be interpreted in a straightforward manner, however, as the interpretation of the results differs by industry, scale, and period of operation. For example, many managers of companies that have operated for more than twenty years in ASEAN countries approve of the lifetime employment and seniority systems, because they feel that only under these systems can they advance personnel training in the long run.

The managers of the more recently established enterprises, particularly those established since the Plaza Agreement, doubt the application of the old style of Japanese management. Such managers do not give any priority to the long-term training of personnel. They are much more concerned with the quick establishment of an export base in the ASEAN nations by directly introducing efficient production equipment with "ready-made" personnel. The "head-hunting" that follows makes trouble with other Japanese companies. We may conclude that the management style of the newly established Japanese companies in ASEAN countries is following the Western style in overseas operations.

The Recognition Gap in Technology Transfer

ASEAN countries seem to be learning from the development experiences of the NIEs. The newly industrializing countries have achieved high economic growth through the strategic policy of export-oriented industrialization, the success of which shows that such growth could be realized because their capacity to absorb higher technology was also high.

The NIEs' experiences demonstrate that only a country with a high technology absorption capacity can promote export-oriented industrialization and make the best use of foreign capital and knowhow. An export-oriented policy should be applied carefully and with the prior examination of a number of prerequisites. For instance, before the application there should exist a certain level of industrial base and many entrepreneurial managers, technicians, and educated workers in the economy.

Observing the successes of the Asian NIEs, the ASEAN members and other developing countries have tried to apply the policy of export-oriented industrialization. But most have not been successful in exporting their manufactured commodities and instead have been faced with the problem of trade deficits due to the increase in imports of the materials, intermediate goods, and capital goods needed for domestic production. The governments of the ASEAN countries came to recognize the importance of technology; they expected (and later requested) that foreign capital projects extend to technology transfer. At present it is common for local governments to provide various incentives to foreign capital projects that can produce exportable commodities through technology transfer. In addition, the recent ASEAN deregulation policies were based on the NIEs' experiences.

Although technology transfer is highly recommended and valued by local governments, a recognition gap between the donors and recipients at times causes misunderstandings. A typical case arises when local government officials and some ASEAN economists believe that the Japanese-affiliated companies are unwilling to carry out technology transfer. Their impression is based on comparison of the practices of the Japanese companies and of U.S. or European companies in ASEAN regions.

The ASEAN authorities seem to understand that technology transfer will proceed when the foreign technical advisors have gone home. But Japanese technical advisors do not go home quickly—they stay for longer periods. This is taken as evidence that the Japanese-affiliated companies are unwilling to give technical training. U.S. and European companies, in contrast, send their technical advisors home quickly, and the promotion of local staff is speedy.

It is important at this point to understand what real technology transfer is. Japanese-affiliated manufacturing companies confidently base their production management methods, and especially their technical training, on OJT. European and American companies, on the other hand, basically utilize written manuals and detailed job descriptions. Since it is easy for workers to see and follow the manual, local people seem to be happier working at U.S. and European companies than at Japanese ones. At Japanese-affiliated companies the workers' job content is ambiguous: Japanese companies do not clearly give workers a detailed job description and work standards. They rely instead on OJT or on the technician's experience, which sometimes leads to misunderstanding and misconceptions between workers and managers. Some local people, including government officials, still consider Japanese companies unwilling to teach any technology to the local people.

The Japanese-affiliated companies' real attitude toward technology transfer is as follows. At the first stage, technical advisors train the employees for the operation. There is no difference at this point between the practices of the Japanese and those of Euro-American companies except for the use of manuals.

The difference appears in the second stage of technology transfer. Most of the Euro-American companies withdraw their technical advisors when the factory is operating well, after which the local employees just follow the manuals without any modification. But in the Japanese companies the technical advisors stay even after a smooth operation has been achieved. They continue to train the workers step by step in maintenance and repair, quality control, introduction of new production methods and new technology, and so forth.

When trouble occurs in Euro-American companies the technicians are flown to the factory to perform repairs, after which they go home. They do not trust the local workers in the repair and R&D fields. Japanese technical advisors, on the other hand, generally stay longer and train workers beyond the level of basic operations because they place great emphasis on being able to respond quickly to changes in model design, production methods, materials, and new product development.

The local plants of Japanese and Euro-American enterprises are thus established on different premises, and this is reflected in their attitudes toward technology transfer and personnel training. Government offi-

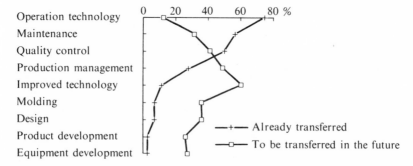

Fig. 6. Stage of Technology Transfer (average for three ASEAN countries).

Source: Yamashita et al. (1989: 38).

Note: The figures are based on a questionnaire survey of Japanese managers of Japan-affiliated companies in Thailand, Singapore, and Malaysia. The percentages are the proportion of total respondents who indicated that the technology in question had "already been transferred" or "would be transferred" in the future.

cials and ASEAN economists should understand the differences between the practices and attitudes held by Japanese and Euro-American companies.

Japanese Managers' Perceptions of Technology Transfer

In order to learn about Japanese managers' perceptions of technology transfer, a questionnaire survey and interview were conducted in Southeast Asia concurrently with the survey on Japanese-style management discussed earlier (Yamashita et al. 1989, 28–40).

One of the results of this questionnaire survey pertains to technology transfer in Thailand, Malaysia, and Singapore (Fig. 6). This survey is distinguished from others in that "technology transfer" was divided into the nine stages shown in Figure 6. Naturally, technology transfer consists of different stages: the first stage is the transfer of operational technology, the second is repair and maintenance technology, the third, quality control (small group activities) technology, which is followed by process management and procurement technology and so on as the degree of technological content increases. We asked the Japanese managers to indicate which stage of technology transfer they had completed by that time and which stage they planned to reach in the future. Seventy-four percent answered that they had completed the first stage, the transfer of operational technology. The figures for repair and maintenance and quality control were 57% and 50%, respectively. For production management the figure dropped to about 28%, for technology improvement it further dropped to 11%, and almost no enterprises had yet done anything about design and new product development.

For the sake of convenience we will call the first five stages of technology transfer the "early stages" of technology transfer in order to distinguish them from the "later stages" which include technological development of new designs, molding, and tools, and development of new products and equipment. The early stages are technologies related to equipment that has already been set up and the affiliated production processes. Japanese enterprises have been teaching these stages to the local employees, whereas the Euro-American companies seem to limit their technology transfer to the stage of operational technology.

The attitude and consideration shown by Japanese managers to the later stages of technology transfer differ among themselves. In the areas of development of new design, molding, tools, new products, and production lines, only a few managers responded that they are proceeding with technology transfer. Such negative responses are based on the managers' evaluation of the technical standards and research environment of the region. The managers have not yet placed their full confidence in the local employees, and consider it to be more efficient at this time to design and develop new products at the headquarters research centers in Japan.

Japanese enterprises should not, however, underestimate the ability of the local employees—they need to better understand the local educational and economic environments. Local employees will soon bridge the technology gap. Thorough personnel training takes more time. Japanese managers, especially at the headquarters, should consider technology transfer in the longer term, and continuously train technical experts and managers.

The Role of Japanese-affiliated Companies and the Creation of a New Corporate Culture

The increase in Japanese direct investment deepens the relationship between Japan and the ASEAN countries. It not only leads to closer economic relations but also has political and sociocultural repercussions. The activities of joint ventures or Japanese-affiliated companies should be reconsidered at this stage of development in order to find a new direction for Japan's future relations with ASEAN countries.

The significance of the role of Japanese direct investment may be summarized as follows. First, Japanese direct investment contributes to industrialization and economic development through job creation, technology and managerial transfer, foreign exchange earnings through exports, and development of related industries. Second, the training of local employees at the Japanese-affiliated companies contributes not only to career development in one company but also to human development in the society in general.[2] Third, by transferring advanced Japanese technologies and managerial knowhow, local managers and employees may change their attitudes and try to modernize their management style and probably their life-style as well. Such changes will have a positive influence on further socioeconomic development in the recipient country.

It is true of course that Japanese companies pursue direct investment in ASEAN countries because it is profitable. They transplant their

---

2. The retirement of trained personnel may be a loss to the company, but not to the society. In addition, when the Japanese company can afford to do so, it can keep them as consultants or partners.

factories to Southeast Asian locations in order to reduce production and operation costs. The merits and significance of Japanese direct invest- ment mentioned above are supposed to be the *accompanying* effects of the profit-making activity of Japanese enterprises.

Among the points that Japanese-affiliated companies in the ASEAN region need to reconsider are that relations between Japan and the Southeast Asian countries are going to be tightened year by year and that therefore the activities of the Japanese-affiliated companies will produce wide and frequent contacts with the local people and society, with the result that undesirable incidents are apt to occur in and outside the Japanese-affiliated companies.

Many small and medium-scale Japanese enterprises have recently started businesses and factory operations in Southeast Asian countries, but many Japanese managers have not yet understood the local people's situations and feelings. Such managers should recognize that Japanese styles of management and thinking may not be accepted by the local people.

Although Japanese-affiliated companies are still welcomed by local governments and play important roles in local industrialization and modernization, the Japanese must be very cautious of their impact and influence on the recipients' economy and society. Anti-Japanese senti- ments have existed since World War II and even earlier.

First, the managers of both Japanese-affiliated companies and their parent companies should be concerned about their activities' influence on the natural environment and the people.

Second, the impact of foreign investment on related industries and the economy as a whole is great, and such investment may even drive out local industries and products. Japanese companies should instead contribute to developing related industries and local subcontracts so as to create job opportunities and new business in the recipient countries.

Third, concerning management practices in Japanese-affiliated com- panies, managers should listen to criticisms and complaints from locals, and particularly to those criticisms regarding slow promotion of local employees, unwillingness to transfer software technology, and so on. Slow promotion of and lower wages for locals may in fact create problems for the Japanese companies themselves in the future. It is said that in Thailand the best students do not want to get jobs in Japanese- affiliated companies; they prefer jobs in such outstanding local compa- nies as Siam Cement, and the second-best students get positions in Euro- American companies. Some of those remaining go to Japanese compa- nies. Human resources are very important for the growth of enterprises, but Japanese-affiliated companies do not get the best new university graduates. For the sake of future development, Japanese-affiliated companies need to reexamine their recruitment systems in Asia.

Fourth, the job descriptions and manuals used in Japanese-affiliated companies are incomplete. The Japanese language is often used during meetings, giving rise to misunderstandings between Japanese managers and advisers and local employees. It is thus necessary for the companies to have clear-cut criteria for jobs and promotions. Moreover, headquarters usually ignore the situations and conditions of the local factories. Top managers at headquarters should listen to managers on the scene and try to adapt to local conditions. It is essential for these enterprises to attempt to reduce conflicts with local people.

Human resource development and human relations are most important considerations for Japanese enterprises. Their business success depends upon whether they can maintain good human relations in local joint ventures and upon how many local staff members they can develop.

The experiences of the Japanese enterprises that have operated in Southeast Asia for more than two decades are very useful. Newly transferring Japanese enterprises can learn from such experiences in human relations, promotion, career development, technology transfer, and other areas.

Japanese enterprises are now expected to look in new directions for management philosophy in their Southeast Asian operations. Because European and American enterprises have continued to produce standardized products using only fixed written manuals, promotion and technology transfer in Euro-American enterprises proceed faster than in Japanese enterprises. The Euro-American transfer, however, is only that of low-level technology to unskilled laborers. Manufacturing is largely carried out through automatic machinery, so the technology that local employees have mastered is nothing more than machine operation.

Japanese enterprises are latecomers in foreign direct investment, but their activities and roles in ASEAN countries are growing, especially since the yen appreciation. It is necessary for them to pay more attention to local peoples. In order to get along with local employees, Japanese enterprises should look for new styles of management and human relations that differ from the Euro-American or even the present Japanese style. If Japanese-affiliated companies can promote a new corporate culture in the ASEAN countries, they can move in new creative directions through their own devices.

2
Japan's Investment and Local Capital in ASEAN since 1985

Pasuk Phongpaichit

This paper looks at the determinants of Japanese investment in the member countries of the Association of Southeast Asian Nations (ASEAN) after 1985 and discusses the possible impact of that investment on domestic capital and some implications for the management of joint venture firms. The study is confined to Indonesia, Malaysia, Singapore, and Thailand.

Japanese direct investment (JDI) in ASEAN during the post-1985 era differs from JDI in the 1960s and 1970s in both scale and character. Figures from Japan's Ministry of Finance show that JDI in ASEAN for the three years 1985 to 1987 totalled US$422 million as compared to an accumulated stock of US$593 million during the previous three decades (Nakakita 1988). Manufacturing investment in the 1960s and 1970s focused mostly on import-substituting industries, producing for domestic markets. Ventures usually involved the assembly of components and parts imported from Japan. The investment was mostly joint venture with local partners. Large trading companies (*Sogo Shosha*) played an important role in matching and organizing the joint ventures and sometimes were directly involved in the local production jointly with the Japanese manufacturers and local partners.

JDI in the post-1985 era is significantly more export-oriented. In Indonesia the number of new export-oriented projects established by Japanese firms had averaged 3.7 projects per year between 1970 and 1984. Between 1985 and 1987, the average jumped to 14 per year. In Thailand the Board of Investment approved 260 Japanese investment projects between 1986 and May 1988. Of these 206 or 79% were classified as export industries, that is, projects that export at least 80% of their products. The Japanese firms involved are both final manufacturers and their subcontractors, including a large number of small and medium-sized enterprises, particularly in such competitive export-oriented sectors as electronics components, electrical machinery, food processing, and automobile parts. This same trend is taking place in the rest of the ASEAN member countries as well.

A result of the new trend is a more complicated production network among Japanese and Japanese joint venture firms. There is an increase in intra-firm trade and an increased local sourcing. A survey by Japan External Trade Organization (JETRO) in December 1987 showed an increased local sourcing by Japanese subsidiaries or joint-venture firms in ASEAN, which increased backward linkages with local subcontractors and material producers. This same study also found that a majority of the firms surveyed reported increases in their exports to Japan in the period since 1985 (JETRO 1986). There are also new forms of investment, involving contractual sales of innovative technology and management by Japanese firms to local producers in return for minority equity shares (Nakakita 1988).

What will be the impact of the new wave of Japanese investment on domestic capital in ASEAN in the next decade? To answer this question properly large-scale empirical research is needed, but it is possible to begin a preliminary discussion by theorizing based on the motivations and other causes of the recent increase in JDI in ASEAN in recent years, as well as by analyzing the responses from the government and the local capitalists.

Determinants of Japanese Direct Investment

The Kojima Thesis and the Western Approach

Kojima (1978) has argued that in the 1960s and 1970s the major factor determining JDI was the change in comparative advantage between Japan and developing Asian countries. This change came largely from Japan or from changes in the supply side. Japan's industrialization in the post-World War II period was dominated by labor-intensive manufacturing. As it became more successful the cost of labor and materials rose, and Japan began to lose its comparative advantage in labor-intensive products. Consequently the Japanese industrial structure shifted to more capital-intensive and high-technology processes, and firms began to relocate the production of labor-intensive manufacturing to developing countries whose comparative advantage lies in having a more abundant supply of labor relative to capital.

Ozawa (1979) employs a similar analysis but emphasizes the importance of the resource constraint within Japan. He argues that Japan is a resource-scarce country and that, in order to prevent this constraint from limiting the growth of the economy, Japan ensures the production of cheap raw materials from overseas by investing directly in countries with an abundant supply of natural resources. Direct investment is necessary because it gives direct control over the production process and prices. According to Ozawa, the Japanese government has an important role to play in promoting foreign investment. Without government assistance (including financial assistance, use of aid to improve infrastructure and to soften possible resentment against Japan in developing countries, other assistance via JETRO, and so on) Japanese investors would not have become so successful in their overseas operations.

Kojima thus explains the predominance of JDI in labor-intensive manufacturing in Asian countries, while Ozawa explains the investment in resource-based industries in some countries (especially in Malaysia, Indonesia, and Latin America).

While these explanations may describe the outflow of capital from Japan to other countries in the 1950s and early 1960s fairly well, the late 1960s began to see changes in the motivation of JDI from Japan.

Over the years more and more of JDI has been occurring in product lines in which Japanese firms have comparative advantage in terms of technological knowhow, marketing or managerial skills as compared to host countries. As Japan moved up the technological scale, it began to exhibit what some academics called "the American types" of investment, that is, investment which is induced by a desire to take advantage of the accumulated technological knowhow (both small and large firms) and of innovative products. More and more Japanese firms have also graduated to become multinational and have acquired the innovation to reduce the transaction costs associated with direct investment. Such developments increase the attractiveness of overseas investment and induce Japanese firms to invest overseas.

To explain the increased flow of JDI in ASEAN during the 1980s, writers thus must discuss not only the impact of the changes in comparative advantage but also other factors, making the increased maturity of and the structural shift in the Japanese economy toward high-tech industries and the trend toward globalization of Japanese firms. The outflow of JDI in recent years is linked closely to the process of industrial restructuring in Japan, a subject which is dealt with in more detail in Dr. Suthy Prasartset's paper in this volume.

The Host Country Demand

There is of course another side to the story—the demand for foreign investment from the host country's perspective.

In the existing literature, factors on the host country's side are often considered under the rubrics of investment climate, locational aspects, availability of natural resources and labor, cultural compatibility, political stability, and so on (Allen 1973a,b,c, 1979; Goldsbrough 1987). Such factors are important to foreign investors as they are rough indicators of the degree of attractiveness of the host country. I would like to go beyond this and focus on the demand for foreign investment from host countries.

In considering the determinants of the demand for foreign investment, two main actors are important: domestic entrepreneurs (domestic capital) and local government. Labor is important in some countries. But in ASEAN at present the labor factor is not yet significant.

We may postulate schematically that demand for foreign investment is a function of that investment's utility to local government and capitalists. For the governments of host countries, the satisfaction or utility of foreign investment inflow includes economic contributions to balance of payments (net increase in capital inflow and exports), employment generation, increase in the rate of growth, upgrading of the technological level of workers and of different economic sectors. Then there are also the contributions that are political in character. Foreign investment may be attractive on the grounds that it can be regulated more easily than domestic private investment. The government could for example stipulate that foreign investment in certain sectors be made in collaboration with state capital (state enterprises), thereby resulting in an expansion of the state sector in the economy vis-à-vis the private sector. Foreign investment could play a role in policies designed to strengthen one particular group. But foreign investment may also be perceived as a threat to state capital, as a potential focus of political tension, or as a distorting influence in domestic factor markets (foreign firms may pay very high wages and thus create a situation of labor aristocracy).

For local capitalists, the utility of foreign investment lies in the profits to be made in the case of joint ventures, in contributions toward the upgrading of technology and marketing, managerial, and enterpreneurial knowhow, and in access to external markets. On the negative side, foreign investment may mean increased competition in the same product markets and competition for scarce resources.

The host country's demand for foreign investment has direct bearing on the motivation and cost calculations of foreign investors. If the host country has a high demand for foreign investment, it can reduce costs and raise profitability for the incoming firms in various ways. It may reduce the costs involved in bureaucratic procedure, the process of finding partners and suppliers, gaining access to infrastructure and information sources. It may relax rules and regulations in favor of foreign investors. All these increase the comparative advantage of the host country vis-à-vis Japan and other recipient countries. They reduce the transaction cost involved in foreign investment and may become an important determinant of the foreign investment flow into the host country.

Domestic Capital, State Capital, Foreign Capital

In any country at any time the key factors affecting the demand for foreign capital are the attitude of domestic capital and the attitude of government, and their relation to foreign capital.

In certain circumstances domestic capital may view foreign capital as a threat, as a competitor. It may then put pressure on government to restrict the inflow, refuse to cooperate in joint projects, and otherwise disrupt or deter foreign investment. In other circumstances, domestic capital may see foreign capital as an ally, a source of technology and strength, and may therefore influence government to facilitate the inflow, and cooperate willingly. Whether domestic capital is warm or cool toward foreign capital is likely to be determined by two main factors: its estimate of the relative strength of domestic versus foreign capital; and its estimate of the extent to which government will protect and promote the interest of domestic capital in the face of foreign competition.

As for the government, there are three main sets of factors that shape its attitude to foreign capital: first, the government's assessment of the impact of foreign capital on the economy as a whole; second, its assessment of the impact of foreign investment on the government's own economic interests, namely, state capital; and third, its assessment of the impact of foreign investment on the political balance, particularly on the political role of domestic capital.

Besides this general state interest, there is also the more specific state interest bound up with state capital. In many developing countries, including those of ASEAN, the state plays an active role in capital accumulation through state enterprises and government participation in joint public-private ventures. Just like domestic capital, this "state capital" interest can view foreign capital as a threat or as a source of strength, depending on circumstances.

In trying to maintain its objectives the state will often face fundamental constraints on its policy options because the interests of domestic capital, foreign capital, and the state itself are in conflict. For instance the demand of private domestic and foreign capital for rational and predictable laws governing the state may be contradictory to the practice of appropriation of state power and resources by officials in a military regime. In a more general context, the state support of large multi-nationals may upset small local enterprises that feel threatened by competition from foreign firms. For these reasons, policy toward foreign investment is rarely simple and straightforward. Indeed it is riven with self-contradiction and compromise. This makes it especially hard to analyze, and some simplification is necessary. In the next section, how the attitudes of governments and domestic business during the period from the 1960s to the mid-1980s molded the demand for foreign capital in each country is examined.

State, Domestic, and Foreign Capital in ASEAN before 1985

From the 1960s to the early 1980s, the ASEAN governments were as a general rule rather lukewarm towards foreign investment. State capital in most of the countries during this period was expanding its scale and influence and was not keen to allow foreign capital to enter its own areas of interest as a competitor. At the same time governments could recognize that foreign capital could contribute benefits, particularly in new technology, additional employment, and raised efficiency levels in domestic firms exposed to competition. Thus even in this period when state capital was dominant, foreign investment was admitted, though usually under restrictive conditions stipulated by the state. Domestic capital was generally opposed to foreign capital inflow and periodically lobbied the state to protect its interests.

Although state capital was ascendent in all four countries during this period, the development of domestic capital and the relationship between state and domestic capital differed greatly from country to country. In the 1980s, these differences would affect the receptivity toward foreign capital inflow.

Indonesia. The demand for foreign capital in Indonesia has been shaped by one major influence: the existence of a large state capital sector. From the 1960s through the mid-1980s, state capital was largely opposed to the inflow of foreign capital, which it viewed as a potential threat to its own position. The weak domestic capital sector also did not feel strong enough to bargain profitably with foreign capital and so supported government policies that preserved the domestic market for domestic capital. In the late 1960s, a foreign exchange crisis coupled with a realignment of internal political forces caused the attitudes toward foreign investment to soften somewhat, but the basic policy orientation remained lukewarm to foreign capital until the mid-1980s.

The predominance of state enterprise (state capital) in Indonesia dates back to the postcolonial period. In the 1950s following independence, Sukarno's military regime nationalized foreign firms. By 1960, 489 Dutch companies had been nationalized, including 216 in plantations, 161 in industry and mining, 40 in trading, and 16 in insurance. Some of the nationalized firms were returned to the previous British and American owners in 1967, but state capital remained important in public utilities, petroleum, mining (such as aluminium smelting), fertilizer production, printing, communications, animal husbandry, transport, construction, trade, forestry, fisheries, real estate, cement, and pulp and paper. In addition 80% of the major bank loans remained under the control of the government, and until the end of 1988 the banking sector was closed to new investment from foreign capital.

The importance of state capital was larger than these statistics of government enterprises suggest. A large number of domestic entrepreneurs were dependent on the state for subcontract work in areas such as construction, procurement of materials, goods, and services. In addition, various departments in the military ran business enterprises. State capital and its allies pervaded the Indonesian economy.

The Sukarno regime was able to push through the nationalization program in the late 1950s for two reasons. First, the regime had inherited a relatively powerful state structure from the Dutch. Second, the regime drew its support from peasant and labor interests, which were very opposed to the old colonial interests and to the Chinese entrepreneurial groups that dominated private capital at the end of the Dutch period. The moderate party that represented the middle class and indigenous petty capitalists tried to persuade the government to transfer some of the ex-Dutch enterprises to the private sector, but it was not successful, largely because the candidates to take over such enterprises were mainly Indonesian Chinese who had become identified with Dutch colonial rule. The military governments under Sukarno justified the state role in business as a means to reduce the power of Chinese domestic capital and to develop the country in the interests of the Indonesian nation.

Domestic capital was divided into Pribumi (Indonesian) and Chinese segments. The Pribumi capitalists tended to be small scale and rather inexperienced. The few medium and large scale enterprises had grown through association with the government and were essentially adjuncts of state capital. They relied heavily on subcontract work from state enterprises and had privileged access to state credit facilities and licenses. Chinese capital concentrated on manufacturing production and, more especially, distribution for the domestic market.

Domestic capital lobbied for government to protect the internal market from any inflow of foreign capital. Government responded by more or less protecting domestic distribution, service industries, and low-level technology manufacturing for the home market. In Suharto's time, businesses that benefited from government protection included both Pribumi and Chinese.

The Indonesian economy encountered severe problems with the balance of payments in the late 1960s. At the same time the advent of the new Suharto regime represented an adjustment in the configuration of political forces. The new regime recognized that the spread of state enterprises had been only partially successful. It also recognized that Chinese capital was vital to the continued growth and prosperity of the Indonesian economy. To solve the balance-of-payments problem and to sustain growth, the government began to admit more foreign investment and set out to reach a modus vivendi with domestic private (including Chinese) capital.

The Suharto regime continued to nurture and extend state capital, which provided a major source of revenue for the government and its supporters. It also continued to maintain a framework of investment regulations and licensing rules for controlling the development of private capital. But to a greater extent than under the previous regime, Suharto promoted the growth of selected business interests that harmonized with the interests of state capital and the interests of the regime itself. These selected business interests were both Pribumi and Chinese. As part of this more pragmatic policy making, the regime was also significantly more open to foreign capital.

Foreign capital was admitted in areas where it offered no threat to the interests of state or to favored domestic capital (that is, businesses that could seek protection from the state, or businesses run by those who were allies of the government in power) and in areas where the country needed the high technology that foreign capital controlled. Even in these areas, foreign capital had to tolerate conditions imposed by the government. In the oil industry, for instance, the government enforced a production sharing contract system, which restricted the foreign partners to 15% of the total output as a return for their investment, expertise, and technology. In some areas of high technology, foreign capital was admitted in joint ventures with domestic capital.

The government relaxed some of the restrictions on foreign investment, but only partially. The Foreign Investment Law of 1967 provided a structure for admitting foreign investment but still preserved sectors such as public utilities, harbors, shipping, aviation, atomic energy, and mass media for state control. In manufacturing it allowed foreign firms to control production processes but explicitly reserved domestic distribution for Indonesian firms. In the years following, foreign investment increased but was always limited by political realities. There were cases of strong resentment against foreign capital on the issue of control of management and technology. In 1974 there were popular protests against the rise in Japanese investment. In response, the government obliged all foreign ventures to reduce the foreign equity share to 80% and to reduce it further to 49% within ten years.

In sum, state capital rose to a dominant position in the post-independence Indonesian economy. It deliberately suppressed the expansion of domestic capital that was independent of state capital. And it strictly controlled the inflow of foreign investment. After the crisis of the late 1960s, the government was forced to become more flexible. The Suharto regime maintained a dominant state sector as a counterweight to the possibility of outright Chinese dominance in the commercial and industrial economy, but at the same time the regime allowed selected business interests, including Chinese, to prosper, usually in alliance with the government and state capital. Foreign investment was admitted to a larger but still limited extent within this overall framework of tight control and careful balancing of conflicting interests. State capital remained dominant, but it was obliged to allow more scope for domestic and foreign capital. The delicate modus vivendi worked out in this period survived into the early 1980s.

Malaysia. As in Indonesia, the government that took over at independence used the strong state structure inherited from the colonial power to extend state capital and to limit the role of domestic capital controlled by ethnic Chinese. But the Malaysian case differs from the Indonesian in one important respect: the relative size and power of the ethnic Chinese community. In Indonesia, the Chinese community is numerically small, and at the time of independence its business interests were still largely limited to domestic distribution. In Malaysia, however, the Chinese represent close to half of the total population, and even at independence their business interests were extensive. The Malaysian government's policies for developing the country on behalf of Bumiputera (that is, indigenous Malay) interests have had to be more forceful and more controversial than in Indonesia. In this context, attitudes towards foreign capital inflow to Malaysia have been more complex.

At independence the new Malaysian government could appeal to Malay resentment against the economic domination by foreigners and against the economic prominence of the ethnic Chinese. There was no immediate large scale nationalization as in Indonesia, but the government did inherit the strong structure of state control established by the colonial power, which included state operation of public utilities, and expanded the activities to include telecommunications, electricity, and water works for the public at large. Then, beginning in the mid-1960s, the role of state capital was substantially expanded. The Companies Act of 1965 permitted state enterprises to participate directly in trade, commerce, industry, and finance.

Under the New Economic Policy (known as NEP) program introduced in the early 1970s, the government extended the scope of state enterprises in order to increase the participation of the indigenous Malay population in business and to reduce the domination by Malaysian Chinese in trading, banking, and most economic activities. At this time Bumiputeras held only 4.3% of total equity in Malaysia, compared to 61.7% held by foreigners and 34% by other Malaysians, most of whom were ethnic Chinese. Under the NEP the government planned to increase the share of the Bumiputeras to at least 30% by 1990. The government also planned to increase the share of Bumiputeras in total non-agricultural employment. Expansion of state capital was a major strategy for achieving both the equity and employment objectives.

New state enterprises were established in banking, steel, oil, airlines, heavy industry, and automobiles. Several government banks were established to promote the development of Malay entrepreneurs. The government inaugurated ventures in cooperation with private Malay partners with the aim of eventually selling out the government share to Malays once the enterprises had proven profitable. Public enterprises were launched with trust agencies set up to hold shares on behalf of the indigenous community. The Industrial Coordination Act of 1975 stipulated that 30% of the equity and employment in enterprises of a certain size (foreign or domestic) had to be Bumiputera-owned.

As far as the government and its Bumiputera allies were concerned, foreign investment was judged to be good or bad depending on the extent to which it promoted the policy goals represented by the NEP. When the NEP was introduced in 1970, 60% of the Malaysian corporate sector was in the hands of foreign capital. Many British firms were bought out by the government or by the business groups associated with the major (Malay) political parties. This buying out offered a quick and relatively painless method for increasing the equity share of Bumiputeras in corporate capital.

By the late 1970s the Malaysian economy was in poor shape. The government achieved its aim of increasing Bumiputera ownership of capital, but it discouraged investment among Chinese entrepreneurs. The rate of growth of domestic investment (mostly from the Chinese) declined, and some Chinese capital fled from Malaysia. At the same time, the new state enterprises established under the NEP tended to be inefficient. And Western foreign capital was discouraged by the prospect of another buyout in the future. The decline in oil prices in the early 1980s tipped the economy into a severe recession. The government continued the NEP but was forced to reevaluate its policy toward foreign investment. The government and allied groups now tried actively to promote foreign investment in ways that would support NEP goals and at the same time promote the overall growth of the economy. This was the background for launching the "Look East" policy in the early 1980s.

The "Look East" policy encouraged the inflow of Japanese and Korean capital in order to promote prosperity and so strengthen the power of the state. The government also structured incentives and imposed conditions intended to ensure that the new capital inflow would not serve as an ally of domestic Chinese capital. It allowed foreign companies to have 100% ownership, thus tacitly discouraging joint ventures. It channeled much of the investment into free-trade zones, which were relatively isolated from the rest of the economy; here they contributed to employment and to the balance of payments without doing much to stimulate the growth of domestic enterprise. And it established joint ventures between Japanese capital and state capital in such enterprises as the Proton car. Thus foreign capital was encouraged primarily to balance out the dominance of Chinese businesses and secondly in collaboration with state capital to crowd out local capital in certain sectors, such as construction and automobiles, that had been Chinese-dominated.

As in Indonesia, state capital rose to a dominant position in Malaysia. Initially it was opposed to competition from either domestic or foreign capital. In the late 1970s and early 1980s, the government was forced to reevaluate its attitude in order to sustain economic growth, but it attempted still to control and manage the inflow of foreign investment in a way that would not undermine the dominant role of state capital.

Singapore. In both Indonesia and Malaysia, the dominant position of state capital tended to restrict the ambit of foreign capital. In Singapore, state capital was even more dominant. Yet in this case it coexisted with foreign capital—indeed, the Singapore government actively encouraged foreign capital inflow. The Singapore case illustrates a situation in which the receptivity to foreign capital may be due to the limited range of options open to a small country. Lack of entrepreneurship and the limited size of the markets compelled the Singapore government to adopt an export-oriented industrialization strategy with heavy reliance on foreign capital and technology.

The Singapore economy in the 1960s relied on entrepôt trade and British military expenditure. The announcement of the British military withdrawal in 1967 threatened to exacerbate an already critical un-employment situation; unemployment was running at over 10%. In that situation the people's expectation of the government was high, and to legitimize its position the government had to take an active part in initiating growth and providing employment. The situation provided a strong rationale for a highly interventionist government. Thus developed the background for the Singapore government's extension of the range of government enterprises far beyond the usual selection of public utilities.

By 1986 there were a total of 608 government-linked companies ranging from department stores to shipping yards. In some areas, such as airlines and shipping, government remained the sole owner until recently. In others, government is a major shareholder. The Develop-ment Bank of Singapore, for instance, is 48% government owned. In joint-venture businesses the government has been active in steel, sugar, and department stores (Yaohan, established partly with Japanese capi-tal) and has taken an equity share in a wide variety of other enterprises.

Despite the extensive network of state capital in the economic life of Singapore, the government has adopted a most positive and definitive policy stand towards foreign capital. From the beginning the govern-ment welcomed foreign capital almost unconditionally. The government actively identified foreign firms that were likely to find Singapore attractive and invited their executives to Singapore to display the facilities available and the government's willingness to receive their investment. It imposed no restrictions on foreign equity participation except in certain industries like banking, publishing, and residential properties; no restrictions on remittances of earnings or repatriation of capital; and relatively minor restrictions on the employment of suitably qualified foreign professionals and skilled workers. The reasons behind the adoption of such a policy lay in the relative weakness of Singapore's domestic capital.

Domestic capital in Singapore was weak in all sectors. In manufacturing, domestic capital was mainly confined to small and medium enterprises working as subcontractors to larger enterprises. Only a few progressed, with the help of the government and links to foreign capital. In 1983, 83% of manufactured exports were produced by foreign firms. In construction, small-scale operations were dominated by domestic capital, but the large scale was dominated by foreign firms. In such a situation the development of domestic capital was very much shaped by the design of government policies. It remained weak.

Thailand. Unlike all the other member states of ASEAN, Thailand was never formally colonized and consequently never passed through the stage of nationalism and independence. The economy was however under some colonial influence from the mid-nineteenth century until about 1927 as a result of the unequal trade treaties with the West. In the other ASEAN states, the colonial period implanted a relatively powerful state structure (bureaucracy, education, public works), and the independence movement ended with this state structure, relatively intact, being taken over by a nationalist government with a purposeful ideology of development and nation-building. It was this process that created the foundations for the extension of state capital. In Thailand during the same period, however, there was some state-building activity in imitation of its colonized neighbors but nowhere near as advanced. And there was a surge of nationalism in the decolonization period, but again it was played in a minor key. The foundations for the extension of state capital were much weaker in Thailand than in the other ASEAN states.

Like Indonesia and Malaysia, Thailand's business activity was dominated by ethnic Chinese, and this domination was resented by the Thai majority who were still mainly engaged in rice farming. From the 1930s to the 1950s, military-based governments espoused economic nationalism and attempted to transfer many Chinese-run businesses to state control. Many state enterprises were set up to replace the Chinese in rice trading and other distributive trades, manufacturing, and banking.

Thus Thailand began the 1950s with commitments to expand state capital and limit Chinese capital, very much along the lines of Indonesia and Malaysia. Yet by the end of the decade, these policies had been abandoned.

The relatively weak Thai state structure proved incapable of managing state capital on a large scale. In the 1960s and 1970s, most of the state enterprises created in the economic nationalist era were sold back to private ownership. Only a handful, including tobacco and petroleum, remained under government control. Any further extensions of state capital were limited to public utilities and enterprises considered vital for the purpose of defense or for national development.

In the absence of the kind of strong religious barriers that exist in Indonesia and Malaysia, the ethnic Chinese in Thailand were able to achieve relatively successful social integration. During the next genera-tion government and the ethnic Chinese business sector gradually worked out a way to coexist and cooperate. As in the other three countries studied, domestic capital in Thailand (mainly Chinese owned) was especially strong in distribution, service industries, and low-technology manufacturing. From the late 1950s, with the help of limited govern-ment protection, Thai domestic capital grew in strength in these areas and also expanded into manufacturing and export production.

Domestic capital developed in Thailand during the 1960s and 1970s in agro-industries, consumer goods industries, textiles and garments, jewellery, and automobile parts. These enterprises were not confined to producing goods for domestic markets but branched out into successful export businesses in jewellery, garments, processed food, artificial flowers, and other consumer goods. Several Thai-owned conglomerates have emerged, such as Siam Cement, Charoen Pokphand, Mitr Phol, and Saha Union. In each case they started in the traditionally strong sectors and then diversified. Siam Cement began in construction but later developed extensive manufacturing interests. Charoen Pokphand began in distribution but grew into a multinational agro-industry. Mitr Phol began as a sugarcane grower and then branched into sugar manufacturing. Saha Union began in distribution but later extended into manufacturing for the domestic market and export.

Among domestic capital, attitudes to foreign capital inflow varied from sector to sector but were generally antithetical. Especially in the areas of traditional strength (service, distribution, low-tech manufacture), domestic capital lobbied strongly for foreign capital to be excluded. In subsectors where domestic capital was strong and strongly organized, such pressure bore fruit. For instance, in banking, which is dominated by ten very powerful families, the Thai Bankers Association was successful in opposing the opening of banking and insurance to foreign companies. In the hotel trade, tourism, and construction, domestic capital lobbied government extensively and won some degree of favoritism with regard to foreign capital.

In manufacturing, the attitude to foreign capital was more pragmatic. In subsectors where Thai domestic capital saw that the only opportunity to gain access to the best technology lay through collaboration with foreign capital, foreign investment was generally welcomed, but pref-erably in a joint venture format that could benefit domestic capital in some way. In subsectors where technology was easily available, foreign capital was viewed as a threat, and domestic capital lobbied hard for government assistance to protect its interest. This has been evident in such areas as textiles and the manufacture of domestic appliances and automobile parts, in which domestic interests have lobbied government to limit promotional privileges to foreign firms.

The Thai government's attitude to foreign capital, therefore, was not influenced by the need to protect or extend the interest of state capital. Rather its attitude was molded by the lobbying of domestic capital interests and by its own estimation of foreign capital's contribution to state goals. In the 1960s, when domestic capital in manufacturing was still relatively weak, the Thai government gave in to pressure from the World Bank and the U.S. government to provide a legal framework for the promotion of foreign investment. As a result, the Investment Promotion Law was passed in 1962. But, significantly, this law applied equally to both domestic and foreign investment. It also required that a majority share in any enterprise be Thai-owned (under a separate agreement, this requirement was waived for American companies). These measures set the tone for the Thai government's attitude to foreign capital through the 1960s and 1970s. In general, the Thai government had no strong objections to foreign investment and provided a general framework for its operation, but it was hardly enthusiastic about encouraging foreign investment and tended to favor domestic capital interest by obliging foreign investors to enter into joint ventures.

In sum, the attitude of state and domestic capital in ASEAN in the 1960s and 1970s was rather lukewarm toward foreign and Japanese investment. In the 1980s this attitude changed, in part due to the recession of the early 1980s.

The Fiscal and Debt Crisis of the 1980s

Economic growth rates in the United States and other major industrialized countries slowed down in the early 1980s as these countries struggled to cope with the second oil price increase. Countries with high unemployment problems resorted to protectionism. Most countries abandoned the fixed exchange rate regime and adopted some form of the floating system, leading to greater fluctuations in the foreign exchange market. All of these reactions contributed to a decline in world trade. At about the same time over-supply of primary commodities depressed commodity prices in the world markets. The economies of the ASEAN countries were severely affected. Growth rates slowed markedly after 1981 and slumped in 1985 and 1986 at the lowest point of the recession.

In Singapore and Thailand the trade deficit widened. In Malaysia, the usual surplus was transformed into a small deficit. Indonesia reduced oil production in line with OPEC policy and saw its usually large trade balance severely reduced. The fall in oil prices after 1984 exacerbated the problems for both Malaysia and Indonesia. In all ASEAN countries, government revenue depended heavily on taxes levied on the import and export trade, so the trade recession affected government revenues. The share of government revenue in GDP declined in Indonesia from 1981 to 1985, remained constant in Malaysia, and increased only slightly in Singapore and Thailand. In certain countries in some years government revenue was actually reduced in real terms.

Most ASEAN countries had borrowed abroad during the low interest period in the 1970s to cover their trade and budget deficits. Indonesia in particular had borrowed heavily. The private sectors had also been tempted by low interest rates to borrow abroad to cover losses or increase capital. In the early 1980s, anti-inflationary macroeconomic policies in the industrial countries led to a rapid rise in the nominal interest rates, and ASEAN countries with large foreign debts were hit hard. The appreciation of the yen after 1985 exacerbated the problem as debts denominated in yen suddenly multiplied in size. Indonesia, which had around a third of its total debt denominated in yen, suffered especially badly.

The combination of decelerating GDP growth, rising interest rates, and rising yen exchange rates increased both the overall debt burden and the debt service ratio. Malaysia's total external debt as a percentage of GDP rose to 62% in 1985 and to 77% in 1986. In Indonesia external debt rose from 37 to 40% of GDP during the same years. In Thailand the absolute debt burden was less acute but the rise equally dramatic. From just 11% of GDP in 1970 the debt burden jumped to 36% by 1986.

The debt-service ratio in Indonesia rose from 8% in 1980 to 19.9% in 1985. In Malaysia during the same period the debt service ratio rose from 2.3% to 22.3%, and in Thailand from 3.4% to 14.7%. Only Singapore kept debt service at a manageable level. For the other three countries, by the mid-1980s debt service had become a major problem. It was also clear that the cause of the problem was the state sector, particularly the inefficiency of state enterprises. In all three countries, over 70% of the total external debt was public debt.

The recession of the mid-1980s thus became a turning point for state capital. The policy of heavy reliance on state capital for development was in disfavor. It had created inefficient industries that had saddled the countries with heavy debt problems. To escape the immediate recession, countries needed a new source of capital. In these circumstances government attitudes to foreign capital had to be revised: whereas it had once been seen as a potential competitor to state capital, it now promised to serve as a tool to aid the state achieve its aim of continued economic growth and continued revenue generation.

Changes in Foreign Investment Policies

Changes in policies toward foreign direct investment in most of the ASEAN countries took place during the 1980s, especially after 1985. All countries adopted some form of "privatization" and "deregulation" of the economy in favor of private domestic and foreign capital.

In Indonesia, the government had ruled in 1974 that all foreign ventures must eventually be transformed into minority holdings. In 1986 this rule was relaxed and foreign firms were allowed to hold up to 95% of the equity of a joint venture company for up to five years on the condition that the increase in foreign equity enhanced the firm's export capacity. The government had also in 1974 excluded all firms with any foreign equity participation from involvement in local distribution. This was revised in 1986 to allow joint venture firms with at least 75% Indonesian equity to engage in domestic distribution. Joint venture firms producing export products were also given access to low-interest export credit. Foreigners were allowed to purchase shares in the Indonesian capital market in December 1987, and in late 1988 various import monopolies were abolished and the wholesale, shipping, and banking industries were reopened for foreign participation. To improve the financial infrastructure and facilitate the operation of export firms, foreign banks were permitted to establish branches outside Jakarta.

The decline in oil prices and the debt crisis made it vital for the Indonesian government to increase exports. It was this economic factor that created the political will to liberalize the economy. Private domestic capital from both Chinese and Pribumi sources welcomed the change.

In Malaysia, several amendments to regulations affecting foreign investment were established in 1986. The government provided exemption from income and development tax for companies engaged in manufacturing new products or undertaking modernization, expansion, or diversification. In addition, the Bumiputera rule for foreign firms was modified: foreign-owned firms were completely exempted from the requirements for Bumiputera shareholding and employment if they were medium-sized or if they exported at least 80% of their output. The government also gave firms until 1990 to apply for permission for 100% foreign ownership as long as they exported at least 50% of their output, employed at least 350 Malaysian workers, had a reasonable proportion of ethnic Malay workers, and did not compete against existing locally produced goods in the local market.

In Thailand, the government in the 1960s had set up a framework for promoting investment, including foreign investment. But until the 1980s the government had never felt an urgent need to promote foreign capital as a means to achieve economic growth. As a result the operation of the investment promotion machinery for foreign firms was allowed to become entangled in bureaucratic red tape. The foreign minority equity rule was strictly enforced. Foreign investors regularly complained, and the World Bank constantly agitated for reform. Nothing much resulted, however, until the recession of 1985–1986 saddled Thailand with a hugh trade deficit and a high debt burden. The government then took a renewed interest in foreign capital. Measures were taken to speed up the procedures for granting promotion. The restrictions on foreign equity share were interpreted more flexibly. Firms that exported 100% of their product could now have 100% foreign ownership. Firms that exported at least 20% of their total output could automatically apply for such export promotion incentives as exemption of business and export taxes on export sales.

To sum up, Singapore had positively encouraged foreign capital inflow since the mid-1960s, but in the other three countries the government's attitude to foreign capital was influenced by its desire to promote state capital and, in the case of Thailand, to nurture domestic capital as well. The world recession, exchange rate adjustments, and oil price drop created a fiscal and debt crisis that undermined the position of state capital. Deregulation, privatization and investment promotion policies were quickly implemented to attract private capital, especially in export industries.

In all four countries, the government reacted to the crisis of the early 1980s by encouraging foreign capital inflow rather than by promoting domestic capital directly. There were several reasons for this choice. First, domestic capital generally lacked the technology needed to compete in international markets and lacked easy access to these markets; in both respects, foreign capital was better equiped. Further, in the case of Malaysia and to a smaller extent Indonesia, a policy of promoting domestic capital would involve high political costs that the governments were not prepared to bear.

Domestic Capital and the Demand for Foreign Investment

While the debt problems of the mid-1980s had a direct impact on the attitude of ASEAN governments to the inflow of foreign capital, the accompanying recession also influenced the attitude of domestic capital in the countries concerned.

First, the difficulties experienced by government had an immediate impact on domestic capital in those countries where domestic capital still depended greatly on links with government and with state capital. Decline in the number and profitability of government-awarded contracts and a slowdown in joint public-private projects prompted major domestic capital interests to reevaluate the prospects of working in joint ventures with foreign capital.

This was particularly visible in Indonesia, the ASEAN country with the most predominating state capital sector, where some of the major business groups associated closely with the government increased the extent of their joint-venture business, particularly in cooperation with the Japanese.

Such joint venture business was not a new phenomenon, but it increased dramatically in scale. The major ethnic Chinese business groups that enjoyed government favor led the trend. The Liem group established assembly projects with Hino, Suzuki, and Mazda and entered into housing development in a joint venture with Marubeni. The other leading ethnic Chinese group, Astra, has joint venture projects in automobile assembly with Toyota, Daihatsu, and Honda and has expanded into manufacture of automobile components in cooperation with Nippondenso, into producing engines for cars with Daihatsu and Toyota, and into manufacture of motorcycles with Honda. The group also has joint ventures with Japanese capital in distribution for Fuji Xerox, Toyota, Honda motorcycles, and Komatsu tractors. The Roda Mas group (Tan Siong Kie, alias Hanafi) is another leading Chinese business group that has prospered in joint investment, allying with Asahi Glass to manufacture glass and plastics and with Sumitomo. Major Pribumi groups have also been active in joint prospects with the Japanese, albeit on a lesser scale than the major ethnic Chinese combines. The Gobel group has joint investments with Matsushita and Osaki Denki Kogyo. The Poleko group cooperates with Toray in synthetic textiles, with Mitsui in a plywood adhesive factory, and with Kao in a chemical factory. The Samudra group and the Mercu Buana group have also invested jointly with Japanese capital.

A second reason for the change in attitude in domestic capital is that during the recession in the early 1980s, producers of consumer goods for the home markets faced decline or stagnant demand as the GNP growth rates slowed down or turned negative in some countries. At the same time, some producers of labor-intensive export products fared much better. This was particularly true of companies able to penetrate the market in Japan, which was far more buoyant than markets in the West. Some of these were joint-venture firms whose foreign partners provided access to technology and external markets. Others were locally owned firms, producing labor-intensive products (such as jewellery, artificial flowers, animal feed, frozen chicken, and canned sea food) in which the firms had a clear comparative advantage.

The success of the export firms, some of which gained technology and access to export markets through the collaboration with a foreign joint partner, created demonstration effects for other firms.

Two major characteristics defined the firms that were able to respond most readily to these demonstration effects. First, they often had a past history of cooperation with the Japanese, usually in assembly and distribution operations targeted at the domestic market. Such firms had already been through the learning process of working with the Japanese and had their business contacts already in place. In many cases it was relatively simple to upgrade from an assembly or distribution operation to manufacture of the same product range for both the domestic and export markets. In other cases, existing Japanese-domestic joint ventures branched out into new product lines in which the host country enjoyed a comparative advantage. And in other cases, domestic firms with existing Japanese joint ventures entered into additional ventures with totally separate Japanese groups. Second, most of the responsive firms were the larger and more developed business combines. They had the management resources to expand quickly for new ventures. And they were attractive partners for Japanese capital on account of their size and influence.

Both of these characteristics were evident in Thai firms. Many of the leading industrialists in Thailand had begun as trading firms selling Japanese and other foreign imports. Pornavalai (1989) reported that of 211 companies under the umbrella of 24 leading business groups in Thailand, 76 have had some business links with foreign firms in the past. Of the 76 companies, 61 have had business links with Japanese firms. Also, most of the large conglomerates in Thailand, regardless of whether they have past experience in Japanese joint ventures, have been keen to enter into joint prospects since the mid-1980s. These ventures cover a wide range—real estate, tourism, automobile parts, electrical machinery, electronics, and petro-chemical and other export products. They are attracted to Japanese collaboration because it offers technology, management knowhow, and access to Japanese and other markets. The country's largest industrial combine, the Siam Cement Group, has since 1980 become increasingly enmeshed in ventures with Japanese capital. It has cooperated with Kubota and Marubeni in manufacture of Diesel engines for agricultural machinery; with Hino in automobile parts; with Toto in sanitary ware and sanitary porcelain; with Toshiba, Mitsubishi, Philips, and a consortium of local firms in color television tubes; and with Asahi Glass in manufacture of bulb glass and color televisions.

The Siam Motors group is another large Thai business combine with a long history of cooperation with Nissan in assembly and distribution of automobiles. It is now extending this joint venture to undertake manufacture of Diesel and gasoline engines, while other companies in the Siam Motors Group are joining with Komatsu to produce construction machinery, with Hitachi to make elavators, and with Daikin to make compression engines. Nissan has already announced plans to use Thailand as a base to supply the markets of Taiwan, Malaysia, Bangladesh, and Pakistan.

Another Thai firm, Charoen Pokphand, provides an example of a firm with no previous Japanese relations that has entered into a joint venture with Japanese capital in the mid-1980s. Begun in 1921 as an import-export firm specializing in agro-products, Charoen Pokphand entered into a joint venture with a U.S. firm in 1970 to import poultry breeding stock. In the 1970s and early 1980s the firm grew into a diversified agro-product combine with operations in Indonesia, Taiwan, Malaysia, China, and Thailand. It embarked in the mid-1980s on a joint venture with Japanese capital to develop quality shrimp stock.

Not all domestic capital was as keen to enter into Japanese joint ventures or to welcome an inflow of Japanese investment. In several ASEAN states, domestic businesses that experienced no direct gain from the Japanese inflow expressed resentment. While large business combines have often been the most open to Japanese investments, smaller business interests have often been the most opposed.

While the large Thai companies have benefited much from collaboration with Japanese capital, it has not come about without tensions, especially in cases where such joint investments that are entitled to promotional privileges come into direct conflict with smaller producers who are already supplying the local markets. These small and medium-sized firms that do not benefit directly continue to see Japanese investment as a threat. In particular, the government's decision to allow 100% Japanese enterprises to enter into some new export businesses and to release up to 20% of their output into the local market has created resentment among competing domestic firms.

In Indonesia, Pribumi entrepreneurs have continued to be suspicious of Japanese investment, but some have begun to look to the possibility of joint ventures with Japanese in export businesses or in tourist businesses as a means to counter the decline in subcontracting business from the government sector. In Singapore, the domestic retail trade has complained against competition from foreign companies and tried to lobby the government for assistance in excluding or limiting foreign √ competition. In manufacturing, small firms have lobbied for government support. In response the government has established a Small Enterprise Bureau within the Economic Development Board to help develop the small-scale sector, not in competition with foreign firms but in support of them through subcontracting arrangements.

In Malaysia the question of support for or opposition to foreign investment has been colored by the investment regulations and the political environment. In general, major Bumiputera business groups have supported foreign investment. Even when allowed to operate as 100%-owned subsidiaries, several foreign firms prefer to take Bumiputera partners as a strategy to reduce business risks. Foreign alliances help merging Bumiputera business groups grow stronger. At the same time, ethnic Chinese capital has found the new regulations, particularly the 1986 modifications to the Industrial Coordination Act, discriminatory. Under certain conditions, foreign firms can be exempted from the rules requiring medium and large firms to have a certain level of Bumiputera shareholding and a certain level of Bumiputera employment; but local firms owned by Chinese capital do not have the same exemption. In certain areas, ethnic Chinese firms find that they now face increased competition from foreign firms or foreign-Bumiputera joint ventures.

The recession of the mid-1980s increased the demand for foreign investment in the ASEAN states. Whereas governments had earlier tended to see foreign capital as a potential threat to the development of state capital, this issue became progressively less relevant as the role of state capital diminished (at different rates in different countries). Meanwhile, the recession of trade and, in particular, the explosive debt problem made foreign investment attractive as a strategy to regenerate growth and reduce the debt burden. In several ASEAN states, official regulation of foreign investment was substantially liberalized in the years 1985 to 1987.

The recession also influenced the attitude of domestic capital. While the impact on governments was sudden and resulted in a dramatic revision of policies in a short space of years in the middle of the decade, the change in attitude on the part of domestic capital followed a gradual and rising trend beginning in the late 1970s. While firms that concentrated on the domestic market bore the brunt of the recession and the exhaustion of prospects for import-substituting growth, firms that had access to still buoyant markets overseas, particularly in Japan, fared better. Many such firms were joint ventures that benefited from the access to technology and export markets.

The firms that responded most readily to the potential advantages of joint ventures for export tended to be large firms with the management capacity for expansion and often with a history of cooperation with overseas capital, particularly Japanese. In many cases firms that had previously undertaken joint ventures in assembly and distribution now expanded into manufacture for both domestic and export markets. In other cases major domestic business interests contracted a whole new series of ventures with overseas capital.

By and large, small-scale domestic capital was less keen on the inflow of investment that increased the scale of competition from foreign concerns and from joint venture concerns involving large-scale domestic partners. In Malaysia and Indonesia, attitudes to foreign investment were also affected by the political context. In both cases the groups that benefited were those supported by the government, either through formal regulation or through networks of joint interests and informal ties, while those that were excluded tended to show resentment.

Future Prospects and Conclusions

In this concluding section the future prospects for JDI and the impact on local capital in the four ASEAN member countries are outlined in the light of the forgoing analysis.

On the supply side, structural change in Japan will continue. Labor, land, and other costs will keep rising. Technological advance will continue. Japan will have fewer labor-intensive industries to relocate; in their place, more firms with specific advantages will go out in the world trying to realize an optimum profit from their accumulated knowledge and innovative technology. Thus we can expect the outflow of Japanese capital to continue, because of both continuing changes in comparative advantage and the growth of oligopolistic firms. In the future the outflow of foreign investment due to growth of oligopolistic firms will become increasingly more important and also the new form of investment.

In a medium-term time frame, given the estimation that the ASEAN member countries will continue to grow at reasonable rates of 6–8% a year, we can expect Japanese firms to continue to want to invest in the region, not only because of natural resources and cheap labor, but also because of ASEAN potential as a market.

But there are possibilities that JDI may divert from ASEAN. There is the possibility of a reverse flow back to Japan as a result of improvement in automation technology, as in the case of high-quality garment manufacturing. There is a possibility of JDI flow diverting from ASEAN to the European Community (EC) following the integration in 1992, to China, and to South Asia. Finally, the building of consensus in Japan against the outflow of foreign direct investment (due to the fear of hollowing out) in manufacturing may stem the JDI outflow.

How likely are these possibilities to be realized in the next five years? Some JDI may be reversed to Japan due to improvement in automation technology. But there is a limit to automation—there will still be many production processes that require labor inputs as well as materials. On the possibility of JDI diverting to non-ASEAN locations, the most likely new locations will be China, Indochina, and South Asia. But increased JDI in those places will also benefit ASEAN, as it will entail increased demand for intermediate and semi-processed materials from ASEAN. As for JDI flow to the EC, much JDI has already gone to the EC in anticipation of the 1992 integration. More will go, but the amount will not be that substantial during the next five years.

On the question of hollowing out: Policy makers and the public may have such fears and want to retain the core production processes of manufacturing industries within Japan. But what the public wants and what the firms want may be two different things. As far as the firms are concerned, as they become more global in their outlook and in their investment planning, borders become less relevant. What matters to them is the growth of the firm. The attempt to maintain the core production processes within Japan may be successful up to a point, but to restrict Japanese direct investment altogether is not possible.

The fear of JDI diversion from ASEAN is not such a serious problem. ASEAN can expect to receive more foreign investment from such other sources as Singapore, South Korea, and Taiwan, which are now experiencing the same problems of high labor costs, rising currencies, and increased maturity of the economy as are found in Japan.

A more interesting question is in what way ASEAN demand for

Japanese direct investment may change. In our approach, state and domestic capital play an active role in the game. The increase in demand for JDI from these two actors helps to facilitate the JDI flow in host countries. Their demand can also affect the form and types of JDI.

First, as long as mutual benefits can be obtained from joint investment and as long as the resentment felt by small and medium size local producers over the issue of competition is not taken up by the government (which suggests that the issue is not yet important enough), then we can expect a high demand for JDI to continue from domestic capital. Over time, however, the demand will also depend on: (a) the possibility of gaining a better bargain from some other source, such as Asian NIEs, Europe, and the United States; and (b) the "quality" of Japanese investment, which will increasingly become more important than the volume as domestic capitalists themselves become stronger and more experienced. Increasingly also, domestic capital will want to have more control over the operation of the joint enterprise. We may expect local capital to want more share in the management of the joint enterprises. Factor (a) may stabilize the demand for JDI. But given the present trends we may expect JDI to be the most important source of foreign capital and technology in ASEAN countries at least for the next five years. With factor (b) operating (especially in Singapore and Thailand) we may expect an increase in the demand for such nontraditional direct investments as licensing agreements and the new forms of investment that involve technology and management tie-ups with lower levels of direct equity participation from Japanese partners. With this development we may expect greater demand for participation in the management of joint enterprises. The demand for the new forms of investment in itself reflects the local capitalists' desire for more autonomy.

Second, regarding the demand for overall flow of JDI, in our framework demand will increase as the perception of the utility of JDI continues to be favorable. So far, for the period considered, the views of the state and the important sections of domestic capital have coincided; both view Japanese direct investment in a favorable light. This facilitates the JDI inflow. Will this continue during the next five years? Up to now JDI has been acceptable to the state and the important sections of local private capital because JDI is contributing to the GNP growth rates. Further, the JDI inflow has contributed much to the wealth of the top echelon of the business sectors. But we must not forget that for Indonesia, Malaysia, and Thailand, where income inequality is high (Gini coefficient of around .5 for Malaysia and Thailand), the enrichment of the top echelon of the business community is going to widen the income gap. Luckily, for 1987–1989 the JDI flow (really flowing in 1987–1988) coincided with the improvements in the commodity prices and the tourist boom. The latter is also true of Singapore. The combined favorable effects of all these impetuses on the economy enabled the increased income to trickle down and reduce the incidence of poverty, though not the growing income gap. The relatively high growth rates allowed the trickle-down effects to take place and blurred the tensions due to income inequality.

If, however, the three large ASEAN economies covered in our study again faced an economic crisis due to a dramatic decline in commodity prices, and/or a stagnation of manufactured export growth, the problems of income inequality might flare up as an economic and political issue. The public could blame an over-dependence on JDI as the major cause of the recession and economic difficulties. In such a situation, groups opposing JDI (small and medium local producers and other groups who resent JDI's presence and competition) will join forces and may become a pressure group, which, if strong enough, may force the government to limit the inflow of JDI.

There is also an issue related to the relations between domestic capital, state capital, and foreign capital. An interesting question at this juncture is what is the likely impact of JDI on the relative strength of state and domestic capital.

Although this subject requires more empirical research, it is not too early to judge. There is evidence that indicates that the new JDI is likely to lead to a significant strengthening of domestic capital. We base our preliminary judgement on the prevailing competitive forces that will compel Japanese firms to use local subcontractors, to train local employees, to provide technical assistance to local suppliers in order to remain competitive in world markets vis-à-vis competitors from Asian NIEs. We also believe in the dynamism of domestic capital in countries like Singapore, Thailand, Indonesia, and Malaysia; we believe in its increasing abilities (gained through the process of learning by doing) to adapt and accumulate management skills and technical capabilities through increasing exposure to Japanese multinationals. The speed and the extent of the process of improvement in technical capabilities, however, varies from country to country depending on the policies of the government and the strength and vitality of domestic capital.

The relevant policy areas are research and development expenditure by the government and assistance to local firms in this area; the skill development of human resources; the competitive environment in which firms operate; and the issue of joint investment versus 100% foreign-owned firms. R&D, the human resource development issues, and the competitive environment are old themes. ASEAN countries will best benefit from JDI if the workforce has a high capacity to absorb technology transfer—and this means an upgrading of the educational levels of the labor force, as well as a stepping up of R&D assistance for local firms. On the competitive environment, the crucial issue is to strengthen the competitiveness of domestic capital by forcing it to compete in the world market rather than to protect it with high tariffs. As Ariff and Hill conclude, foreign investment works best in an environment where free trade is operative, not in protected situations.

The policy issue of joint investment versus 100% foreign-owned firms is relatively new. During the 1960s and 1970s, most JDI was in joint ventures with local capital for the reason that local equity is in the majority operative in most countries. The Japanese comply because such collaboration could reduce the risk elements involved in operating in alien situations. In the era of the new wave of JDI, small and medium firms in export-oriented industries from Japan would like to retain 100% foreign ownership. Host countries comply for fear that a continued stringent equity rule may turn away Japanese investment at the time when the economies need it. Such open policy has an advantage in that it does not discourage firms with special specific advantages. But 100% foreign firms, producing for exports by assembling components and parts imported from their own subsidiaries from all over the region, tend to resort to transfer-pricing among themselves in order to get around government regulations and taxation. The venture is profitable for the firm. But from the economy's point of view the society may not be getting the best deal out of the investment. One or two of these firms are acceptable. But too many may prevent domestic capital from gaining the benefits of transfer of management expertise and other technological knowhow and of profit-sharing, which is possible under the alternative of joint-venture arrangements. This is an area that deserves attention. On the evidence of the lobbying power of domestic capital in Thailand and in Indonesia, it may be argued that in the medium term, domestic capital itself, as it becomes stronger, will keep a check on this. Over the short term, however, the government may overlook the issue because of the acute need for foreign capital to cope with balance of payments problems and unemployment.

The retreat of state capital in the mid-1980s and the ascendancy of private domestic and foreign capital has important implications for the prospects of political development in the countries covered in our study.

The economic recession (and in the case of Malaysia and Indonesia, the fall in oil prices) causes the state to be in retreat. But the situation could reverse again if circumstances allow the state sector to grow anew and to become a major impetus in the economy. The liberalization policies and the pressure for the contraction of the state sector after 1985, however, quickly permitted the domestic capital sector as well as the middle class to grow and expand rather rapidly—and they cannot be cut back. The modern bourgeoisie is here to stay, and it will in the long term become an important social force in balancing the former power of the state, which in some countries still lies with the military. Unless the region faces a dramatic economic recession again, it will become increasingly more difficult for a nondemocratic government to maintain itself in power.

In the 1960s and 1970s JDI was criticized as being exploitative and as having a limited impact on industrial development efforts of ASEAN countries. In the 1980s this image is changing. The impact that this new investment has already had on local capital indicates the more positive contribution that Japan's investment can have on ASEAN's efforts to promote industrial development and the economic well-being of its populace. The picture painted here is not without problems. The future depends very much on the role of governments and the ability of ASEAN to sustain consistent high economic growth over a long period—at least another decade. As local capital is strengthened, Japanese investors will face tougher partners. They will have to be prepared to share the control of the joint enterprises in terms of both production and financial management.

Comment

Tetsuo Abo

Professor Pasuk presents an important view of Japanese direct investments in ASEAN countries during the 1980s from a macroeconomic
perspective, with special focus on the "demand side" of foreign direct
investment (FDI)—that is, demand from the local government, domestic capital, and the local public for investment by Japanese firms (in
response to the supply of Japanese capital).

Analysis of FDI or the multinational enterprise (MNE) is usually
conducted primarily from the "supply side" of foreign firms, focusing
on the determinants of FDI, where locational aspects are taken up as
an attractive feature of the host country. But Professor Pasuk emphasizes
the importance of the environment that has been produced by local
economic and political conditions, and which has played a significant
role in accelerating a "new form" of FDI since the 1970s.

This emphasis is, in a sense, similar to that of our joint research
project entitled "Local Production of Japanese Automobile and Electronics Industries in the United States—Application and Adaptation of
Japanese Management," which, like Professor Yamashita's project, has
been assisted by the Toyota Foundation. The application aspect refers
to the transfer of the comparative advantages of the MNE to the host
country, so that "application" corresponds to the supply side. On the
other hand, we also emphasize the necessity or inevitability of "adaptation" to local economic and social conditions, which corresponds to
the demand side, and we want to find a special relationship between
application and adaptation.

At any rate, Professor Pasuk has illuminated vividly how nationalistic
and protectionism-oriented local governments and domestic capital in
ASEAN countries have traditionally changed. Since the early 1980s both
sectors have demanded Japanese FDI in correspondence with the supply
side conditions of Japanese firms.

The following questions concerning the paper may contribute to
further productive discussion.

First, we can foresee some results of the response of the supply side to the demand for FDI. Here the demand is to have export-oriented firms or technologies introduced in order to achieve a balance of payments surplus, which Professor Yamashita calls "quick establishment of the export base."

Such a demand may result in hardware-oriented technology transfer, then a sizable increase in imports of machines and equipment, key parts and components from Japan and other countries, and finally balance-of-payment burdens, just as in the case of the Asian NIEs. The demand also may result in a considerable increase in the number of "coordinators" (not necessarily top managers) brought in from Japan in order to secure high quality and efficiency. Many Japanese coodinators are being sent overseas, even to the United States. This is the human aspect of technology transfer, which, I believe, is the critical condition for Japanese multinational firms, in contrast to Western ones.

Second, the paper succeeds in explaining consistently the cause of the sharp increase in Japanese FDI in ASEAN countries in the 1980s as an interaction between demand and supply. Professor Pasuk, from a macroeconomic perspective, considers both cost factors (lower wage rates and so on) in host countries and technological development and structural change in the Japanese economy as the background of Japanese FDI. But quantitative aspects of such production factors as costs do not constitute sufficient conditions to explain why Japanese firms are increasingly investing in ASEAN countries as opposed to, say, South Asia, Latin America (FDI has already been initiated in Mexico), or even in Africa. In this regard I think that the special quality of human resources in East Asia should be taken into account as an important factor on the demand side.

Additionally, I partly agree with Professor Pasuk's criticism of Professor Kojima's theory in that Professor Kojima disregards, just as U.S. models do, the development of Japanese FDI—in a word, his thesis is normative. But at the same time I should point out that the theses put forth by Professor Kojima or Professor Ozawa are not necessarily much different from such American models as the product life cycle theory. In my understanding, however, the macro theory based on American types of investment would not be sufficient to illuminate completely the characteristic behaviors of Japanese-type multinationals, which have been setting up their manufacturing plants in the East Asian countries, not simply because of cheap labor, but also because of socio-cultural familiality with Japan. This means that the micro level, qualitative differences of production factors such as human resources should be incorporated as one of the comparative advantages in the theory of multinational enterprise.

Finally, one of the most interesting points in Professor Pasuk's paper concerns the similarities and differences between the four ASEAN countries studied. Both are far more impressive than I had thought, initially assuming as I had that both similarities and differences might be closely related to the manners of existence of ethnic Chinese people in ASEAN countries.

3

The Global Context and the New Wave of Japanese Investment in Thailand

Suthy Prasartset

The Global Context of Internationalization of Capital

The evolution of the economic relationship between Japan and Thailand cannot be properly grasped without placing it into the global context of the internationalization of capital. In the following discussion we will briefly outline such a process from a world-system perspective. Through the operation of the law of accumulation and the continuing development of productive forces, the capitalist system tends to expand beyond national frontiers to integrate socio-economic formations outside it, a process that eventually brought about the emergence and consolidation of the world capitalist system or transnational capitalism of the contemporary historical period.

Among contemporary writers, Baran (1957), Frank (1967, 1969), Amin (1974, 1975), Wallerstein (1974, 1980), Cardoso (1972), and Dos Santos (1969) have, with varying emphases, analyzed the process of accumulation on a world scale in the following aspects: a) its historical development, especially its cyclical movements in the long-wave of economic upswing and downswing; b) its structural transformation, especially in the tendency toward new international divisions of labor; and c) continuing differentiation into center and periphery formations owing to the law of uneven development with its resultant unequal relationship in the world capitalist system.

Other writers have also discussed this phenomenon and proposed interesting and penetrating theoretical insights for an analysis of the present phase of global accumulation in which the transnational corporations play a dominant role. Murray (1971) and Hymer (1972) designate this contemporary phase of capital accumulation as the "internationalization of capital," while Polk (1973) conceives it as the "new international production." Palloix (1975, 1977) draws attention to

55

the process of self-expansion of capital on a world scale, especially the internationalization of the circuit of the productive capital. On the other hand, Frobel, Heinrichs, and Kreye (1980) have explained and analyzed this new phenomena as the trend toward "the new international division of labor." Sunkel and Fuenzalida (1979) alternatively explain it as the process of transnationalization and the formation of transnational capitalism.

Although the world capitalist system had undergone a long-term historical transformation in terms of the long-wave of economic upswing and downswing, it was during the latest wave of economic upswing in the years 1945–1970 that the environment was congenial for the rapid growth of modern corporations. This new and viable institutional form of capital, which emerged from the organizational innovation of the last economic downturn, has expanded dramatically and grown into the transnational corporation, which now has a dominant role in the world capitalist system. Again, the outcome of the struggles in both the center and the periphery had been fully revealed during the 1945–1970 period: the rise of new hegemonic power (the United States) and the collapse of the second wave of formal colonialism that had established itself firmly before the First World War. Relative stability and peace under the hegemony of the United States brought about a relatively stable regime of free trade under the arrangements of GATT and the support of such multilateral institutions as the World Bank (IBRD) and the International Monetary Fund (IMF) (Bergesen 1980).

It was during this period of expansion that the internationalization of the circuit of productive capital took place on a large scale and with a long-term perspective. During this period also all circuits of capital became internationalized concurrently. The transnational corporations (TNCs) as the most powerful institutional form of capitalism in the present historical epoch have embraced all circuits of capital within their ambits in their internationalization: that is, the circuit of commodity capital (C......C) the circuit of money capital (M......M) and the circuit of productive capital (P......P). The internationalization of the first circuit is evident in the trade figure, which surpassed $300 billion in 1972. It is striking that the intra-firm trade of the TNCs accounted for about 30% of world trade in the same year. The two figures have since grown tremendously. On the other hand, the book value of international investment, which stood at $165 billion in 1971 for the center (for example, $86 billion for the United States, $24 billion for Britain), is a clear manifestation of the internationalization of the circuit of money capital.

The internationalization of the circuit of productive capital is estimated from the foreign production of the various "national capitals" at no less than $330 billion for 1971. Palloix further emphasizes that the internationalization of this circuit of capital is growing even more rapidly than world trade. In a similar vein Polk (1973:17, 20) also argues that the internationalized production has been growing faster than the non-internationalized sectors and that this trend will continue into the twenty-first century.

Regarding international relations, the eventual outcome of the anti-colonial struggles, especially after the Second World War, was a new system of multilateral arrangements that were initiated and proliferated through the support of such newly formed "international" institutions as IMF, IBRD, and GATT. Since then a new system of global international division of labor based on a center-periphery relation has been largely forged, transformed, and proliferated by these powerful institutions in close collaboration with the state apparatus of the hegemonic powers and allies and the transnational corporate conglomerates.

This process involves a new division of labor between the center and the periphery: what Frobel, Heinrichs, and Kreye (1980) characterized as the tendency toward the new international division of labor (NIDL). The emerging new model of accumulation in the postwar period increasingly necessitated a further integration of the periphery into the world capitalist system through the NIDL process. According to Frobel et al. (1980: 45) this process designates the tendency that (a) undermines the traditional bisection of the world into a few industrialized countries on one hand and a great majority of developing countries integrated into the world economy solely as raw material producers on the other; and (b) compels the increasing subdivision of manufacturing processes into a number of partial operations at different industrial sites throughout the world, where the division of labor should be understood as an ongoing process and not as a final result.

This means that for the first time in centuries the peripheral countries have now become manufacturing sites on a tremendous and growing scale. Concomitantly the production process had the potential to be increasingly fragmented into a variety of partial operations to be performed worldwide at different locations—and that is what has happened as part of the process of worldwide reorganization of industrial production stemming from changed conditions for the advanced industrial countries regarding capital expansion. The changed conditions include:

1. The existence of a worldwide industrial reserve army or an inex-

haustible supply of unemployed cheap labor in the periphery
2. An efficient transport, communication, and information technology that renders the industrial location and the control of production increasingly less dependent on geographical distance
3. The possibility of a far-reaching subdivision of production processes into fragments that will enable even unskilled laborers to perform otherwise complex operations after a short period of training
4. Demographic changes causing chronic labor shortages and structural changes in the industrial sector as a result of technological transformation in the central countries, making several manufacturing processes obsolete and internationally non-competitive and consequently requiring such industries to be relocated overseas where conditions are more favorable.

NIDL has therefore brought about "world market-oriented production" in the periphery, which comprises "both production for the domestic markets of the host countries (so-called import substitution) and production for markets traditionally supplied by the industries of the advanced countries themselves (so-called export production)" (Frobel et al. 1978: 24).

The global expansion of capital led by the TNCs has been fundamentally premised on certain forms of institutional and legal arrangements at a global level, what we might appropriately designate as the "global superstructure." According to Frobel et al. (1980:37) the elements of global superstructure include: the rudiments of institutionalized multilateral or bilateral cooperation in monetary and trade policies (IMF, GATT); tax agreements to avoid double taxation; treaties for investment protection; increased compatibility of training and education in international military cooperation; and "neutral" international organizations that pave the way for transnational capital under the guise of supplying technical and managerial expertise for "development" (IBRD, UNIDO, FAO).

Such international organizations were created basically to carry out at the transnational level functions that individual corporations could not perform. IMF and IBRD, in particular, often set conditions on loans in order to press governments of developing countries to follow certain monetary, fiscal, and tariff policies that are consistent with the interests that they represent. These organizations' activities consequently constitute a control mechanism that is aimed at further integration of the periphery into the world system through the process of NIDL.

The process of NIDL results not only from the relocation of the transnational capital productive facilities to new sites in the Third World but also from the promotional policies of the host countries. In order to carry on import-substituting industrialization and later export-oriented industrialization, restructuring of existing institutions and establishment of new ones is needed. Such was the case in Thailand during the Sarit regime around 1960. According to James Petras (1979) the conditions essential to integration into the world capitalist system and thereby to facilitation of the process of global accumulation include the following activities:

1. "State-building"—creating the formal machinery of government in order to secure the groundwork for effective exploitation; the creation of a sound army and police force is crucial to this process
2. Eliminating or containing internal dissidents
3. Minimizing external competition
4. Creating the economic infrastructure through loans and "aid."

In the process of state- or institution-building, U.S. agencies and IBRD have played the key role (Bell 1978).

Examining the process as it unfolded in Thailand, we can identify three related aspects of state-building: 1) that which facilitates the process of capital accumulation; 2) that which maintains legitimacy; 3) that which maintains existing social relations.

We will deal only with the first aspect in what follows. The first aspect of state-building in Thailand included the establishment of such institutions to facilitate capital accumulation as the Budget Bureau, Board of Investment, National Economic Development Board, Ministry of National Development, and Industrial Finance Corporation. These new government agencies were created during the years 1959–1963 in order to "rationalize capitalist development" (Bell 1978: 61). To provide manpower for such agencies, the U.S. transnational philanthropic foundations had been active in financing the training of Thai officials in U.S. universities, "where they absorbed the social science theory and ideological perspective of their U.S. counterparts" (Bell 1978: 62).

The U.S. agencies and philanthropic foundations were later responsible for establishing such education programs and institutes in Thailand as the agricultural programs formulated by the Agricultural Development Council at Kasetsart University, the National Institute of Development Administration, and so on. Through the U.S. training and such local institutions the Thai technocrats and academicians absorbed the value system consistent with the transnational corporate interests, especially regarding adherence to the ideology of developmentalism, consumerism, and militarism, or the doctrine of national security (Prasartset 1985). These ideological practices, as expressed concretely in public policies, are facilitating the process of accumulation led by the transnational capital in partnership with the local bourgeoisie and hence are enhancing the process of transnationalization of the Thai social formation. Indeed, these institutions provide the economic and social infrastructure for such an accumulation process.

It is obvious from the preceding discussion that a favorable socio-economic and legal environment had come into being through the close collaboration between the Thai state and the international organizations, providing an attractive climate for the expansion of global accumulation and the further integration of Thailand into the world capitalist system. In this regard Japanese investors have been in a more advantageous position to avail themselves of such open and favorable state policies towards foreign capital.

Restructuring and Internationalization of Japanese Capital

The internationalization of Japanese capital is a recent phenomenon, beginning only after Japan's postwar success in reconstructing a viable economy with solid industrial bases. In fact Japanese overseas investments before and during World War II were either much damaged or completely liquidated by the end of the war. But by the early 1970s Japan had reemerged as a leading investor in Asia, ranking by 1972 after only the United States and the United Kingdom in foreign direct investment in Asia (Ozawa 1979: 77).

It is also interesting to note that throughout the 1950s Japan was mostly preoccupied with reconstructing its own economy. At that time Japan had to depend heavily on the West, especially the United States, for capital, technology, and markets. Only after the early 1960s, when Japan was able to achieve sustained economic growth, did it begin to look to other Asian countries, especially those so-called NICs and those in ASEAN, for additional markets and sources of new investment and raw material supplies.

The attitude of the people in such Asian countries were however still much affected by wartime memories of Japanese soldiers, and nationalist sentiments remained very strong. In this regard the United Nations First Development Decade, which started in 1960, did much to dispel the entrenched feelings of nationalism at the time. Several Asian countries were then keen to undertake an outward-looking industrialization strategy for national development. Among the early recipients of

Japanese foreign direct investment were of course Taiwan, South Korea, Hong Kong, and Singapore, to be followed later by ASEAN countries.

In the latter half of the 1960s Japan suffered such an acute shortage of young workers in factories in labor-intensive operations that wages rose rapidly. Moreover, the small- and medium-sized firms were not at all attractive to the young workers as their working facilities were still traditional. Such firms were most severely affected by the situation and forced to look for labor forces and new industrial sites in such neighboring countries as Taiwan, Korea, and so on.

This expansion process was reinforced by Japan's Ministry of International Trade and Industry (MITI) policy of relocation of noncompetitive industries to Asian countries where economic and social conditions for production were more favorable than those in Japan. As a consequence, "the labor-intensive, low-productivity, and low value-added end of Japan's dual industrial structure has been pushed out of Japan to developing countries, particularly in Asia," which can be testified to by the fact that the value-added labor ratio for Japanese manufacturing affiliates in Asia in 1972 was only 46% of that in Japan, while the same ratios for North America and Europe were 342% and 146% in that order (Ozawa 1979: 82). The process of the internationalization of Japanese capital has thus come into being.

The Japanese capital internationalization process has been explained by several scholars, each of whom has presented an interesting perspective. According to Ozawa (1979: 69), Japan's drive toward internationalization of capital was "motivated by the uncertain supplies of overseas resources and by the irremovable scarcities of labor and industrial space at home." This had been the situation since the late 1960s, by which time Japan had achieved great success in world trade and an accumulation of surplus capital that was available to invest in profitable fields overseas.

The pattern of the internationalization of Japanese capital was unique, however, and cannot be explained by Western economists' theories. Ozawa (1979: 69) described such explanations as micro-oriented theories that concentrate on the growth process of the national firms, which, after acquiring "superior economic efficiency" (à la Harry Johnson) or "techno-structure" (à la John Kenneth Galbraith) expand overseas for enhanced operating capacity.

The factors that really lead to overseas expansion of Japanese firms are, on the contrary, macro-oriented in nature, for instance, emerging factor scarcities, increasing uncertainty associated with imports of key resources, and more especially the declining competitiveness of Japan's labor-intensive industries (Ozawa 1979: 69–70). More important, Western firms before going overseas operate within an oligopolistic structure in their home market. Their Japanese counterparts, on the other hand, operate within a "relatively competitive" market structure. Ozawa (1979: 73) pointed out that Japanese overseas investment might be best explained in terms of "the expanded factor-endowments model, which emphasizes the motivation of those sectors to transfer corporate production to developing countries where factor endowments are more favorable."

In explaining the situation of the late 1960s, Ozawa also mentioned such other factors as appreciation of yen, rising labor and energy costs, problems of environmental decay, and industrial site shortages, all of which encouraged Japanese firms of all sizes to relocate production facilities to appropriate overseas locations. The relocation decision was made not so much to secure competitive advantage over local firms as to escape from the so-called Ricardo-Hicksian trap, a situation in which unalterable scarcity of key inputs is certain to prevail. This helps to explain the suddenness and simultaneity of the massive rush of Japanese companies to expand abroad, a trend that began in the late 1960s.

What, one might now ask, were the factors that enhanced small and medium Japanese firms' capacity for internationalization at a time when they had not yet developed their own technostructures with good planning systems and "collective intelligence"? Such facilitating factors include:

1. The organizational and financial assistance of the Japanese government and the Sogo Shosha (general trading companies)
2. Widespread practices of mutual help and collaboration within and between different industrial groups regarding their overseas operations and collective economic power
3. The "administrative guidance" of MITI
4. The global information network of the Sogo Shosha

All these factors, according to Ozawa, together constitute what he appropriately designated as a macro-technostructure, in contrast to Galbraith's firm-specific technostructure (Ozawa 1979: 75).

Miyohei Shinohara (1982) gives another penetrating explanation of the process of internationalization of Japanese capital, synthesizing the views of both Japanese and Western scholars. He also examines the process's impact on Japan in a discussion of what he calls the "boomerang effect" and the Japanese response to it. He describes the pattern of industrial development in postwar Japan as the "Akamatsu-Vernon cycle." Akamatsu (1961) had depicted a product cycle by referring to this pattern:

Imports → Domestic Production → Exports

Raymond Vernon (1966), on the other hand, described a pattern of product cycle by placing domestic production at the beginning, reflecting the American reality of the 1950s:

Domestic Production → Exports → Foreign Investment

Shinohara (1982) synthesized the two theories into this pattern:

Imports → Domestic Production → Exports
→ Foreign Direct Investment

While Japanese foreign direct investment had increased significantly since the late 1960s, discussions went on about the "boomerang effect" from such overseas investments. Boomerang effects include not only the acute competition from "reversed imports" of low-cost products manufactured in countries to which Japan had earlier exported capital and technology but also such countries' growing inroads against Japanese goods into third country markets. This effect had by the early 1970s made itself felt in the textiles, printing and publishing, electronics, and shipbuilding businesses, especially from South Korea and Taiwan (Shinohara 1982: 14).

Japan's reaction to the boomerang effect was not to resort to trade protectionism but to opt for the internationalization of the industrial structure. As Shinohara (1982: 14) aptly put it, "The goal of developing self-contained modern industries and strengthening their international competitive position across the board was relevant to Japan's trade and industrial structure before 1970. But now attention should be focused on how to carry out such an international industrial adjustment."

This new direction was charted by the Industrial Structure Council's report "The Basic Direction of Trade and Industry in the 1970s." The report also prescribed the "knowledge-intensive industrial structure" as the vision of the industrial structure of the 1970s. This is the hallmark of the international aspect of the new industrial policies, in which an across-the-board emphasis on international competitiveness for all industries shifted to one on industrial transfer or international industry adjustment.

Japan has thus since the early 1970s planned for the internationalization of industrial structure, relocating those branches that were losing international competitiveness to NICs and later to ASEAN countries while at the same time concentrating more on R&D-intensive industries (computer, aircraft, industrial robots, atomic power, large-scale integrated circuits, refined chemicals, ocean development, and so on), high processing industries, fashion industries, knowledge industries, and all kinds of highly sophisticated technologies.

The restructuring of the industrial system in such advanced industrial countries as Japan, with the resulting overseas relocation of less competitive industries, has been largely responsible for the relatively rapid industrialization in NICs and later in ASEAN countries. This is testified to by the fact the revealed comparative advantage in export (RCAX)[1] for labor-intensive manufactured products in NICs and ASEAN countries has increased while the Japanese RCAX for the same product group has correspondingly declined. For Thailand in particular we will see that the RCAX for labor-intensive manufactures (textiles, clothing, leather and footwear, furniture and wood products, rubber and plastic products, and miscellaneous) increased markedly from 1970 to 1980, rising from 0.574 to 1.681, which means that it changed from a comparatively disadvantaged position to one of increasing comparative advantage (index value > unity). In contrast, Japan's RCAX for capital-intensive manufactured products and machinery has increased significantly, reflecting a process closely integrated through the international input-output relationship (Shinohara 1982: 210). Thus the NIDL process has been strengthened and is gathering strong momentum.

The NIDL process is affirmed by structural changes in the composition of exports and imports from trading partners, reflecting also the changes in the production structure. We will examine such changes at three levels: the level of the advanced industrial country Japan; the level of the newly industrialized countries; and the level of such so-called near-NICs as the ASEAN countries, excluding Singapore.

According to Yamazawa and Watanabe (1988: 208), Japan's export structure during 1970–1980 was marked by a predominant share of chemicals, steel, and machinery. Such a pattern was similar to those of the EC and the United States.

In examining the export structure of Japan in more detail we will see drastic changes in the composition of industrial branches and hence the technological transformation in Japan. Export of textiles dropped drastically from 30.2% in 1960 to 4.8% in 1979, while that of machinery, including automobiles and ships, jumped from 13.7% in 1955 to 25.5% in 1960 and further to 61.3% in 1979, a remarkable achievement unparalleled by other industrial countries. If we take into account both heavy and chemical industries, their shares in the total exports exhibited

---

1. RCAXi = (Xih/Xi) / (Wh/W)
    where Xi, (Xih) = the i–th country's export of all commodities (commodity group h)
    W, (Wh) = the world total trade of commodities (commodity group h)
    Source: Yamazawa and Watanabe (1988: 209).

dramatic growth, rising from 38% in 1955 to 85.8% in 1979 (Shinohara 1982: 14). Chemicals and machinery have of course since become the most important exports.

Japan's imports were virtually dominated by primary products, mostly mineral fuels whose shares expanded throughout the 1970s. Imports also included other labor-intensive manufactures.

NICs had small shares of primary product exports but larger shares of labor-intensive manufactures. During the 1970s the shares of labor-intensive manufactures decreased while those of electric machinery, precision instruments, and others increased.

NICs imports comprised large shares of primary products, on the one hand, and chemicals, metal products, and machinery on the other. The latter's share tended to decline but still accounted for more than a third of all imports in 1980.

The four ASEAN countries' exports were dominated by raw and processed primary products. Their shares, however, decreased during the 1970s while those of electrical machinery and textiles have gradually been rising. ASEAN's imports were dominated by chemicals, steel, and machinery.

In the process of the internationalization of Japanese capital, however, the developing countries were not the only focus of concern. In fact, by the mid-1970s Japan's manufacturing industries had significantly increased their direct investment in advanced countries as well, especially in mechanical and electrical machinery, transportation equipment, and other processing and assembling activities. This trend has continued strongly especially since the early 1980s when a rapidly rising tide of protectionism swept these countries. The *endaka*, the sharp rise in the yen exchange rate since 1985, has accelerated this trend.

Since the mid-1980s, moreover, the industrial restructuring process in Japan has occurred not only in the manufacturing sector, as formerly was the case, but has spread over entire industries, including trade, agriculture, construction, transport and telecommunication, distribution, and finance and other services. This is due mainly to changing economic, social, and technological environments, both global and domestic, including such factors as the *endaka*, protectionism, international pressures for deregulation and privatization, strong competition from the Asian NICs, and the arrival of the electronics age and highly information-oriented social relations that are shaping a new structure of demands and products, the aging of Japanese society, and so on (EPA 1988: 163–71).

In the next section we will focus on a single aspect of the process of the restructure and internationalization of Japanese capital—the restructuring of manufacturing industries that resulted from the *endaka*, and how it influences the growth and composition of direct foreign investment in Thailand.

The New Wave of Japanese Investment in Thailand

General Trend of Japanese Direct Investment in Thailand

Although Japanese direct investment in Thailand has increased significantly over time, only since 1985 has it exhibited a dramatic leap forward, rising from an annual average of 1,354 million baht during 1978–1985 to 3,049 in 1986 to 14,591 in 1988. The *endaka*, since the Plaza agreement in late 1985, was mostly responsible for such a great influx of Japanese capital into Thailand.

Regarding the overall role of Japanese direct investment in Thailand, Japan along with the United States has played the dominant role in foreign direct investment (FDI) in Thailand. According to Thailand's Board of Investment statistics, Japanese FDI as of June 1988 accounted for 40% of the projects approved and 46% of the projects starting operation. The corresponding figures for American FDI are respectively only 10% and 11%.

The Bank of Thailand's statistics on net inflow of FDI show that Japan has since 1986 consistently ranked as the number one investor, followed at a widening distance by the United States (Table 1).

The United States, on the average during 1978 to 1985, was still the number one contributor (with a share of 31% to the net inflow of FDI in Thailand. Japan (with a share of 28%) ranked as number two. However, since 1986 the Japanese share has surged, reaching 52% in 1988, while that of the United States dropped to only 11% and second place. The *endaka* clearly has contributed greatly to the surge of the new wave of Japanese FDI in Thailand.

Structural Changes in Japanese FDI in Thailand

The major feature of Japanese FDI in Thailand is the great leap in the level of investment, which as mentioned earlier shot from an average of 1,354 million baht in 1978–1985 to 3,269 in 1987 and to 14,591 in 1988. Apart from the great leap in level, important structural shifts in the sectoral preference of Japanese FDI exist.

Structural changes in sectoral distribution of Japanese FDI are shown in Table 2. During 1978–1985 Japanese investors placed major emphasis

Table 1. Shares of Japanese and American Direct Investment in Thailand.
(%, million baht)

	1978–1985 (av.)	1986	1987	1988
Japan	27.7	44.1	36.2	51.7
United States	31.2	18.7	20.0	11.3
All countries	100.0	100.0	100.0	100.0
Total (million baht)	4,894	6,908	9,044	28,244
% Growth	—	41	31	212

Sources: Bank of Thailand.

Table 2. Structure of Japanese Direct Investment in Thailand.
A. Composition of JDI in Thailand   (%, million baht)

	1978–1985 (av.)	1986	1987	1988
Financial institutions	1.3	2.1	13.7	4.7
Trade	24.5	34.7	–11.3	7.9
Construction	37.7	28.3	27.1	9.1
Mining & quarrying	0.1	0.1	0.0	0.0
Agriculture	0.7	4.7	3.8	1.2
Industry	31.7	23.1	57.3	72.1
Services	4.0	7.1	9.4	5.0
Total (%)	100.0	100.0	100.0	100.0
Total in million baht	1,354	3,049	3,269	14,591

B. Composition of JDI in Thai Industrial Sector

	1978–1985 (av.)	1986	1987	1988
Food	–5.3	7.9	–0.7	3.1
Textiles	23.1	10.5	0.9	3.0
Metal, based & non-met	28.3	–14.9	12.0	15.6
Electrical appliances	28.3	45.5	44.1	44.5
Machinery & transport	13.2	–5.2	8.3	6.3
Chemicals & paper	9.8	5.8	15.9	3.4
Petroleum products	0.5	0.0	0.0	19.3
Construction materials	0.4	0.0	–0.1	0.0
Others	1.9	50.4	19.7	4.8
Total (%)	100.0	100.0	100.0	100.0
Total in million baht	429	703	1,874	10,518

Sources: Calculated from data supplied by Bank of Thailand.

on three sectors: construction (37.7%), manufacturing (31.6%), and trade (24.5%).

This dramatic shift in sectoral preference occurred since the *endaka*. The attention of Japanese investors since 1986 has been mainly directed toward manufacturing. In spite of the huge increase in the level of investment, the share of Japanese FDI in this sector rose sharply to 57% in 1987 and further to 72% in the following year, thus almost dwarfing the shares of other sectors.

Within the manufacturing sector, the major focus of Japanese FDI during 1978–1985 was on metal and non-metallic products (28.27%), electrical appliances (28.25%), textiles (23.1%), and machinery and transport equipment (13.2%). Since the *endaka* the major emphasis has been on electrical appliances, mainly electronic component parts, and machine parts and accessories.

A contrasting sharp drop was registered in the textiles subsector, decreasing consistently from over 20% during 1978–1985 to only about 3% in 1988. This reflects a major shift in the product cycle. Japanese investors in Thailand are phasing out of such old labor-intensive industries as textiles and shifting to such new labor-intensive industries as electronic parts and components assembly. Other product lines also tend now to demand more skill-intensive work than formerly was the case.

Motives for Japanese FDI in Thailand

Various motives exist for Japanese FDI in Thailand, and they seem to be changing over time. The rapid industrial structural changes in Japan have indeed entailed such changes. In a study quoted by Wai Jamornmarn (1987: 17–18) the major reasons for overseas investment (after 1971) by Japanese small and medium firms were (multiple answers): 1) low wages (49.2 %); 2) good market prospects (47.5%); 3) cheap raw materials (25.4%); 4) subcontracting (23.7%); and 5) demand and support from the host countries (18.6%). According to Somsak Tambunlertchai (1987:4) the motives are: 1) to maintain and develop Thai markets by investing in import-substitution industries; 2) to take advantage of promotional privileges granted; 3) to circumvent high tariff rates and quotas; 4) to compete with other firms in the same lines of business; and 5) to make use of cheap and relatively well-disciplined labor.

The MITI Survey of Small and Medium Industries of July 1985, as quoted in Phongpaichit (1987:12), reveals the following motives regarding Japanese investment in ASEAN countries (multiple answers): 1) to utilize cheap labor (55%); 2) to secure the market of host countries

(50%); 3) to export to Japan (28%); 4) to secure raw materials (28%); 5) to export to third countries (25%); 6) to export technology (25%); 7) to follow parent companies (15%); and 8) to utilize promotional privileges (10%).

The three most predominant motives for Japanese small and medium industry investment in ASEAN countries and in Thailand are, in descending order, to utilize cheap labor, to secure local markets, and to establish export platforms to either Japan or third countries. The first and the third motives are actually complementary and foremost, especially since the *endaka* came to occupy central stage in Japan's international economic relations. During the last two years the great influx of Japanese investment in Thailand owed to the *endaka*, and now the predominant motive has shifted to that of seeking a production platform for export from Thailand. This will be discussed in detail in the following sections.

The Nature of Ownership and Control of Japanese FDI

Regarding the control of joint-venture firms, a huge gap exists between the nature of share holding and the real controlling power.

A 1980 survey by Thailand's Board of Investment (BOI) revealed that only two of 134 Japanese-involved firms were 100% Japanese—the majority ranged from about 30% to 50% ownership.

The Bank of Thailand's survey of promoted joint-venture firms in the same year put the figures for the pattern of ownership distribution as: Japanese, 40.2%; Thai, 57.4%; and others, 2.4%. BOI figures for 1986 show that the situation did not change much: Japanese, 45.1%; Thai, 52.2%; and others, 2.6%. And BOI data for 1987 up to June 30 shows: Japanese, 33.3%; Thai, 65.9%; and others, 0.8%. The pattern of these figures indicates the high share of Thai firms in textiles (83%) as compared to the Japanese (16.8%).

BOI data for the promoted firms for the whole of 1988, however, shows that the Japanese share rose to 72.7% while the Thai share dropped to 23.2%. The sector comprising mechanical, electrical, and electronic machinery and components, in particular, registered an above average Japanese share of 82.7%.

Regarding firm level, it is generally accepted that majority equity participation does not guarantee dominant control by the partner in joint ventures (UN-CTC 1978: 66). Neither the Japanese side nor the Thai side can easily be blamed when dummy shareholders are used to make the joint-venture firm a Thai company, that is, a Thai majority-owned company.

At a 1987 seminar organized by the Japanese Studies Project of Thammasat University, a prominent and knowledgeable Thai business-man commented that though a large number of joint-venture firms with 60 or 70% Thai equity participation exist, they are still under Japanese control. He mentioned that in some industries the Thai partners were suffering declining shares and complained that Japanese banks also contribute to Japanese dominance in the joint-ventures because they are much less cooperative toward or even withhold credit lines from firms that register marked increases in Thai shares.

This comment is consistent with the observation by a Western scholar who described how the Japanese partners dominate joint ventures through credit leverage, especially for the imports of machinery, equipment, and parts. Weinstein (1976: 390) states that the "joint ventures in Thailand rely [heavily on] loans for the import of plant, equipment, raw materials. These loans normally are procured by the Japanese side and sometimes are possible mainly because the parent Japanese company stands behind them. Often the loans come directly from the parent company itself, which enables the company to earn interest at the expense of its subsidiary. Heavy use is also made of supplier's credits."

In another study it is also noted that Japanese partners "have frequently exercised considerable powers of direction over even minority-owned subsidiaries by their insistence on retaining powers of decision over operational and managerial policies" (UN-CTC 1978: 63).

The Thai businessman mentioned above thus went on to propose that the Thai state limit the maximum equity participation of foreign firms and see to it that the Thai share be adequately increased in due time.

On the other hand, another businessman participating in the seminar argued with confidence that the new generation of Thai businessmen must learn how to cope with their Japanese partners in spite of their weaknesses vis-à-vis the foreign partners.

New Wave of Relocation of Small Japanese Firms in Thailand

The sharp yen appreciation (amounting to more than 70%) that began in 1985 has caused such severe problems for smaller Japanese firms that they have had to speed up relocation overseas, especially in ASEAN countries—and Thailand has come to be considered a very favorable relocation site. With the new wave of Japanese investment in Thailand during the past two years a new pattern of foreign investment in Thailand has emerged: the prime objective of the direct investment is not so much access to the Thai market as the securing of cheap labor costs and an export platform to third markets, as well as the export of certain products and parts to parent or affiliated firms in Japan.

An analysis of the pattern of Japanese FDI in Thailand follows. Figures are calculated from statistics, which reflect on the *endaka*, kindly supplied by the Board of Investment of the Royal Thai Government. The period concerned covers only 1986, 1987, and 1988 to the end of May. Additional data is given in squared brackets just for the sake of information and without analysis for the sake of consistency.

Number of Firms and Distribution by Sectors

The number of Japanese investment projects approved by the BOI during the period concerned follow a generally increasing trend. The number of firms approved by the BOI in 1986 was 34; in 1987, 114; in 1988 (May), 100; [and in 1988 (Dec.), 264.] It will be noticed that the number of firms jumped from just 34 in 1986 to over 100 in two years.

The firms' distribution by sector is set out in Table 3. The sectors are defined as follows: sector 1 = agricultural products and commodities; 2 = minerals, metal and ceramic products; 3 = chemicals and chemical products; 4 = mechanical and electrical equipment; and 5 = other manufactured products.

It is readily seen that Japanese firms direct most of their attention to

Table 3. Number of Japanese Projects Approved by BOI, 1986–1988.

	Sector 1	Sector 2	Sector 3	Sector 4	Sector 5	Total
1986	7	2	2	9	14	34
1987	6	6	2	33	67	114
1988 (Jan.–May)	9	8	4	26	53	(100)
1988 (June–Dec.)	35	21	15	101	92	264

Source: Board of Investment (BOI), Thailand.

sector 5, which includes all kinds of manufactured goods not specified in sectors 1 to 4. Among the more important products in this sector are textiles, automotive wiring, extruded aluminum bar, acrylonitrile styrene resin, storage batteries, plastic parts, steel sheets, plastic toys, footwear, furniture, and others. Surprisingly sector 5 also includes some such products as electrical construction material and automatic filling packaging machines. In total, sector 5 received about 41 to 58% of the total investment.

Sector 4, mechanical and electrical equipment, attracted the second largest number of investments, receiving roughly about one quarter of the total investment. The composition of this sector is more homogeneous than that of sector 5.

Size of Employment

The new wave of small and medium firms' investment in Thailand has contributed significantly to the growth of manufacturing employment (Table 4).

Table 4.   Total Size of Employment, by Number of Employees, 1986–1988.

(unit: persons)

	Thai	Japanese
1986	5,079 (100%)	120 (100%)
1987	13,118 (258%)	353 (294%)
1988 (through May)	20,852 (410%)	439 (366%)
1988 (through Dec.)	66,454 (for both Thai and Japanese)	

Source: BOI, Thailand.

The average size of Thai employment per firm shows a fluctuating trend, from 149 in 1986 dropping to 115 in 1987 and then jumping to 208 in 1988. In view of the earlier finding that the average firm size tends to decline, and if the size of employment per firm shows an increasing trend, as it did 1988, we may conclude that the new Japanese investment tends to go into more labor intensive sectors.

Size of Investment Capital

The average size of investment seems to be declining over time as the new wave of relocation of small and medium firms to Thailand has taken place in earnest.

Table 5.   Average Total Size of Investment, 1986–1988.

(unit: million baht)

	Total	Average
1986	14,353	422
1987	16,666	146
1988 (May)	14,296	143
1988 (Dec.)	76,749	291

Source: BOI, Thailand.

Investment (in million baht) in 1986 seems to be concentrated in larger firms (figures in parentheses are Japanese shares):

Thai Plastic & Chemical Co., 3,103 (20%)
Thai Honda Manufacturing Co., 784 (60%)
Thai Suzuki Motor Co., 1,472 (48.9%)
Siam Yamaha Co., 970 (13%)
Thai Ferrite Co., 597 (48%)
Sharp Appliances, 639 (100%)
Thai Silk Reeling Industries, 520 (20%)
Nissan and Siam Motor, 1,471 (16%)
Toyota and Siam Cement Co., 1,222.5 (8%)
Isuzu, Mitsubishi, Mazda, Ford, Mr. Wan Chansue, 1,667 (10%).

Owing to the investment contributed by these firms, the average size of investment in 1986 registered an average of 422 million baht as compared with 146 and 143 in the following two years.

The trend in the distribution of firm size, as measured by size of investment funds, is shown in Table 6.

Table 6. Distribution of Firm Size, by Size of Investment Funds, 1986–May 1988. (%)

Year \ Capitalization	Small (1–100 million baht)	Medium (101–200 million baht)	Large (201+ million baht)
1986	56%	6%	38%
1987	67	12	20
1988 (May)	65	22	13
Average 1986–88 (May)	65	15	20

Source: BOI, Thailand.

The majority of investing firms (65%) are in the small size category. For the period of years concerned, the shares of medium firms have increased from 6 to 22% and those of the large firms decreased consistently from 38% in 1986 to 13% in the first half of 1988.

Pattern of Equity Participation

The pattern of Japanese share holding is shown in Table 7.

The percentage of Japanese foreign investment share holding tends to increase over time, at the expense of Thai ownership. If the firms with only 1–24% Japanese control are defined as being firms under Thai

Table 7. Japanese Share Holding, 1986–May 1988.

(no. of projects)

Year \ Share	1–24%	25–49%	50–74%	75–100%	N.A.	Total
1986	12	10	4	8	—	34
1987	11	48	7	48	—	114
1988	10	26	12	36	16	100

Source: BOI, Thailand.

control, then it is seen that Thai control of the joint venture firms tends to decline over time. The share of Thai-controlled firms in 1986 was 35% but declined to 9.6% and 11.9% in 1987 and 1988 respectively.

In contrast, if the firms with 75–100% equity participation by Japanese investors are defined as being firms under Japanese control, then the opposite trend is observed for Thai-controlled firms. The Japanese-controlled firms increased their share in the total from 24% in 1986 to 42% and 43% in the following two years. It is interesting that the firms with Japanese equity participation in the area of 25–74% remained constant at around 45% during the three years under review.

Distribution of Capital Intensity by Sector and by Degree of Japanese Ownership

As Thailand is a labor surplus country and also a host to foreign investment, it is important to investigate the nature of the promoted projects in order to know whether and in what sector they are labor intensive or capital intensive and whether the degree of foreign ownership influences the technological choices made in the joint-venture firms.

The distribution of capital intensity by sector. The distribution of capital intensity by sector is shown in Table 8. In this analysis we want to identify the relative degree of capital intensity or, conversely, the degree of labor intensity. The figures given in Table 8 are the ratio of investment funds (in million baht) divided by the corresponding project's expected employment number. In this sense the lower ratio reflects lower capital intensity, or more labor intensity, and vice versa. We use the following criteria: those firms with capital intensity of up to 0.6—meaning that an investment fund of Bt. 600,000 is needed to create an employment of one person—are labor intensive; those with 0.7 to 1.0 are fairly neutral; those with a ratios of 1.1 to 3.0 are capital intensive; and those with a ratios of over 3.1 are highly capital intensive.

The findings in Table 8 are consistent with the fact that most of the

Table 8. Distribution of Capital Intensity by Sector.

(no. of projects)

Intensity \ Sector	1	2	3	4	5
0–0.3	9	4	1	22	62
0.4–0.6	4	2	3	18	19
0.7–1.0	2	1	1	11	23
1.1–3.0	5	6	2	9	27
3.1+	2	3	1	8	3
Total	22	16	8	68	134

(as percentage)

0–0.3	40.9	25.0	12.5	32.4	46.3
0.4–0.6	18.2	12.5	37.5	26.2	14.2
0.7–1.0	9.1	6.3	12.5	16.2	17.2
1.1–3.0	22.7	37.5	25.0	13.2	20.2
3.1+	9.1	18.8	12.5	11.7	2.2
Total	100.0	100.0	100.0	100.0	100.0

Note: Capital intensity shows the relation between investment capital and Thai employment; a ratio of 0.6 means an investment fund of Bt. 600,000 is needed to employ one person in the relevant project.
Source: BOI, Thailand.

Table 9. Distribution of Capital Intensity by Size of Investment.

(no. of projects)

Sector \ Size (in million Baht)	1–20	21–100	101–200	201–500	500+
1	6	12	2	0	2
2	2	5	5	3	1
3	0	7	0	0	1
4	6	29	17	7	9
5	36	58	14	17	9
Total	50	111	38	27	22

Source: BOI, Thailand.

projects measured are relatively smaller in investment size, and accordingly they are more labor intensive. This is confirmed by the data in Table 9, which sets out the distribution of the degree of capital intensity by size of investment funds. These figures show a positive relationship between the size of investment funds and the degree of capital intensity.

All sectors except sector 2 (mineral, metal, and ceramic products) were characterized by labor intensity, as over half of the projects exhibited intensity ratios of less than 0.6. Only about 37% of the projects in sector 2 were in the labor intensive category, while more than half, not surprisingly, were in the capital intensive and highly capital intensive categories. The respective labor intensity ratios are as follows: sector 1 = 59%, sector 2 = 37.5%, sector 3 = 50%, sector 4 = 59%, and sector 5 = 60%.

Regarding the capital intensive categories, it is interesting to note that the percentage distribution of the projects with a ratio of above 1.0—meaning that an investment fund of about 1 million baht is needed to create one employment opportunity—in each sector is as follows: sector 1 = 32%, sector 2 = 56%, sector 3 = 38%, sector 4 = 25%, sector 5 = 22%.

Distribution of Capital Intensity by Degree of Japanese Ownership. The distribution of capital intensity of BOI-promoted projects by degree of ownership is set out in Table 10. In the following discussion we determine which type of ownership is more labor intensive, a technical structure that is suitable for such labor-surplus economies as Thailand. Based on information from Table 10, the varying degrees of capital intensity of the Thai majority-owned firms and the Japanese majority-owned firms are compared in Table 11.

As mentioned above, firms with capital intensity ratios of up to 0.6 are considered labor intensive. It is interesting that both the Thai and Japanese majority-owned firms exhibit approximately the same technical features: about 60% of both are labor intensive (60% and 62% respectively). This is the only point of similarity. Nine percent of the Thai majority-owned firms are highly capital intensive (over 3.0) while only 3% of the Japanese are. The same pattern is true in the capital intensive category (1.1–3.0): about 20% of Thai firms are capital intensive while only 14% of the Japanese are.

A similar pattern of distribution regarding degree of capital intensity was also exhibited for the Japanese majority-owned and Thai majority-owned firms.

Therefore we may conclude that the difference in degree of ownership does not make much difference in terms of technical choices as reflected in the distribution of capital intensity by degree of ownership. However,

Table 10. Distribution of Capital Intensity by Japanese Share Holding.
(no. of projects)

Share (%) Intensity	0–24	25–49	50–74	75–89	90–100
0–0.3	17	28	8	4	34
0.4–0.6	4	15	5	3	16
0.7–1.0	4	11	3	7	12
1.1–3.0	7	20	4	3	10
3.1+	3	8	2	0	3
Total	35	82	22	17	75

Source: BOI, Thailand.

Table 11. Comparison of Capital Intensity by Thai and Japanese Majority
Ownership.

Capital Intensity	Thai Majority Ownership (N=35)	Japanese Majority Ownership (N=92)
up to 0.6	60%	62%
0.7–1.0	11	21
1.0–3.0	20	14
3.1+	9	3

Note: Majority ownership is here defined as 75–100% ownership.

although the majority of firms in both the Thai majority-owned and
Japanese majority-owned categories are labor intensive, a higher share
of the former are capital intensive.

Distribution of Size of Investment by Sector

The distribution of size of investment by sector is shown in Table 12. For
the sake of comparison, we adopt the following criteria: firms with investment capital of up to 100 million baht are considered small; those with
investment capital of between 101 and 200 million baht are medium;
and those with investment capital above 200 million baht are large.

Sectors 1 (agricultural products and commodities), 3 (chemicals and
chemical products), and 5 (other manufactured products) are mostly

Table 12. Distribution of Investment Size by Sector.

(no. of projects)

Size (million Baht) / Sector	1	2	3	4	5
1–20	6	2	0	0	36
21–100	12	5	7	29	58
101–200	2	5	0	17	14
201–500	0	3	0	7	17
500+	2	1	1	9	9
Total	22	16	8	68	134

Source: BOI, Thailand.

concentrated in projects with investment capital of less than 100 million baht; about three quarters of the projects in these sectors are in the "small" category. These projects tend to have a relatively smaller size of investment than those in the other sectors as well as less than average percentage investment than those projects in the medium and large categories.

About one quarter of the projects in sector 2 (mineral, metal, and ceramic products) and sector 4 (mechanical and electrical equipment) are in the large investment capital category, about one third to one quarter of the projects are in the medium category, and less than one half are in the small category.

In sum, the average size of investment in sectors 1, 3, and 5 is much smaller than that in sectors 2 and 4.

Distribution of Japanese Equity Participation by Sector and Size of Firm

In this section the degree of Japanese ownership in a particular sector and whether the new wave of Japanese investment in Thailand favors a certain sector or sectors are investigated. The nature of Japanese ownership, that is, firm size as measured by the amount of investment capital, is also examined.

Distribution of Japanese Equity Participation by Sector. The distribution of the degree of Japanese equity participation is set out in Table 13. The following criteria are adopted for this analysis: firms with Japanese share holding of up to 24% are considered as being in the high-Thai-ownership category; those with between 25% and 49% are in the more-Thai-ownership category; those between 50% and 74% are in the more-

Table 13. Distribution of Japanese Share Holding by Sector.

(no. of projects)

Share (%) \ Sector	1	2	3	4	5
0–24	6	2	3	4	20
25–49	8	6	4	23	41
50–74	2	1	0	8	11
75–89	1	1	0	4	11
90–100	5	4	0	23	43
Total	22	14	7	62	126

Source: BOI, Thailand.

Japanese-ownership category; and those with 75% or more are in the high-Japanese-ownership category.

High-Thai-ownership is found mostly in sectors 3 and 1, in that order. Sectors 3, 1, and 2 show higher levels of more-Thai-ownership than do the other two sectors, but it is interesting to note that the percentage of firms with more-Japanese-ownership ranged between only 0.0 and 12.90 in all sectors.

More significant is the fact that the firms in the high-Japanese-ownership category show a significant share of projects in all sectors except sector 3. Sectors 4 and 5 have about 43% of the projects in the high-Japanese-ownership category while sectors 2 and 1 respectively tally about 36% and 27%.

Examining the figures for 1987 and 1988, however, we see a rising trend of increasing Japanese ownership in sector 5, from 33 to 47%, and in sector 1, from 17 to 44%.

Distribution of Japanese Equity Participation by Size of Firm. The degree of ownership in joint enterprises by size of investment capital is shown in Table 14. In the small category, the high-Japanese-ownership firms accounted for about 35% and the high-Thai-ownership firms for only 14% of the total. However, the more-Thai-ownership firms accounted for 38% while the more-Japanese-ownership firms accounted for only 11%.

Among the medium firms, the high-Japanese-ownership firms accounted for 58%—much more than the share of the high-Thai-ownership firms, which had only 9%. This difference is not offset by the percentages found in the other categories of ownership.

Table 14. Distribution of Japanese Share Holding by Size of Investment.

(no. of projects)

Size (million Baht) Share (%)	1–20	21–100	101–200	201–500	500+
0–24	7	15	3	3	7
25–49	14	45	9	8	6
50–74	6	11	2	1	2
75–89	5	4	5	3	0
90–100	16	30	14	7	6
Total	48	105	33	22	21

Source: BOI, Thailand.

Among large firms, the share of the high-Japanese-ownership firms was highest, accounting for 37% of the total. The share of the high-Thai-ownership firms was only 23%. The more-Thai-ownership firms accounted, however, for about 32% of the total, comparing favorably with the more-Japanese-ownership firms, which weighed in with only a 6% share.

On the whole, the shares of the high-Japanese-ownership firms were greater than those of the high-Thai-ownership firms in all firm size categories, but Japanese investors seemed especially to dominate the medium firms.

Conclusion

The Japanese-Thai economic relationship develops within the context of the transformation of the world capitalist system. The law of accumulation, among other forces, comprises the competitive drive through technological innovation that sustains an outward expansion of national economic activities that ultimately integrate socio-economic terrains far beyond the commonly accepted "national boundary." In the age of transnational capitalism, national boundaries are increasingly drawn with fading ink. The mechanism of transnational capitalism has shaped a world capitalist system of hierarchical economic configurations.

Within the more advanced countries an inherent tendency toward restructuring of industrial activities exists, resulting in a shift to higher levels on the technological ladder or to the high-tech and knowledge-intensive industries. In the process the need to relocate the so-called non-competitive industries will be intensified; the internationalization of capital has therefore started in this context. In Japan such a tendency has been developing rapidly; the *endaka* served only to trigger the ongoing industrial restructuring process, which requires site relocation in the course of charting a new division of labor among nations, especially Japan and the ASEAN countries.

This study is a small attempt to explain the nature of Japanese industrial relocation in Thailand. Although further research is needed to confirm our findings, we offer the following concluding remarks.

It is important to note that while the internationalization of Japanese capital has brought about rapid industrialization in the host countries, the nature of "compressed development" simultaneously carries with it several problems, in particular those associated with socio-economic adjustments in the host country. Such problems include: a) monopolistic industrial structures that result from transplantation of relatively large firms and the host country's relatively small domestic market; b) intensified need for intermediate and capital goods tends to bring about chronic deficits in the trade balances (Yamazawa and Watanabe 1988: 219), and, more importantly, the transplanted industries are often highly import-dependent; c) a tendency toward greater ownership and control of local industries by foreign investors; which in turn causes d) shortages of production factor supply and infrastructural services in the host countries, thereby upsetting planned resource allocation; and e) a shift to the host countries of some industrial processes that cause increased pollution and health hazards.

Comment

Akira Suehiro

My first comment is connected to a new movement of Japanese multinational electronics firms to Thailand and other Asian countries, which seems to indicate well the emergence of the "new international division of labor" that Dr. Suthy introduced in the first part of his study.

Dr. Suthy's presentation of the current situation of Japanese FDI in Thailand (Table 2 of his paper) is based on Bank of Thailand data, which, unlike BOI data, indicates the actual movement (net inflow) of foreign (Japanese) capital in the all industries. (BOI data refers only to manufacturing, the modern-type agricultural sector, and a part of the service sector.) Two major trends in Japanese investment in Thailand since 1986 can easily be drawn from the data in Table 2: (1) the manufacturing sector is coming to play a more and more important role in recent FDI; and (2) among the manufacturing sectors, the electrical and electronics industry have come to occupy the lion's share of FDI due to the active movement of Japanese MNCs.

The case of Sharp Corporation will serve as an example to explain how the Thai electrical and electronics industry has quickly been integrated into a new strategy of foreign capital, especially that of Japanese MNCs following the *endaka*. During the 1960s the five leading Japanese firms (Matsushita, Sanyo, Toshiba, Mitsubishi, and Hitachi) began production operations for such products as radio receivers, color and black and white television sets, refrigerators, and electronic rice cookers. Importantly, all of these products were intended for sale only in the domestic market. No Japanese MNCs had started assembly of exportable products as of the mid-1980s, in contrast to the American firms that had already manufactured and exported integrated circuits (ICs) since the early 1970s.

After the yen appreciation, however, Japanese electronics firms (assemblers and electronic parts manufacturers) gradually began coming to Thailand in order to establish export bases. Sharp Corporation, which started production of electronic ovens in 1986, is a most typical case. What is notable here is that Sharp presently has four major production-export bases for electronic ovens in England, the United States, Thailand, and Japan. In England and the United States the plants are engaged exclusively in production of large-sized electronic ovens for their own markets, while the new Thai plant engages in the production of lower-priced, standardized products for export to the United States, Asia, and the Middle East. The latter type of products originally was assembled in Japan, but operations completely shifted to Thailand in 1986. Sharp's Japanese plant meanwhile changed its production line to more high-technology electronic ovens employing ICs intended for export to the world market including the United States. At the same time Sharp also began to reorganize its overseas activities in Asian countries into a more region-based production system in line with the head office's global strategy. For instance, Sharp enhanced three major Malaysian plants that produce color televisions and AV sets for export. Sharp's color television plant in Malaysia (producing two million sets per year) is now expected to become one of the largest exporters in the world. Thus a distinct division of labor in major products emerges among the Asian countries and among the regions (Japan, the United States, the EC, and Asia) under the leadership of the parent company. The same pattern is observed in other leading Japanese electronic MNCs since the yen appreciation.

As the case of Sharp clearly shows, the development of the electronics industry in Thailand (or Malaysia) is crucially determined by the movement of Japanese MNCs rather than by the local governments' industrial and investment policies. The answers to such problems as which types of products shall be produced or which level of technology shall be introduced into Thailand are now determined by the global strategy promoted by Japanese MNCs. Such changes in the reorganization process of the Thai electronics industry may well indicate that a firm's level of activities is based on the idea of the "new international division of labor" as described by Dr. Suthy.

My second comment is related to the changing pattern in ownership structure of recent Thai–Japan joint ventures in Thailand. In Dr. Suthy's observation, the Thai-controlled firms have experienced a swift reduction of position in a group of joint-ventures in major industries during the course of the foreign investment boom whereas 100% Japanese-controlled firms have enlarged their market shares and destroyed smaller local businesses. This new trend is apparently caused by the Thai government's new investment policies, in which foreign investors are permitted to keep 100% ownership as long as they maintain a 100% export performance.

Basically I agree with this observation but at the same time I have to point out the fact that the new investment boom of foreign capital provides opportunities not only for Japanese MNCs to establish a strong stake in Thailand but also for existing (or newly rising) local industrial groups to enlarge and diversify their production lines. A typical case of local opportunity growth is the Siam Cement group, which successfully advanced into such technology-intensive industries as electric tubes for color televisions (with Mitsubishi Electric) and automobile engines (with Toyota Motor). Several leading industrial groups have realized the reorganization of production systems from import substitution to export expansion mostly in cooperation with foreign groups under the local groups' leadership, as seen in the cases of the Saha Union, Saha Phattana, CP, and Srifuengfung groups. Dr. Suthy seems to stress one side of the problem of the increasing economic power of foreign capital in Thailand. But the question of what is taking place among the local industrial groups or their capability in introducing foreign technology and market development knowhow will become the increasingly important issue in the examination of the impact of FDI on future Thai industrial development.

My last comment is related to the methodology employed in the study of economic relations between Japan and Thailand after 1986. Dr. Suthy discusses this topic by restricting the scope of his study to the bilateral trade and investment problems. At the same time he specifically points out in the second part of his study that rapid increases in overseas investment of Japanese capital is essentially caused by Japan–U.S. trade conflicts and international adjustment of foreign currencies among the leading industrialized countries. If this is so, then the scope of study surrounding the discussion of Japan–Thai economic relations should be extended to a more global one.

Indeed, the increasing manufactured exports from Thailand since 1987 are closely related to two major factors: (1) the improvement of international competitiveness in Thai industries due mainly to the value appreciation of yen, Korean won, and Taiwan yeun against the U.S. dollar; and (2) the influx into Thailand of export-oriented Japanese firms that had faced difficulties in further expansion of direct export to the United States. The Thai–U.S. trade conflicts that surfaced in 1989 therefore reflect economic problems between Thailand and Japan. In this sense the world economy approach is now required even in studying bilateral trade and investment problems, which is precisely the point that Dr. Suthy himself insists on in the first part of his paper.

4
Japanese Foreign Direct Investment and Japanese-Style Management in Singapore

Lim Hua Sing

Foreign direct investment (FDI) has contributed greatly towards ✓ Singapore's rapid economic development.[1] Foreign investment commitments have dominated (in value) investment commitments to Singapore's manufacturing sector with the lowest of 65.6% and the highest of 86.1% in the 1980s. During the period 1975–1984, foreign-owned establishments (with more than 50% of foreign capital investment) comprised 23% of establishments, but generated 55% of employment, 73% of gross output, and 65% of capital expenditure (Krause et al. 1987: 24–25). The United States, Japan, and Europe have been the ✓ predominant investors in Singapore. These three were responsible for 99% in 1988 and 97% in the first quarter of 1989 of total FDI in Singapore's manufacturing sector. In the 1980s, the United States had been the largest investor during the period 1980–1985 but was overwhelmed by Japan during the period 1986–1988. In 1980, Japan's investment commitments to Singapore's manufacturing sector were just 27% of that of the United States. The drastic yen appreciation in 1985 prompted Japan's investment in Singapore and in 1986 Japan exceeded the United States with a new record of 42%, leaving the United States behind with 37% and Europe with merely 18%.

The Japanese presence in Singapore has accordingly attracted much

---

1. There are quite a number of works dealing with this topic. For example: You Poh Seng and Lim Chong Yah, eds., *Singapore: Twenty-five Years of Development* (Singapore: Nan Yang Xing Zhou Lianhe Zaobao, 1984); Walter Galenson, ed., *Foreign Trade and Investment: Economic Growth in the Newly Industrializing Asian Countries* (University of Wisconsin Press, 1985); Lawrence B. Krause et al. *The Singapore Economy Reconsidered* (Singapore: Institute of Southeast Asian Studies, 1987); Lim Chong Yah et al., *Policy Options for the Singapore Economy* (Singapore: McGraw-Hill Book Company, 1988); and Lim Hua Sing, *Singaporu no taigai keizai kankei* (Singapore's foreign economic relations), in Toshio Watanabe et al., eds., *Ajia NIEs Soran* (On the Asian NIEs), (Enterprise Press, 1989).

attention. The adaptation to Singapore of Japanese-style management in Japanese companies in Singapore has become a great concern of not only the Singapore government but also the Japanese investors.

The aim of this paper is, therefore, twofold: first, to examine the characteristics and recent development of Japanese DFI in Singapore, and second, to analyze the possibility of adapting the Japanese-style managerial system in Japanese enterprises to the heterogenous society of Singapore.

Investment Motivators for Japanese FDI

Two comprehensive surveys have been conducted by Japanese organizations concerning the investment motivation of the Japanese in Singapore.

Survey I

This survey[2] was conducted just before the drastic yen appreciation began in September 1985. Issues such as "political stability" and favorable "economic infrastructure" are somehow excluded in this survey. Japanese firms regard Singapore as an important base of entrepôt trade, especially for exporting their manufactures to third countries, and as an important production base for supplying industrial parts and components (the combined affirmative responses to these two questions amounted to 33% of the total number of responses received). Singapore is also regarded by the Japanese firms, as expected, as an important information center, due to its strategic location and well-established transport and telecommunications system. Affirmative responses to these questions comprised 31% (282 cases) and indicated the most important motivation for Japanese investment in Singapore. This is straightforwardly reflected in the rapid increase of Japanese liaison offices and branch offices in Singapore during the period 1979–1984. Besides, it is interesting to note that out of 282 cases, 196 cases (70%) were non-manufacturers (Table 1). It is believed that, because a large proportion of Japanese liaison offices and branch offices is set up by non-manufacturers, one of their main activities must be related to information gathering and data analysis aiming for regional and global

---

2. This survey was jointly conducted during August–October 1985 by the Japan Singapore Association (JSA), the Japan Trade Centre (JTC), the Japan Embassy (JE), and the Japanese Chamber of Commerce and Industry (JCCI). These four Japanese institutions are based in Singapore.

Table 1. Japanese Investment Motivations in Singapore, 1985.

Investment Motivation	Manufacturer	Non-Manufacturer	Total
Low labor cost	14	6	20
As a consumption market	43	59	102
Supply of industrial parts & components	62	30	92
As a base of entrepôt trade	54	154	208
Preferential tariffs	52	22	74
Information center	86	196	282
Financial center	—	11	11
Hardly any merit	21	13	34
Others	25	55	80
Total	357	546	903

Source: Nihon Shingaporu Kyokai (Japan Singapore Association), *Shingaporu no Nikei Kigyo* (Japanese Business Activities in Singapore) (Tokyo 1986), 13.

Note: This survey was conducted in August–October 1985. It was based on multiple responses. The category "Financial Center" was initially not included in the questionnaire survey; the 11 cases recorded here were responses given by the non-manufacturers that are included in "others."

business expansion. Industrial restructuring and drastic economic changes in Singapore and in the region have prompted Japanese firms to treat the region more seriously. From time to time Japanese firms are keen to make timely decisions conducive to business expansion. With this in mind, Japanese firms perceive Singapore as the most reputable information center, despite the fact that operational costs in the country are the highest among Southeast Asian countries.

The survey also indicates that Japanese firms are rationally concerned about the supply of industrial parts and components in Singapore (92 cases, 10%). Obviously, Japanese manufacturers in Singapore realize that a sufficient supply of high-quality and sophisticated industrial parts and components for its high-technology and knowledge-intensive industries is one of the important factors in doing business in Singapore. Had this survey been conducted after the drastic yen appreciation in 1985, when the Japanese economy had started to feel the impact, the additionally stimulated eagerness in looking for a supply of industrial parts and components, especially for the Japanese electrical and electronics industries, would have been reflected. This may be due to two reasons: first, Japanese firms in Singapore will reduce imports of industrial parts and components from Japan due to the high yen; second, procurement of industrial parts and components in Singapore's local markets will increase to coincide with Japanese firms shifting their production operations to Singapore.

Survey II

This survey has been conducted annually by the Toyo Keizai Shimposha. The survey reveals that over the period 1983–1989, Japanese motivation to invest in Singapore has been centered around: (a) increasing sales in Singapore and third countries; (b) utilization of the local labor force and reduction in operating costs; (c) collecting information; and (d) benefitting from the protective policies adopted by the Singapore government (Table 2). Singapore has also been regarded by Japanese firms as an important production base and center for exploring international markets, as indicated in the previous survey.

Japanese manufacturing industries in Singapore benefitted not only from the procurement of industrial parts and components from Japanese supporting industries in Singapore, but also from non-Japanese supporting industries, of Singaporean or other nationalities, though to a much lesser extent. Singapore's small and medium-sized businesses (SMBs) (mostly Chinese) are perceived as the least developed among the Asian newly industrializing economies (NIEs), due mainly to Singapore's heavy reliance since the separation from Malaysia in 1965 on multinational corporations (MNCs) and on developing public enterprises. Singapore's SMBs have consequently played a limited supplementary or supporting role to Japanese firms. Singapore's highly trained workforce and well-developed economic infrastructure, however, have ensured that the country develops high-tech, high-value-added, and knowledge-intensive industries. Labor-intensive industries are being phased out from Singapore. Some Japanese firms are therefore forced to relocate their production to neighboring countries in Asia.[3] A Singapore objective, especially after 1979 when it started restructuring toward export-oriented, high-value-added, high-tech, knowledge-intensive activities, has been to attract Japanese firms with advanced technology. Similar firms with advanced technology of other nationalities have also been attracted to Singapore. It is likely that the supply of industrial parts and components to Japanese manufacturing industries in Singapore

---

3. For instance, in 1987 Taiko Electronics, Sanyo Electronics Singapore, Singapore Kobe, Matsushita Electronics Pte., and Fujitsu Singapore shifted from Singapore to Malaysia. In 1988, Tanshin (Pekas Nanas) shifted from Singapore to Malacca.

Table 2. Japanese Investment Motivations in Singapore, 1983–1989.

Investment Motivation	1983 Cases	1983 %	1984 Cases	1984 %	1985 Cases	1985 %	1986 Cases	1986 %	1987 Cases	1987 %	1988 Cases	1988 %	1989 Cases	1989 %
To ensure raw material supply	13	2.7	11	2.1	10	1.8	9	1.5	9	1.5	9	1.5	12	1.9
Easier to produce here due to the availability of abundant resources	8	1.7	8	1.6	8	1.5	9	1.5	10	1.7	12	2.0	12	1.9
Utilization of labor force; reduction of operating cost	86	18.0	81	15.8	88	16.0	93	15.4	91	15.4	95	15.6	103	16.0
Can benefit from the protective policies adopted by the Singapore government	64	13.4	68	13.2	70	12.7	73	12.1	69	11.7	69	11.3	73	11.4
To expand sales to markets in Singapore and to third countries	234	49.1	266	51.8	289	52.5	310	51.4	301	51.0	310	51.0	317	49.3
To collect information	71	14.9	79	15.4	85	15.4	96	15.9	95	16.1	92	15.1	95	14.7
To solve the export difficulties due to trade frictions	1	0.2	1	0.2	1	0.2	4	0.7	6	1.0	8	1.3	11	1.7
Royalty	N.A.	–	N.A.	–	N.A.	–	9	1.5	9	1.5	13	2.1	20	3.1
Total	477	100.0	514	100.0	551	100.0	603	100.0	590	100.0	608	100.0	643	100.0
Major Export Destinations for Manufacturers														
Japan	30	12.5	31	11.9	35	12.5	38	12.2	43	13.5	47	13.8	52	14.8
Local markets	123	51.3	141	54.0	150	53.4	171	54.6	173	54.4	185	54.4	188	53.6
Third countries other than Japan	87	36.2	89	34.1	96	34.1	104	33.2	102	32.1	108	31.8	111	31.6
Total	240	100.0	261	100.0	281	100.0	313	100.0	318	100.0	340	100.0	351	100.0
Major Sources of Industrial Raw Materials Import														
Japan	71	52.2	83	50.9	89	51.5	96	49.2	100	46.7	120	46.7	127	45.5
Local markets	47	34.6	59	36.2	63	36.4	74	38.0	83	38.8	95	37.0	104	37.3
Third countries other than Japan	18	13.2	21	12.9	21	12.1	25	12.8	31	14.5	42	16.3	48	17.2
Total	136	100.0	163	100.0	173	100.0	195	100.0	214	100.0	257	100.0	279	100.0

Source: Compiled and computed from Toyo Keizai Shimposha, Kaigai Shinshutsu Kigyo Soran (Japanese Overseas Companies, Facts and Figures) (Tokyo, various years).

will be partly substituted for by newly established Japanese and non-Japanese supporting industries in Singapore. Table 2 reveals that Japanese firms are optimistic (37% in 1989) about securing or acquiring the necessary supply of industrial raw materials (that is, industrial parts and components) in Singapore. It is surprising, however, that despite drastic yen appreciation imports of industrial raw materials from Japan have remained at fairly high levels during 1986–1989 (Table 2).

√   Protective policies, preferential tariffs, and the utilization of the labor force are considered important motivators for investment by Japanese firms. The concept of protective policies is rather vague from the macroeconomic viewpoint—it seems to refer to overall efforts made by the government to create a favorable environment in order to attract FDI; from the microeconomic viewpoint it seems to refer to various incentives and benefits given by the government, including incentives to pioneer industries and to expand established enterprises, investment allowances, warehousing and servicing incentives, international consultancy services, foreign loans for productive equipment, incentives for research and development, venture capital incentives, and royalties, fees, and development contributions.[4] The package of protective policies has undoubtedly facilitated Japanese FDI in Singapore.

Taking advantage of preferential tariffs in Singapore was also considered by Japanese firms as an important motivator for investment. As early as 1971, Japan had its first yen revaluation and the application of the General System of Preference (GSP), which had seriously affected Japanese labor-intensive industries (such as textile, lumber, and sundry processing industries) in their export drive (Sekiguchi 1983: 246–48). Furthermore, prompted by increasing wage rates, higher energy prices, and higher prices for some natural resources, Japanese firms were forced to pursue radical industrial restructuring and overseas investment. By January 1989, Japanese firms were to a large extent entitled to the GSP, despite the fact that over the past few years protectionist tendencies have escalated due to the continuation of the worldwide economic recession. Some manufactures produced in Singapore, however, have been excluded from the GSP. The United States graduated Singapore from the GSP in January 1989, and such other countries as Canada, European countries, Australia, and New Zealand are restricting imports of Singapore's manufactures by reducing Singapore's benefits

---

4. For more information, see Peat Marwick, *Singapore Zeisei, Kaikei Seido, Kaisha-ho no Gaiyo* (Taxation, Accounting and Company Law in Singapore) (Singapore, July 1986), 23–35.

from the GSP. American MNCs in Singapore suffered seriously from the protectionist measure, and Japanese firms were also affected. It is expected that manufactures produced in Singapore will be increasingly excluded from the GSP. Consequently, it is believed that Japanese firms have excluded the GSP as a motivator for investment in Singapore since January 1989. Japanese firms can, however, make themselves entitled to various preferential tariffs extended by the Singapore government when they shift their production operations to Singapore.

The quality of the labor force in Singapore has also been an important attraction for Japanese FDI. Singapore's educational level is comparatively higher among the ASEAN countries despite the fact that its labor quality in the manufacturing industries is the lowest among the Asian NIEs. Singapore is said to have lacked middle-level managerial staff. Upgrading the quality of unskilled labor and creating a stratum of middle management are therefore crucial to Singapore's economic development. Singapore is, however, suitable for developing high-value-added, high-tech, and knowledge-intensive industries because it has sufficient engineers, professionals, and high-level managerial staff. Singapore could recruit, as it has done before, professional personnel from all over the world whenever needed. By and large, high-value-added, high-tech, and knowledge-intensive industries in Singapore have not, compared to other Southeast Asian countries, encountered any difficulty in recruiting professional personnel.

It should be pointed out that high labor cost in Singapore is one of the obstacles to attracting FDI. By 1985, Singapore's labor cost was the highest not only among the ASEAN countries but also among Asia's newly industrializing economies (NIEs).[5] Compared to Japan's labor cost,[6] however, Singapore appears to be attractive to Japanese firms. Besides, after the Economic Committee's recommendation on wage restraint and reform in February 1986, wages in Singapore were effectively restrained.[7] Singapore regained its international competitiveness thereafter. The National Wages Council (NWC) had further recom-

---

5. In 1984, the hourly wages of production workers of Asian NIEs were: Singapore US$2.37, Taiwan US$1.90, Hong Kong US$1.40, and South Korea US$1.32.
6. In 1984, the hourly wages in manufacturing industry in the selected countries were: U.S.A. US$9.17, Canada US$8.18, Japan US$5.91, the Netherlands US$5.44, and the U.K. US$4.91.
7. Besides wage restraint, the following measures had also been taken. First, to reduce employers' Central Providence Fund (CPF), contributions were decreased from 25% to 10%. Second, corporate taxes were reduced from 40% to 30%. Third, to introduce an across-the-board investment, allowance of 30% on investments in machinery and equipment was made.

mended that wage restraint continue to be exercised in 1987. In the end, Singapore succeeded in rapid recovery in 1987, and the economic growth from 1988 appeared promising.[8]

By 1986, the average wage of Singapore workers in manufacturing industries was the highest among the ASEAN countries including China. Among the Asian NIEs, however, Singapore was lower than Korea and Hong Kong. Singapore was about one-seventh that of Japan. Therefore, from the viewpoint of Japanese firms, operation costs in Singapore are still manageable.[9] Japanese firms are usually good at technical innovation, improvement of manufactures, and the collection of business knowhow. Within the investment environment in Singapore, Japanese firms are seen to be able to achieve these goals comfortably. Labor cost, which is estimated to comprise 10–15% of the production costs of machinery industries, is therefore not a decisive factor in determining the competitiveness of manufactured goods produced (Nomura Research Institute 1987: 7). Moreover, since Japanese DFI in Singapore is becoming increasingly capital and knowledge intensive, less and less manpower (especially unskilled workers) will be required. As long as Singapore can provide sufficient engineers, managerial staff, and other professional personnel, Japanese firms are likely to increase their business activities in the country.

Industrial Distribution and Type of Ownership

The precise number of Japanese-affiliated firms by sector in Singapore is difficult to ascertain for the reason that, in recent years, the Singapore government (Economic Development Board) has ceased to disclose detailed breakdowns, which is said to be due to industrial secrecy and

---

8. The Finance Minister of Singapore, Dr. Richard Hu, predicted that the Singapore economy would chalk up 3 to 4% growth for 1987 and 6% from 1988 (*Straits Times*, May 25, 1987, p.1). As a matter of fact, Singapore succeeded in having an 8.8% and 11.0% economic growth in 1987 and 1988 respectively.

9. In October 1985, the Japan Chamber of Commerce and Industries (JCCI) in Singapore submitted a report based on a questionnaire survey of Japanese manufacturing industries in Singapore to the Singapore government. The report urged the government to look into four areas of concern: high operation costs, inadequacy of the labor force and the working attitude of employees, support of industry, and economic policies (centered around high wage policy and restrictions on foreign workers) of the government. Since then, problems pertaining to high wage and operation costs in Singapore have been effectively remedied. Japanese firms in Singapore have now faced the problems of the working attitude of employees (that is, mainly job-hopping) and the inadequacy in nurturing supporting industries in Singapore.

sensitivity. A list of Japanese-affiliated firms by sector in Singapore can instead be gathered from the Registrar of Companies (ROC) in Singapore. Such a list lacks accuracy, however, for two reasons. First, some firms have not actually started their businesses although they have registered with the ROC. Second, some firms evacuate or cease activity without informing either the ROC or the local Japanese official representatives (for example, the Japanese Embassy in Singapore). In addition, paid-up capital of Japanese firms has always been smaller than authorized capital. Comprehensive statistics pertaining to the Japanese FDI in Singapore therefore cannot be acquired from the ROC.

Industrial Distribution

Statistics available here are from two sources. One is the regular surveys conducted by Japanese institutions in Singapore.[10] The second is the Ministry of Finance in Japan. There are discrepancies between the two. The figures from the Japanese institutions are said to include approximately 90% of Japanese firms that responded to the surveys. Firms that have evacuated or ceased activities have been excluded from the surveys. The Ministry of Finance figures include cases of investment that have registered with the Ministry. It is believed that a single firm may have more than one case of investment due to business expansion. Furthermore, the dates and capital investment registered with the Ministry of Finance sometimes may not correspond to the actual Japanese FDI in Singapore.

These two sources are nevertheless thus far considered the most reliable and provide us with a pretty clear picture of industrial distribution of Japanese firms in Singapore.

Source One:

Table 3 reveals Japanese investment by industry in Singapore in 1970, 1980, 1982, and 1985.[11] The following features can be identified. First, in the manufacturing sector, Japanese firms have a very high concentration in electronics and electrical fields.[12] In 1970, the textile industry

---

10. See footnote 2.
11. Japanese institutions (JSA, JTC, JE, and JCCI) in Singapore conducted questionnaire surveys on Japanese firms these years.
12. In 1986, there were 166 leading foreign-affiliated firms invested in electronics and electrical products in Singapore. The breakdown includes the U.S. 71, Europe 40, Japan 44, Australia and New Zealand 7, and others 4. Singapore deserves its status as an important production base for electronics and electrical industries for multinational corporations (MNCs) in Asia.

Table 3. Development of Japanese Investment, by Industry, 1970, 1980, 1982, and 1985.

Industry	1970		1980		1982		1985	
	No. of Enterprises	%	No. of Enterprises	%	No. of Enterprises	%	No. of Enterprises	%
Manufacturer								
Food & Beverage	3	3.0	9	1.3	10	1.3	11	1.6
Textile & Textile Products	5	5.0	8	1.1	5	0.6	2	0.3
Ferrous & Non-ferrous Products	6	6.0	37	5.2	36	4.6	25	3.7
Petroleum & Chemical Products	9	9.0	35	4.9	36	4.6	25	3.7
Machinery	1	1.0	14	1.9	13	1.6	23	3.4
Electronic & Electrical Products	3	3.0	85	11.8	87	11.1	77	11.4
Transportation Machinery	2	2.0	9	1.3	17	2.2	5	0.7
Other Manufacturing	8	8.0	45	6.3	50	6.4	44	6.5
Subtotal	37	37.0	242	33.7	254	32.3	212	31.4
Non-Manufacturer								
Construction & Engineering	9	9.0	78	10.9	77	9.8	64	9.6
Foreign Trade & Commerce	23	23.0	198	27.6	223	28.4	138	20.4
Transportation & Warehousing	6	6.0	48	6.7	61	7.8	55	8.1
Other Non-manufacturing	20[a]	20.0	111[a]	15.5	121[b]	15.4	161[c]	23.8
Subtotal	63	63.0	476	66.4	532	67.7	464	68.6
	100	100.0	718	100.0	786	100.0	676	100.0

Source: Figures for the years 1970 and 1980 from Nihon Shingaporu Kyokai (Japan Singapore Association), *Shingaporu no Nikei Kigyo* (Japanese Business Activities in Singapore) (Tokyo, 1986), 13.
Figures for 1982 from Japan Trade Centre (Singapore), *Japanese Affiliated Firms in Singapore* (March 1983), 164.
Figures for 1985 from Japan Trade Centre (Singapore), *Japanese Affiliated Firms in Singapore* (March 1986), 166.

Notes: a. Indicates services firms, etc.
b. Indicates services firms comprising 34 wholly owned subsidiaries, 37 joint ventures, 8 branch offices, 25 representative offices, and 17 others.
c. Includes 44 liaison offices of manufacturers, 3 fishery and marine products firms, 1 mining firm, 61 services firms, 5 real estate firms, and 47 non-manufacturing firms (instead of 44 as stated in the reference source).

together with the ferrous and non-ferrous industry, and the petroleum and chemical industry attracted substantial Japanese FDI.[13] However, the importance of Japanese FDI in the textile industry has diminished drastically — from 5 in 1982 to on 2 in 1985. Japan has shifted her investment in Singapore from the relatively low-tech and labor intensive industries to capital and skill-intensive industries. Second, the Japanese investment in Singapore's non-manufacturing sector has been gaining momentum. The ratios of manufacturing to non-manufacturing sectors during the years 1970, 1980, 1982, and 1985 were 1:1.7, 1:3.0, 1:3.1, and 1:3.2 respectively. The number of manufacturing industries has been overwhelmed by that of non-manufacturing industries. In addition, among the non-manufacturing industries, foreign trade and commerce have attracted substantial Japanese FDI. This is a reflection of Singapore's position as a trade and commercial center in the Asia-Pacific region.

Between 1970 and 1985, the number of Japanese firms increased sixfold in foreign trade and commerce, sevenfold in construction and engineering, and ninefold in both finance and insurance and transportation and warehousing. If other "non-manufacturing" is included, the number of non-manufacturing firms had increased 7.4 times, from 63 firms in 1970 to 464 firms in 1985. If however we confine Japanese business activities to the years 1982 and 1985, data provided in Table 3 reveal a different picture. First, overall, the number of non-manufacturing firms decreased except for those belonging to "other non-manufacturing." The number of construction and engineering firms decreased from 77 in 1982 to 64 in 1985; foreign trade and commerce from 223 to 138; finance and insurance from 50 to 46; and transportation and warehousing from 61 to 55. On the other hand, during the same period, the number of Japanese firms in Singapore's manufacturing sector also dropped from 254 to 212. In relative terms, Japanese FDI in Singapore's manufacturing and non-manufacturing sectors combined decreased from 786 in 1982 to 676 in 1985. In absolute terms, Japanese investment commitments in Singapore increased 3.3 times from US$ 73.7 million in 1982 to US$ 244.1 million in 1985 (Economic Development Board 1985–86: 18). Japanese FDI in Singapore is becoming more and more capital and technology intensive. Labor-intensive industries that are unable to automate or mechanize in time are forced to liquidate or to shift to neighboring ASEAN countries. The persistent

13. A study suggests that Japanese firms in Singapore were heavily concentrated in textiles and electronics in the early 1970s. Japanese firms were also heavily invested in textiles and electronics in Malaysia in 1978.

worldwide economic recession and particularly the sluggish economic situation in Singapore in 1984–1985 had threatened the survival of Japanese-affiliated firms with lower productivity, efficiency, and competitiveness. This group of Japanese firms appeared to be composed of textiles, ferrous and non-ferrous metals, transportation machinery, and electronics and electrical industries in the manufacturing sector; and construction and engineering, foreign trade and commerce, and transportation and warehousing firms in the non-manufacturing sector. During the period of Singapore's economic downturn in 1984–1985, Japanese firms in such areas as ferrous and non-ferrous, petroleum and chemicals, electronics and electrical, construction and engineering, and transportation and warehousing appeared to be badly affected.

Source Two:

The Japanese Ministry of Finance has provided the breakdown of Japanese FDI in Singapore for alternate years during the period 1981– 1987. Despite the possible shortcomings mentioned earlier, this source provides us with up-to-date Japanese cumulative investment, in both manufacturing and non-manufacturing, in Singapore in 1981, 1983, 1985, and 1987.

The following features can be observed in Table 4.1. First, both in relative and absolute terms, Japanese FDI in Singapore increased substantially during the period 1981–1987. Second, Japanese DFI in Singapore's manufacturing sector has been predominant but has shown a decline proportionately to non-Japanese FDI. Third, both in relative and absolute terms, Japanese FDI in Singapore's non-manufacturing sector has shown a substantial increase. Fourth, more and more Japanese firms are setting up branch offices in Singapore; their numbers increased from 77 at the end of 1981 to 106 at the end of 1987.

The breakdown of Japanese DFI in Singapore's manufacturing sector is shown in Table 4.2. The following features can be observed. First, Japanese FDI in Singapore's manufacturing sector increased substantially during the period 1981–1987. In relative terms, the cases of Japanese FDI increased 1.7 times, from 527 at the end of March 1981 to 894 at the end of March 1987. In absolute terms, FDI increased 2.3 times, from US$686 million to US$1,550 million during the same period. Second, Japanese FDI has been concentrating in chemicals, machinery, electrical and electronics, and to a lesser extent, transport equipment. The greatest amount of Japanese FDI at the end of March 1981 was in electrical and electronics and constituted one-fifth of Japan's total investment in Singapore, but chemicals had become the recipient

Table 4.1. Japanese Cumulative Investment in Singapore, 1981–1987.

Sectors	By End of March 1981			By End of March 1983			By End of March 1985			By End of March 1987		
	Cases	Amount (US$ million)	%	Cases	Amount (US$ million)	%	Cases	Amount (US$ million)	%	Cases	Amount (US$ million)	%
Manufacturing	527	686	73.5	706	1,006	73.0	826	1,352	70.1	894	1,550	60.3
Non-manufacturing	424	211	22.6	554	327	23.7	711	520	27.0	833	951	37.0
Branch Office	77	32	3.4	86	41	3.0	101	52	2.7	106	64	2.5
Real Estate	27	5	0.5	27	5	0.3	27	5	0.2	27	5	0.2
Total	1,055	934	100.0	1,373	1,382	100.0	1,665	1,929	100.0	1,860	2,570	100.0

Source: Compiled and computed from Okura-sho (Ministry of Finance), *Zaisei Kinyu Tokei Geppo* (Statistics on Finance, Monthly Bulletin) (Tokyo, various issues).

Table 4.2. Japanese Cumulative Investment in Singapore's Manufacturing Industry, by Major Industry Groups, 1981–1987.

Industry	By End of March 1981			By End of March 1983			By End of March 1985			By End of March 1987		
	Cases	Amount (US$ million)	%	Cases	Amount (US$ million)	%	Cases	Amount (US$ million)	%	Cases	Amount (US$ million)	%
Food	21	10	1.5	28	21	2.1	38	31	2.3	40	33	2.1
Textile	29	11	1.6	30	17	1.7	32	17	1.3	35	18	1.2
Wood & Pulp	11	11	1.6	11	11	1.1	11	11	0.8	14	14	0.9
Chemical	61	82	12.0	136	275	27.3	187	477	35.3	199	494	31.9
Metal & Non-metal	67	37	5.4	74	43	4.3	76	48	3.6	83	60	3.9
Machinery	90	123	17.9	111	183	18.1	120	259	19.2	129	337	21.7
Electrical & Electronics	130	138	20.1	170	172	17.0	201	205	15.2	219	254	16.4
Transport & Equipment	20	114	16.6	24	114	11.3	24	114	8.4	25	127	8.2
Others	98	160	23.3	122	173	17.1	137	190	14.1	150	213	13.7
Total	527	686	100.0	706	1,009	100.0	826	1,352	100.0	894	1,550	100.0

Source: Same as Table 4.1.

Table 4.3. Japanese Cumulative Investment in Singapore's Non-manufacturing Industry, by Major Industry Group, 1981–1987.

Industry	By End of March 1981			By End of March 1983			By End of March 1985			By End of March 1987		
	Cases	Amount (US$ million)	%	Cases	Amount (US$ million)	%	Cases	Amount (US$ million)	%	Cases	Amount (US$ million)	%
Agriculture & Forestry	3	1	0.5	4	1	0.3	6	1	0.2	6	2	0.2
Mining	—	—	—	—	—	—	3	3	0.6	3	3	0.2
Construction	50	17	8.1	59	19	5.9	68	29	5.6	70	30	0.2
Commerce	219	56	26.5	289	82	25.1	380	115	22.1	437	187	19.6
Finance & Insurance	18	12	5.7	24	20	6.1	30	83	16.0	63	287	30.1
Services	N.A.	N.A.	—	64	62	19.0	86	90	17.3	97	143	15.3
Transportation	N.A.	N.A.	—	20	39	11.9	39	82	15.8	53	152	16.0
Real Estate Business	N.A.	N.A.	—	4	8	2.4	7	11	2.1	10	40	4.2
Others	134	125	59.2	90	96	29.4	92	106	20.4	94	107	11.2
Total	424	211	100.0	554	327	100.0	711	520	100.0	833	951	100.0

Source: Same as Table 4.1.

of the most Japanese FDI by the end of March 1983. Japan's investment in chemicals constituted approximately one-third of Japan's total FDI in Singapore at the end of March 1987.

The breakdown of Japanese FDI in Singapore's non-manufacturing sector is shown in Table 4.3. It is clear that, first, Japanese FDI in Singapore's non-manufacturing sector increased substantially during the period 1981–1987. In relative terms, the cases of Japanese FDI doubled, from 424 at the end of March 1981 to 833 at the end of March 1987. In absolute terms, FDI increased 4.5 times, from US$211 million to US$951 million during the same period. Second, Japanese FDI has been concentrating on finance, insurance, commerce, transportation, and services. Japanese FDI in finance and insurance increased 24 times, from US$12 million at the end of 1981 to US$287 million at the end of March 1987, and constituted approximately one-third of Japanese FDI in Singapore's non-manufacturing sector at the end of March 1987.

Type of Ownership

Do Japanese investors prefer joint ventures or subsidiaries when they invest in Singapore or elsewhere? The answer to this question is contentious for many reasons.

It depends, first, very much on investors' overall competence and efficiency, which include capital availability, management knowhow, technology, and familiarity with the host country (in terms of such factors as culture, commercial practices, market network, and so on.). In the 1960s and early 1970s, a large proportion of Japanese FDI in Asia was believed to be confined to labor-intensive industries and small and medium-sized industries. In terms of capital availability, management knowhow, and technology, such industries are unavoidably in a weaker position compared to big businesses or MNCs of other nationalities. Under such circumstances it is quite rational for Japanese investors to search for business partners mainly from the host country.[14]

Second, the preference of Japanese investors is related to the nature of Japanese FDI. It is argued that an export-oriented type of investment has a better chance of obtaining approval for 100% ownership than an import-substitution type of investment (Yoshihara 1976: 64). By 1965,

---

14. A questionnaire survey conducted in Singapore reveals that Japanese firms have acquired their business partners through the following routes: exporters or importers in Singapore (57%); the Singapore government (11.4%); Japanese trading companies or trading partners in Singapore (2.9%); banks (5.7%) and others (22.9%). The date of this survey is not stated; however, it is likely that it was conducted in April 1974.

the strategy for industrial development in Singapore was based primarily on policies advocating import substitution. Therefore, an import-substitution type of investment, as long as it could make an impressive contribution to the creation of job opportunities and technological advance, was generally entitled to 100% ownership. The import-substitution type of investment, however, appeared to have difficulty in getting 100% ownership approved after 1965 (the year when Singapore was separated from Malaysia), as Singapore then shifted to promotion of export-oriented industries. Singapore switched its industrialization strategy from import substitution to export orientation in 1967. Import substitution industries became unattractive as they were restricted to products involving merely assembly (Lim Hua Sing 1983: 7). Import substitution industries were discouraged as Singapore lost its domestic markets in Malaysia after 1965. Japanese firms, which considered Singapore as a production base in aiming for regional and international markets, were then entitled to 100% ownership without much difficulty.

And last, Japanese investment preference is related to the Singapore government's involvement and participation. It is a well-known fact that the Singapore government has been actively involved in domestic economic activities.[15] A thorough study of government cooperation with Japanese firms and the development of such kinds of joint ventures is still not available. It is however clear that the Singapore government has a wide range of equity shares in Japanese firms, in both the manufacturing and service sectors.[16] Government participation in foreign firms is due to several reasons: strategic importance, prospects of development, and technology transfer are the main considerations in the government's decision whether to set up joint ventures with foreign firms. The government obviously has the final say despite the fact that a substantial proportion of foreign firms is keen to have 100% equity shares.

A survey conducted in Singapore in April 1974 revealed that 39.4% of Japanese firms preferred joint ventures; 48.5% declined to set up joint ventures (including those who wanted to set up subsidiaries but were rejected by Singapore); 6% had no specific preferences; and the

---

15. For a more detailed discussion, see Linda Low, "Public Enterprises in Singapore," in You Poh Seng and Lim Chong Yah, eds., *op. cit.*, 253–87.
16. To cite a few examples, the government has equity shares in Hitachi Electronic Devices (S) Pte. Ltd. (government equity holdings, 30%), Jurong Shipyard Ltd. (79%), Mitsubishi Singapore Heavy Industries Pte. Ltd. (49%), Petrochemical Industry of Singapore (20%), and Yaohan Singapore Pte. Ltd. (16.7%).

remaining 6% belonged to the "others" category (Ichimura 1980: 12–13). It is interesting that among the ASEAN countries, Singapore was the only country where Japanese firms chose subsidiaries over joint ventures (Ichimura 1980, 12– 13). Singapore's economic development has been heavily reliant on foreign investments and, compared to other ASEAN countries, it has less rigid rules and regulations that restrict equity shares of foreign firms. Japanese firms gave up their intention to set up subsidiaries in Indonesia, Malaysia, Thailand, and the Philippines as they knew that 100% ownership applications would not be accepted in most of those cases.[17]

The number of Japanese industries by sector and type of possession in 1982 is shown in Table 5. The following features may be derived. First, the number of 100% Japanese-owned companies is significant. The number of Japanese wholly-owned subsidiaries (271 firms), branch offices (101 firms), and liaison offices (127 firms) combined constituted 63.5% of the total number of Japanese firms in Singapore in 1982. In the manufacturing sector, we find a high concentration of these three types of companies in trade and commerce. In the non-manufacturing sector, the wholly-owned subsidiaries have concentrated particularly on the electronics and electrical industries. Second, next to the wholly-owned subsidiaries, joint ventures have still remained an important feature of Japanese FDI in Singapore. Aside from the comparatively high concentration in transportation, warehousing, and the chemical industries, joint ventures have particularly been significant in trade and commerce (65 firms) and, to a lesser extent, in electronics and electrical sectors (19 firms). Third, as a result, Japanese firms in Singapore have concentrated on trade and commerce (233 firms; 28% of Japan's total companies in Singapore in 1982), and, to a lesser extent, on electronics and electrical sectors (87 firms; 11%). Compared to the information gathered in Table 5 survey (which was conducted in May-September 1982), data shown in Table 6 indicate that Japanese-affiliated firms in Singapore decreased by 110 firms (14%) in August-October 1985. This

---

17. Among the ASEAN countries, both Indonesia and Malaysia have applied "Pribumi" and "Bumiputera" policies that limit foreign equity shares to 49%. Thailand and the Philippines have practiced rigid regulations, which were partly due to strong nationalism, that restrict foreign firms' ownership. However, in recent years, the ASEAN countries are allowing more and more foreign firms to have 100% of the equity shares provided that they meet certain requirements and specifications (for example, capital requirement, export-oriented industry with a fixed number of employees, investment in certain type of industries, and so on) set by the respective countries.

Table 5. Number of Companies, by Industry and Type of Possession, May–September 1982.

Industry	Wholly Owned Subsidiary	Joint Venture	Branch Office	Liaison Office	Others	Total
Total (%)	271 (34.5%)	250 (31.8%)	101 (12.8%)	127 (16.2%)	37 (4.7%)	786 (100%)
Finance	5	9	15	9	—	38
Insurance	—	3	3	6	—	12
Transportation & Warehousing	10	32	2	16	1	61
Construction & Engineering	11	21	36	7	2	77
Other Services	34	37	8	25	17	121
Manufacturing						
Food & Beverage	3	6	—	1	—	10
Textile & Textile Products	2	2	—	1	—	5
Ferrous & Non-ferrous Metals	13	13	—	8	2	36
Chemical Products	10	17	—	9	—	36
Transportation Machinery	5	5	2	5	—	17
Electronic & Electrical Products	57	19	2	8	1	87
Industrial Machinery	8	5	—	—	—	13
Other Manufacturing	27	16	2	2	3	50

Source: Japan Trade Centre (Singapore), *Japanese Affiliated Firms in Singapore* (March 1983), 164.

was a reflection of the worldwide economic recession and in particular the sluggish economic situation in Singapore. Singapore suffered a decline of 1.8% in real GDP in 1985 after experiencing consistently high economic growth for the two decades following 1965. Japanese-affiliated firms in Singapore suffered at different levels. From 1982 to 1985 the number of Japanese firms engaged in trade and commerce decreased from 223 to 138; in construction and engineering from 77 to 64; in transportation machinery from 17 to 5; and in electronics and electrical products from 87 to 77. These are some notable casualties that have arisen in key industrial sectors where Japanese firms have a high concentration. Singapore's economic climate can thus partly be judged from the performance and vicissitudes of Japanese-affiliated firms in these industrial sectors.

If we compare the two surveys of Tables 5 and 6 closely, the following features can be identified. First, the number of joint ventures decreased by 33% (82 firms), from 250 to 168, whereas the number of wholly-owned subsidiaries decreased by only 11% (31 firms), from 271 to 240. Judging by the casualty rates, joint ventures seemed to be more vulnerable or inflexible than the wholly-owned subsidiaries during times of economic downturn in Singapore. Especially in the trade and commerce sectors, the number of Japanese joint ventures decreased by as much as 60% (39 firms), from 65 in 1982 to merely 26 in 1985, whereas the number of wholly-owned subsidiaries decreased by merely 12% (10 firms), from 86 to 76, during the same period. It is believed that if no restrictions are imposed by Singapore, which has been that country's consistent policy, an increasing number of Japanese investors will prefer 100% shares in their future investments in Singapore. Second, the overall number of branch offices increased marginally from 101 to 105 whereas the number of liaison offices decreased slightly from 127 to 110. It is not easy to explain the change, as all of these offices are in Japanese-owned firms that exclude a third party's capital involvement. If we limit our observation to the trade and commerce sectors, it is not surprising to notice that the number of branch and liaison offices both decreased quite abruptly from 31 to 17 and from 30 to only 6 respectively due to the sluggish economy of Singapore. Perhaps one contributing factor for the overall decline was the setting up of a large number of branch offices and the closing down of liaison offices in the finance and insurance sectors. This is reflected in the fact that the number of liaison offices decreased abruptly from 15 to 6 and the number of branch offices in the finance and insurance sectors increased from 18 to 23. It remains unknown, however, to what extent liaison

Table 6. Number of Companies, by Industry, August–October 1985.

Industry	N.A.	Joint Venture	Wholly Subsidiary	Branch Office	Liaison Office	Others	Total
Manufacture							
Food and Beverage	0	4	5	0	1	1	11
Textile and Textile Products	0	1	0	0	1	0	2
Wood and Pulp	0	2	2	0	0	0	4
Petroleum and Chemical Products	0	14	9	1	1	0	25
Steel and Non-steel Products	0	11	5	3	6	0	25
Machinery	0	5	12	1	3	2	23
Electronic and Electrical Products	1	14	52	5	2	3	77
Transportation Machinery	0	2	2	0	1	0	5
Other Manufacturing	0	2	2	0	1	0	5
Liaison Office of Manufacturers	0	0	0	0	44	0	44
Subtotal	1	63	109	15	59	9	256
Non-manufacture							
Agriculture and Forestry	0	0	0	0	0	0	0
Fishery and Marine Products	0	0	1	0	2	0	3
Mining	0	1	0	0	0	0	1
Construction & Engineering	0	16	8	36	2	2	64
Trade and Commerce	1	26	76	17	6	12	138
Finance and Insurance	0	7	10	23	6	0	46
Services	0	21	18	5	4	13	61
Transportation and Warehousing	2	25	6	2	18	2	55
Real Estate	0	2	1	0	1	1	5
Other Non-manufacturing	0	7	11	7	12	10	47
Subtotal	3	105	131	90	51	40	420
Grand Total	4	168	240	105	110	49	676

Source: Japan Trade Centre (Singapore), *Japanese Affiliated Firms in Singapore* (March 1986), 183.

offices in the finance and insurance sectors have been upgraded to branch offices in Singapore. Nevertheless, the upgrading exercise should have taken place due to the important role played by Singapore as a financial center in the Asia-Pacific region. Japanese investors have undoubtedly expanded their activities in the finance and insurance sectors. Third, as expected, Japanese-affiliated firms suffered a serious setback[18] during the period 1982–1985. Japanese firms decreased by 14% from 786 in 1982 to 676 in 1985. The industries most affected during this period appear to be ferrous and non-ferrous (from 36 to 25), petroleum and chemical (from 36 to 25), transportation machinery (from 17 to 5), electronics and electrical (from 87 to 77), trade and commerce (from 223 to 138), and construction and engineering (from 77 to 64). Obviously, Japanese-affiliated firms in trade and commerce suffered the most serious setback during this period. The overall decline in manufacturing industries has naturally adversely affected the performance of those firms dealing with trade and commerce.

Employment in Japanese Enterprises

One of the most important contributions of Japanese FDI in Singapore pertains to employment opportunities generated by Japanese firms. In 1980, 718 Japanese-affiliated firms in Singapore provided 70,323 employment opportunities to Singaporeans and guest employees mainly from Malaysia, together with 2,909 Japanese and 171 other expatriates. Employees working for Japanese firms formed 6.7% of Singapore's total workforce.[19] In 1982, 786 Japanese firms provided 70,870 employment opportunities to Singaporeans and guest employees from Malaysia. In

18. They have always been casualties in Japan's foreign direct investments, especially in Asia. The reasons for and significance of Japanese casualties in the 1970s have been examined by Ichimura Shinichi, ed., op. cit., 183–201. The latest study further shows that during the period January 1985–December 1986, the number of withdrawals by Japanese-affiliated firms overseas amounted to 191 cases. The breakdown is as follows: Asia, 65 cases (34%); North America, 41 cases (21.5%); Latin America, 26 cases (13.6%); Africa, 24 cases (12.6%); Europe, 20 cases (10.5%); and others, 15 cases (7.9%). The industrial groups are as follows: commerce, 36 cases; transportation, 26 cases; textiles, 18 cases; finance and insurance, 17 cases; agriculture and fisheries, 15 cases; and others. The highest casualties are seen in the manufacturing sector, which amounted to 67 cases (35.1% of the total). See Toyo Keizai, op. cit., 7.
19. In 1980 the total workforce in Japanese firms was 73,403 persons (Nihon Boeki Shinko-kai, op. cit. [July 1981],183) whereas Singapore's total workforce was 1,093,400 persons (Department of Statistics, Economic and Social Statistics, [Singapore 1960–1982, 1983], 32).

Table 7. Number of Employees, by Type of Ownership, 1981.

	Local	Japanese	Other Expatriate	Total
Wholly Owned Subsidiary	28,377	969	51	29,401
Joint Venture	37,824	868	72	38,764
Branch Office	3,088	760	9	3,857
Representative Office	231	206	—	437
Others	803	106	35	944
Total	70,323	2,909	171	73,403

Sources: Nihon Boeki Shinko-Kai (Japan External Trade Organization) and
    Kaigai Keizai Joho Senta (Overseas Economic Information Centre),
    Shingaporu ni Okeru Nikkei Shinshutsu Kigyo no Gensei (The Present
    Situation of Japanese Affiliated Firms in Singapore) (publisher un-
    known, July 1981).

addition, 3,250 Japanese and 69 expatriates were also employed in these
firms. They formed 6.2% of Singapore's total workforce.[20]
    The number of employees by type of ownership in 1980 is shown in
Table 7. Japanese joint ventures employed 38,764 workers (52.8% of the
total workforce in Japanese firms), whereas Japanese wholly-owned
subsidiaries employed 29,397 workers (40.1%). Table 8 further reveals
that 54,692 persons (74.5%) were employed in the manufacturing
sector, which comprised 16.9% of Singapore's total manufacturing
workforce.[21] Viewed from this aspect, it can be argued that some
electronics and electrical industries were highly labor intensive. In 1982
the labor situation in Japanese manufacturing industries had remained
almost unchanged. It is shown in Table 9 that 48,546 workers (68.5%)

20. Nihon Boeki Shinko-kai, op. cit.; Department of Statistics, op. cit. At the end of 1984,
    757 American firms in Singapore employed 71,130 workers, which formed 6.1% of
    Singapore's total workforce, up from 5.5% in 1982 ("American Investment: Singapore,"
    Embassy of the U.S.A., unpublished paper [Singapore, June 1985], 8). 1000 Ameri-
    cans were employed in 757 American firms in 1984 compared to 2,909 Japanese who
    were employed in 718 Japanese firms in 1980 and 3,250 Japanese who were employed
    in 786 Japanese firms in 1982. Accordingly, it is clear that Japanese firms had a higher
    proportion of nationals compared to their American counterparts.
21. A similar feature can also be found in American firms in Singapore. At the end of
    1984 slightly over two-thirds of the workforce were employed in the American
    manufacturing industries, which comprised 17% of Singapore's total manufacturing
    workforce. In addition, the bulk of the manufacturing employees were engaged in
    the electronics industry (Embassy of the U.S.A., op. cit., 8).

Table 8. Number of Employees, by Industry, 1981.

	Local	Japanese	Other Expatriate	Total
Finance	734	109	1	844
Insurance	212	14	3	229
Transportation & Warehousing	739	98	8	845
Foreign Trade & Commerce	3,827	474	11	4,312
Construction & Engineering	8,391	693	22	9,106
Other Services	2,990	335	50	3,375
Manufacturing (total)	53,430	1,186	76	54,692
Food & Beverage	671	22	10	703
Textile	1,697	18	3	1,718
Ferrous & Non-ferrous	4,526	105	12	4,643
Chemical	1,769	103	13	1,885
Transportation Machinery	4,087	102	—	4,189
Electronic & Electrical	27,728	527	22	28,277
Industrial Machinery	6,236	161	—	6,397
Other Manufacturing	6,716	148	16	6,880
Total	70,323	2,909	171	73,403

Sources: Nihon Boeki Shinko-Kai (Japan External Trade Organization) and Kaigai Keizai Joho Senta (Overseas Economic Information Centre), *Shingaporu ni Okeru Nikkei Shinshutsu Kigyo no Gensei* (The Present Situation of Japanese Affiliated Firms in Singapore) (publisher unknown, July 1981).

were employed in the manufacturing sector, which comprised 14.4% of Singapore's total manufacturing workforce. Again, the bulk of the manufacturing employees was engaged in the electronics and electrical sectors, which comprised 48.8% of the total workforce in the manufacturing sector.

In 1988 Japanese firms in Singapore employed 69,179 persons (5.4% of Singapore's total workforce), of which 67,441 persons (97.5% of the total workforce in Japanese firms) were Singaporeans and guest workers other than Japanese, and 1,738 persons (2.5%) were of Japanese origin (Table 10). The following additional features can also be identified. First, in contrast to the incremental growth in Japanese FDI in Singapore, the total workforce employed by Japanese firms is diminishing. Second, the manufacturing sector comprised 79.6% of the total workforce employed in Japanese firms. Third, electronics and electrical industries

Table 9. Number of Employees, by Industry, May–September 1982.

Industry	No. of Companies	Total No. of Employees	Local	Guest Employees				
				Total	From Malaysia	Countries other than Malaysia	Japanese	Other Expatriate
Total	786	70,870	56,709	10,842	7,411	3,411	3,250	69
(%)		(100.0%)	(80.0%)	(15.3%)	(10.5%)	(4.8%)	(4.6%)	(0.1%)
Finance	38	1,036	2	2	—	155	3	3
Insurance	12	204	187	2	1	1	15	4
Transportation & Warehousing	61	1,348	1,087	130	8	122	127	12
Trade & Commerce	233	6,158	5,369	101	83	18	676	6
Construction & Engineering	77	10,524	6,688	3,132	1,885	1,247	698	21
Other Services	121	3,054	2,548	162	144	18	323	
Manufacturing (total)	254	48,546	39,954	7,313	5,288	2,025	1,256	23
Food & Beverage	10	649	535	90	52	38	24	—
Textile & Textile Products	5	188	154	26	17	9	8	9
Ferrous & Non-ferrous	36	4,591	3,203	1,205	969	236	174	6
Chemical Products	36	1,888	1,408	289	242	47	185	1
Transportation Machinery	17	5,578	4,355	1,100	459	641	122	6
Electronic & Electrical Products	87	23,466	20,131	2,840	2,223	617	489	—
Industrial Machinery	13	5,080	4,433	582	394	188	65	6
Other Manufacturing	50	7,106	5,735	1,181	932	249	189	1

Source: Japan Trade Centre (Singapore), *Japanese Affiliated Firms in Singapore* (March 1983), 166.

Table 10. Number of Employees in Japanese Industries in Singapore, 1988.

	Local	Japanese	No. of Executives and Directors
Manufacturing (total)	54,087	982	218
Food & Beverages	651	45	11
Textile	841	5	3
Wood Products	832	14	1
Pulp & Paper Products	128	2	1
Publishing & Printing	1,603	13	6
Chemical	2,732	141	42
Rubber & Leather	786	21	5
Ceramics & Quarrying	691	15	7
Iron & Steel	407	11	4
Non-ferrous metal	1,635	39	11
Metal Products	2,198	36	11
General Electricity	5,887	115	15
Electronic & Electrical Products	29,887	435	81
Transportation Equipment	2,443	34	8
Precision Equipment	1,531	22	6
Others	1,835	34	8
Commerce	7,899	389	137
Finance & Insurance	572	152	60
Real Estate	29	4	3
Transport	1,235	78	29
Services	2,349	48	20
Construction	1,126	72	35
Others	93	10	2
Unknown	51	3	—
All Industries	67,441	1,738	504

Source: Toyo Keizai Shimposha, *Kaigai Shinshutsu Kigyo Soran* (Japanese Companies, Facts and Figures) (Tokyo, 1989), 150.

(including general electricity) had 36,324 employees (66.0% and 52.5% of the total Japanese manufacturing industries and the total Japanese industries, respectively, in Singapore). Fourth, in the non-manufacturing sector, commerce industries constituted the largest share, with a total number of 8,288 employees (12.0% of the total workforce in Japanese firms in Singapore).

Japanese manufacturing industries, especially electronics and electrical, require a large number of guest workers mainly from the Malay Peninsula. As early as 1968 the Singapore government relaxed its immigration policy in order to attract foreign workers. The number of foreign workers in 1973 constituted one-eighth of Singapore's total workforce. The number of foreign workers has since fluctuated but foreign workers have not disappeared from Singapore's labor market scene. Despite the fact that the Singapore government has discouraged the influx of foreign unskilled workers due to industrial restructuring particularly after 1979, the number of foreign workers still comprised 7% of Singapore's total workforce in 1980.[22] In the manufacturing sector, the corresponding figure was as high as 46%. It is clear that securing a sufficient supply of foreign workers is crucial to the development of Singapore's manufacturing industries, but the compulsory employers' Central Provident Fund (CPF) contributions and the heavy levy imposed by the government on employers of foreign workers have greatly perturbed investors and stimulated their protest.[23] The ultimate aim of readjusting CPF[24] and imposing a heavy levy is said to be to encourage investors to mechanize and automate their facilities. If, however, the labor-intensive nature and low productivity of the Singapore facilities are maintained, investors will be forced to liquidate or shift to neighboring countries, where cheaper labor is available.

Japanese-Style Management in Singapore

A Move to Introduce Japanese-style Management
In the early 1980s the Singapore government started to look into the

---

22. The Singapore government declined to disclose the number of foreign workers from 1980 on.
23. Both employer and employee contribute to CPF. From the employees' viewpoint, the more CPF paid by their employers the better, as it ultimately belongs to the employees. CPF contributions have been adjusted again and again by the government. Employers' contributions were reduced from 25 to 10% in 1986, after Singapore's economic downturn in 1984–85. It was readjusted from July 1, 1989 to 15% as Singapore experienced 8.8% and 11.0% GDP growth rates in 1987 and 1988 respectively. The levy, paid by employers to the government, brings no benefits to the employees. Since 1 July 1989 employers have been asked to pay S$240 to the government if they employed a foreign worker; this is said to be aimed at restricting avoidable employment of foreign workers.
24. The Singapore government has also argued that as employers' CPF contributions were cut soon after the economic downturn in 1984–85, and as Singapore has continued to experience high GDP growth rates employers' contributions were raised again in 15% from July 1, 1989.

possibility of introducing the Japanese-style managerial system (which usually refers to a combination of a lifetime employment system, a seniority wage system, and an in-house union into big enterprises, especially Japanese enterprises in Singapore. The government's rationale rested on three basic reasons. First, Japan's rapid economic development was perceived by the Singapore government as a developmental model. Second, Japanese FDI in Singapore was perceived as crucial to Singapore's industrial restructuring toward high-tech, high value-added, and knowledge intensive activities. Third, the number of Japanese affiliated enterprises in Singapore has remained at a high level among foreign enterprises.

Under the Singapore government's initiative, a comprehensive feasibility study was carried out through the following three measures. Japanese experts on management or productivity were invited to serve as advisers or consultants to the National Productivity Board (NPB); with the assistance of the NPB research staff, a number of books on Japanese management were published by these experts under NPB sponsorship. Japanese experts and academicians were invited to give lectures on Japanese managerial systems; such lectures were initiated mainly by the Economic Development Board (EDB) and the Trade Development Board (TDB) together with the NPB. Government officials were sent to Japan to study Japanese management; they gathered first-hand information from companies, factories, and government organizations in Japan.

Through such thorough and comprehensive studies, the Singapore government was quick to realize that Japanese managerial systems were not applicable to Singaporean enterprises, even to Japanese-affiliated enterprises. No official reasons were given for this conclusion, as discussed in the following section.

The Impracticability of Adapting Japanese Managerial Practices to Singapore

The Singapore government had neither publicly nor officially announced that it was looking into the possibility of introducing Japanese management systems into Singaporean enterprises. Any subsequent official announcement pertaining to such a scheme's impracticability thus was unnecessary. Through bits and pieces of views and opinions as expressed by government officials in Singapore's local newspapers, however, it was revealed that the Singapore government had at one time seriously studied Japanese management. Although debate regarding the issue disappeared from the local mass media soon after, later arguments suggested that Japanese managerial practices without modification and rectification would not be applicable in Singapore.

The reasons for the impracticability of applying Japanese management systems — without modification and rectification — in Singapore can perhaps be derived from the following aspects of Singaporean culture.

First, Singapore is a society strongly influenced by Western culture. Singaporeans are said to be individualistic and economically pragmatic as are people in the Western countries. Job-hopping for better remuneration and career advancement is particularly common in Singapore. Remaining in the same job for a long period may be perceived as the result of an employee's inefficiency or incapability. In addition, the pledging of one's loyalty to a single company for life is totally unimaginable for most Singaporeans. A lifetime employment system is therefore impracticable and inapplicable in Singapore.

Second, Singapore is a heterogeneous society, with a population comprised of 76% Chinese, 15% Malays, 7% Indians, and 2% Eurasians and others (1988 census). (Although they are much influenced by Confucianism and qualify as part of the "chopsticks culture," Singaporean Chinese are also very much influenced by the West.) The nature of Singaporean society—with its diverse races, religions, and cultures—makes the implantation of the lifetime employment system and the seniority wage system impossible. In addition, as mentioned in previous chapters, Singaporean enterprises, particularly manufacturing industries, employ substantial numbers of foreign workers (mainly from Malaysia) on a contract basis and expect such employees to commute every day or to leave Singapore when the contracts expire. This further adds to the impracticability of the lifetime employment and seniority wage systems in Singapore. Japan, on the other hand, is basically a homogeneous society, a nation of one people and one culture, despite the existence of approximately 0.7 million Koreans and 60–70,000 Chinese. Members of the "chopsticks culture" and very much influenced by Confucianism, the Japanese are loyal to their companies, and so the lifetime employment system and the seniority wage system are practicable in Japan.

Third, Singapore has a very large number of multinational enterprises of different nationalities. As mentioned earlier, Singapore has attracted multinational enterprises not only from Japan but also from the United States and the European Economic Community. In recent years Asian NIEs (from Korea, Taiwan, and Hong Kong) also increased their investments in Singapore. Even if Japanese managerial systems could be implanted in Japanese enterprises in Singapore, multinational enterprises of other nationalities might not follow suit. Mid-career employment, for example, discouraged in Japanese enterprises, are acceptable, not to say encouraged, in Western enterprises. Furthermore, Japanese enterprises may provide on-the-job training for their employees, but the trained employees may well be absorbed by Western enterprises at a later stage. Employees sent by Japanese companies to Japan for training may job-hop after returning to Singapore. Local employees are of course bonded, but Japanese employers always find it too troublesome to take the oath breakers to court. It can be seen, then, that Japanese managerial systems can never be practiced solely by one enterprise of a particular nationality without the group consent of all the enterprises of other nationalities in Singapore.

What modifications and rectifications would make the practice of Japanese managerial systems in Singapore possible to some degree? Japanese enterprises using modified Japanese-style managerial systems in Singapore have constituted a substantial amount of FDI in that country. The extent to which the Japanese-style management has been practiced in Singapore will now be discussed in more detail.

Characteristics of Japanese-style Managerial Systems

Japanese-affiliated enterprises have applied a rather loose form of Japanese-style management system, in general observing the following practices.

(1) Japanese employers usually do not sign contracts with their employees, in contrast to the practice of local private, public, and Western enterprises, which often sign contracts for, say, one to three years with their employees. Successful local staff of Japanese enterprises become fulltime employees after a six-month probation period. Such employees are allowed to work until the retirement age of 55 (it has recently been proposed to extend it to 60) if they do not commit any serious mistakes or offenses.

(2) Midcareer employees are generally not recruited. Managerial staff are promoted from the rank and file.

(3) Wages are basically figured by seniority. The longer the period an employee has worked, the higher are his or her wages. Wage increments or incentives are given once a year according to the employees' performance and the company's profits. The National Wages Council (NWC) provides guidelines to the public and private sectors every year. Wage increments, incentives, and bonuses are adjusted and determined accordingly although these guidelines are said to be noncompulsory.

(4) In practice, managerial staff are not allowed to join unions. Singapore's largest trade union, the National Trade Unions Congress

(NTUC), has a central committee that is staffed by high-ranking ministers and government officials. NTUC member unions are determined not by the profession of individuals but by enterprise (for example, Singapore Bank Union). The relationship between trade unions and enterprises has been harmonious. Labor disputes have been settled and wage adjustments made through collective bargaining. In-house unions are not implanted in Japanese enterprises, despite the eagerness shown by the government to do so, because the relationship between employees and employers is harmonious.

(5) To a certain extent, on-the-job training and job rotation is applied. Employees, especially on the managerial staff, do not usually stay in one department or section for a long time. Employees are trained by working in different departments or sections, which differs distinctly from non-Japanese enterprises. Japanese enterprises prefer their employees to have comprehensive experience while non-Japanese enterprises demand specialization.

(6) Japanese enterprises demand overtime. Rank-and-file employees are entitled to an overtime allowance (OT allowance). Managerial staff (officers and above) are not entitled to OT allowance, but a "meal allowance" (usually S$10) is given if they work until 8:00 P.M.

Several reports (some prepared by JETRO in Singapore) and some public opinion hold that—in terms of the working environment, remuneration, and career advancement—Japanese enterprises are less attractive as compared to their Western counterparts. Furthermore, public enterprises in Singapore appear to be very attractive to university graduates. Among Japanese university graduates in Singapore, 28% are working for the Singapore government and in the public sector, and 25% for Japanese enterprises (including joint ventures). Entrepreneurial activities and non-Japanese enterprises have absorbed 20% and 17% respectively (Table 11).

After the phenomenal yen appreciation in 1985, Japanese FDI in Singapore increased remarkably. Japanese enterprises in Singapore are looking for increasing numbers of Japanese university graduates as well as for graduates of the National University of Singapore and the Nanyang Technological College. Japanese enterprises nevertheless appear to be less appealing than Western multinational corporations and public enterprises. Numerous posts in the Japanese enterprises remain unfilled, and job-hopping continues to be a common phenomenon. An additionally modified and rectified Japanese-style management is needed in order to adapt to the diverse races, religions, and cultures of Singaporean society.

Table 11.   Occupational Distribution of Japanese University Graduates in Singapore, 1989.

	(%)
Government and Public Sector	27.97
Japanese Enterprises (including joint ventures)	24.90
Entrepreneurial Activities	19.92
Non-Japanese Enterprises	16.86
Others	10.34

Source: Wong Len Poh, "The Roles of Japan Alumni in Singapore," paper presented at the 8th ASCOJA Conference in Thailand, Sept. 30–Oct. 3, 1989 (September 1989).

Conclusions

The twin engines of Singapore's rapid economic development, particularly after 1965, have been FDI and the Singapore government's active involvement in economic activities. Among direct foreign investors, the Japanese are becoming more and more important. The United States used to be the single largest investor in Singapore but since 1986 has been surpassed by Japan. Japanese FDI, together with American and European FDI, is indipensable to Singapore's objective of restructuring its economy into a high-tech, high value-added, and knowledge-intensive one. There are indications that some Japanese electronics and electrical industries, prompted by the 1985 yen appreciation, have expanded their activities in Singapore.[25] Singapore has become an important production base for Japanese manufacturing industries, especially for high-tech and high value-added industries.

Japanese nonmanufacturing industries have also increased invest-

25. It is reported that AIWA and Kenwood, both audio product manufacturers, built additional plants to cope with rising demand. Matsushita also announced plans for a seventh factory, to build facsimile machines, first of its kind in the country. Yokogawa Electric Corporation extended its operation beyond software development for process computer systems to manufacturing as well. SMC established a world-scale pneumatic components plant, Teraoka Seiko invested in both the manufacture of electronic scales and software for system integration, and Hoxan transferred to Singapore its automated solar cell manufacturing facilities. Sony Corporation established a precision component production and engineering support facility, its only such facility outside of Japan. Sony also set up its operational headquarters in Singapore, the first Japanese operational headquarters in Singapore. (See Economic Development Board, *Yearbook 1987/88* [Singapore], 27–28).

ments in Singapore. Japanese FDI since 1985 in Singapore's finance and insurance, commerce, service, and transportation sectors has particularly attracted attention. This trend seems to be further strengthened as Singapore's financial and commercial roles in the Asian and Pacific region gain momentum. The Singapore state's role in economic activities continues to remain paramount despite the fact that the government has hastened the implementation of its policies regarding the privatization and promotion of local enterprises. Singapore's local enterprises, mostly Chinese, have performed soundly in banking, finance, and other service sectors, but have been least effective in the manufacturing sector. The predominant proportion of Chinese enterprises in Singapore are SMBs and are highly labor-intensive. Together with some Japanese labor-intensive industries, they are faced with increasing operational costs (additional employers' CPF contributions and foreign workers' levy), and they will be forced to liquidate or shift to neighboring countries if they are unable to upgrade or automate their facilities in a timely fashion.

Some Japanese manufacturing industries (even some electronics and electrical industries) in Singapore are still quite labor-intensive and require substantial numbers of non-Singaporean workers, mainly from the Malay Peninsula. Such industries are increasingly shifting these high-labor intensive operations to other ASEAN countries or to China, where cheap labor is readily available—and the trend will probably continue, as the Singapore government is unlikely to stop imposing higher employers' CPF contributions and heavy foreign worker levies while it aims at expanding high-tech, high value-added, and knowledge-intensive activities.

Singaporeans have shown more eagerness to work in Japanese enterprises due to the remarkable influx of Japanese FDI in Singapore in recent years. In terms of remuneration and career advancement opportunities, however, the Japanese enterprises still appear to be less attractive compared to Singapore government institutions, public enterprises, and Western multinational corporations. The Japanese-style managerial system without modifications and rectifications is not suitable for such heterogeneous societies strongly influenced by Western cultures such as Singapore. Due to the growth of Japanese FDI in Singapore, a substantial number of employees, both managerial and rank and file, is severely needed by Japanese enterprises. Japanese investors should therefore modify and rectify their managerial systems in a more positive way in order to meet the requirements of Singapore's labor market. Japanese-style management must be internationalized and localized if it is to make greater positive contributions toward Singapore's rapid economic development.

Comment

Takeshi Mori

In his perceptive paper on Japanese business activities in Singapore, Professor Lim offers an insightful illustration of the significance of foreign capital in the development of the Singapore economy, salient features of Japanese investment, and the management style of Japanese affiliates in Singapore.

Although much of the paper is devoted to a discussion of Japan's direct investment in Singapore, Professor Lim has made very important observations on Japanese management. In his view, Japanese culture is very much influenced by Confucianism and ethnic homogeneity, which have been essential factors in the evolution of Japan's lifetime employment and seniority wage systems. Accordingly, because Singaporean society is multiracial and multicultural, those two systems cannot be implanted in Singapore. Another of Professor Lim's observations should particularly arrest the attention of Japanese management: "In terms of working environment, remuneration, and career advancement, Japanese enterprises are less attractive compared to their Western counterparts" and to public enterprises. The following remarks are intended partly to supplement and partly to modify Professor Lim's views by elaborating on some other related aspects of his comments.

In my view the economic policy and philosophy adopted and implemented by the Singapore governmental party (People's Action Party) since the independence of 1965 and characteristics of the labor market subsequently developed are more important reasons for the infeasibility of applying the lifetime employment and seniority wage systems in Singapore than is the racial and cultural multiplicity of Singaporean society.

When Singapore was forced, primarily by the racial conflict between ethnic Chinese and Malay, to part from Malaysia and become an independent nation the situation was full of uncertainties and difficulties. "Although the Indonesian confrontation ended in June 1966, the relation with Malaysia was still tense. Internally, with communist agitation, strikes and industrial action were rampant. Then in July 1967, Singapore suffered another blow: the British Government announced its intention to withdraw all its military forces east of Suez by 31 March 1971."[1]

The basic issue was survival. The government of Singapore believed that government interventions were necessary and desirable for citizens to make a living. Goh Keng Swee, the deputy prime minister wrote: "The laissez-faire policies of the colonial era had led Singapore to a dead-end, with little economic growth, massive unemployment, wretched housing and inadequate education. We had to try a more activist and interventionist approach."[2] The government has by now meticulously penetrated innumerable aspects of the social-economic life of Singapore—population control, housing, education, compulsory savings, industrial relations, wage policy, traffic management, press freedom, marriage of women with college degrees, and so on. At the same time the government promotes an ethos of rugged individualism that emphasizes self-sufficiency over collectivism particularly at the traditional clan level where nepotism leads to serious inefficiencies.

1. Ow Chin Hock, The Role of Government in Economic Development: The Singapore Experience," in Lim Chong Yah and Peter J. Lloyd, eds., *Singapore Resources and Growth* (London: Oxford University Press, 1986), 227.
2. Goh Keng-Swee, "A Socialist Economy that Works," in Devan Nair, ed., *Socialism That Works: The Singapore Way* (Federal Publications, 1976), 84.

Part II

JAPANESE-STYLE MANAGEMENT AND TECHNOLOGY TRANSFER

5
Review of Studies on Japanese-Style Management

Nobuo Kawabe and Tatsuo Kimbara

With the development of the Japanese economy during the past four decades, the management systems of Japanese companies began to attract much attention both inside and outside the country. It has become a topic of both scientific and practical interest on which a number of research studies have been done. The object of study is called Japanese-style management or Japanese management, and the researchers ask questions like: what is Japanese management anyway, what are its characteristics, how does it work, and what are the reasons for its success. Moreover, as Japanese business began investing in foreign countries, a new question was raised: how can it be applied to different cultural environments?

Here, we give a brief review of studies on Japanese management in order that the arguments found in the following chapters may be better understood. The first section lays out the main issues and concepts in the literature. The second section explains four approaches to Japanese management study. In the third section problems for future research are discussed.

Main Issues and Concepts

The origin of the Japanese management system dates back to quite an early time in terms of Japanese value systems and human relations (Hirschmeier and Yui 1975; Yoshino 1968). But it is the general view that Japanese-style management of modern corporations was partly formed in the big businesses of the 1920s (Odaka 1965), when Japan achieved an industrial revolution and witnessed the formation of the large modern corporation.

Different schools of Japanese management already existed by the 1950s. Those schools that specialized in studies on Japanese human relations and the labor market formed one of the mainstreams (Okochi

1952; Sumiya 1964). In most of the studies of this period Japanese management was viewed as a matter of industrial relations. Various influences derived partly from the German school of social politics and partly from the Marxist school. The severe troubles accompanying labor union activities in those days were regarded as being due to the backwardness of the society. The researchers concentrated on such factors as lifetime employment, the seniority system, periodic recruitment of school leavers, the internal promotion system, enterprise unions, and so on with the aim of clarifying the backward features of Japanese management.

Abegglen (1958), in contrast, evaluated the same factors as positive ones for the development of the Japanese economy. His analysis had a strong impact on the Japanese scholars, who mostly specialized in managerial studies, and they began to regard those factors affirmatively, while at the beginning the traditional factors were viewed rather negatively and as related to the backwardness of Japanese capitalism by dominant theorists of the time. Abegglen's revelation of the role of traditional labor practices in economic development became a turning point for the study of Japanese management. The Japanese scholars succeeded in organizing a second mainstream in the field of study, one that has had a stronger impact on the study of Japanese management in accordance with the economic growth of the country.

At that time researchers and top managers were not sure whether Japanese management could be maintained in the future. Although the economy achieved rapid growth in the 1960s and early 1970s, it was not until 1967 that Japan, with serious doubts about its competitive position in the world market, liberalized capital investment. A number of studies on Japanese management were undertaken after the 1950s with the rise of interest in Japan's economic development.

Since then, many studies have been done from various viewpoints and based on concepts and subjects in different dimensions including industrial relations, employment systems, inter-organizational relations, strategy and structure, interpersonal relations, culture and value systems, and international management. In fact, Japanese management is a multi-dimensional field of study.

The main issues discussed in the studies are summarized as follows. The first issue concerns the basic principles underlying Japanese management and organization (Hazama 1963; Iwata 1977)—how and why it functions. Human resources management is one of the key factors emphasized in explaining Japanese management and organization. Groupism or collectivity-orientation is often pointed out as the basic principle of organizing. It is a psychological characteristic that shows group cohesiveness, loyalty to a particular organization, and a sense of value-sharing among members. Compared to other countries' use of employment contracts that specify employees' functions, a wider commitment to the organization by members is broadly seen in Japan, where duties and authority are not specified in the form of a functional contract. In addition, long service to one organization strengthens the involvement beyond a functional one and changes the expected roles of individuals. Researchers explain such a behavior pattern in terms of paternalism, value systems, or culture.

The second issue is related to Japanese management practices. Such employment systems as lifetime employment and the seniority system are among the main topics discussed. The lifetime employment system implies a practice in which an employee will not be discharged without extraordinary reason until retirement age. It is not a contract but an implicit consensus between labor and management. The seniority system offers periodic wage increases every year and promotion based primarily on seniority. Other topics include enterprise unions, cooperative industrial relations, and such decision-making systems as *ringi*. Researchers used to concentrate on the analysis of industrial relations and employment practices, but this issue is now viewed as being apparently interrelated with the first issue of human resource management, as groupism is viewed as having an effect on the formation of the lifetime employment system. Production management methods like quality control (QC) and the Toyota production system are newly regarded as important factors (Monden 1983; Ishikawa 1981) as well.

Third is the comparison of Japanese and Western management practices (Azumi 1979; Yoshihara et al. 1981; Kagono et al. 1983), which focuses on similarities and differences of strategy and structure in Japanese and Western management, on company goals and objectives, and on the results that Japanese management brings in terms of performance. Before performance study appeared, the performance of the economy was implicitly regarded as if it were equivalent to organization performance; managerial performance was rarely analyzed in the majority of previous studies.

Fourth, as foreign investment by Japanese companies increases companies face problems in transferring portions of their management practices and skills to the local operations. The international management of the Japanese company emerged as a topic of central interest (K. Hayashi 1985; Kobayashi 1980; Yoshihara et al. 1983). Questions studied include which functions and practices of Japanese management are applicable to the foreign operation; what are the best ways to manage local people in the organization; and how can resources from both company and host country be effectively mixed? The experiences of many companies provide evidence for these inquiries and offer an opportunity to test the existing theory of Japanese management. Actually, all the above issues regarding companies' international activity are interrelated even though most of the analyses focus on one at a time.

Four Study Approaches

A simple classification of the numerous studies of Japanese management into four approaches will be helpful in identifying the main issues discussed in the following chapters.

The Socio-Cultural Approach

The socio-cultural approach puts the focus on analysis of psychological characteristics, interpersonal relations, and cultural aspects within organization, and the features of the management system are thereby explained. Such dichotomies as groupism and individualism are often used to contrast organizational characteristics in Japan and Western countries, though not in such simple terms.

Hazama (1971) described the Japanese company as managed like a traditional family in which the head of the family behaves as a paternal master. The principle underlying this description is called management paternalism or management familism, but as the family ties that existed in prewar days changed, this management system came to be called welfare corporatism.

The pattern variables offered by Parsons (1951), Bellah (1957), and Odaka (1984) have explained the Japanese way of management as being "particular" and "achievement-oriented" and American management as being "universal" and "achievement-oriented." That is, they regarded particularistic achievement in which expectations of active achievement arise within the particular relational context to be characteristic of the pattern of the Japanese system, as opposed to universalistic achievement with general standards. And they applied these pattern variables to what they called developing countries' "status-oriented" systems. In one of the following chapters Japanese joint-venture management in Thailand is analyzed from this point of view with regard to human resource management, technology transfer, and the labor market.

According to Iwata (1977), the behavior of Japanese people is explained by one of its most significant psychological characteristics:

groupism. Groupism is distinguished from management paternalism because it is seen in the postwar as well as the prewar period. In Iwata's model, diffusion of individual duties is present so that an individual easily adjusts his behavior to the needs of the group. He focuses on the analysis of psychological characteristics as a principle of organization. His analysis is quite consistent and fundamental, but some questions remain, including why is such a psychological characteristic formed, and why does the diffusion of duties in the group occur?

When Ouchi (1981) examined productivity in the United States and Japan, he reached the conclusion that an important reason for Japanese high productivity is not technology but a special way of managing people. He identified two types of management style: the A type (American) and the J type (Japanese). He recognized that the most effective management style stresses the management of people, as is typical in Japanese companies.

Ouchi subsequently proposed a new way of management, called Theory Z management, by which U.S. companies can integrate the important features of Japanese experience into American management. He refers to a "Theory Z organization," which has developed naturally in the United States but which has many characteristics similar to firms in Japan, including such common practices as long-term employment, internal promotion, and long-term evaluation of individual performance.

Leading businessmen sometimes express the view that human resources are a key factor in management and the company's most important resource. This perception is commonly seen in big Japanese corporations in which the achievement of a separation between ownership and management is the most advanced among capitalistic countries. Top management emphasizes a feeling of "family" among organization members, who share similar values and goals. As a result, considerable egalitarianism is seen in the organization. Under the seniority promotion system, the differential in positions is likely to change.

The socio-cultural approach thus emphasizes the psychological characteristics of the individual and the cultural aspects of organization. From a managerial viewpoint, the question of why some companies fail in the market and others succeed, though both exist in a similar cultural context and utilize similar systems, still remains. An approach needs to be developed that will explain the diversity of corporate and individual behavior in the same socio-cultural environment.

One of the results of studies that emphasize Japanese socio-cultural conditions is their contribution to the testing of management theory as developed in the context of Western socio-cultural conditions and the good opportunity they have provided for extending existing theories.

The Institutional Approach

The institutional approach focuses on the institutional aspects of Japanese industrial relations and the employment system. Lifetime employment, a wage and promotion system based on seniority, and enterprise unions were once thought of as the three pillars of Japanese management.

The first generation of institutionalists of this type tended to analyze these factors critically, but they did go so far as to believe that such factors were unique to Japan. The next generation of analysts, who mostly specialized in managerial problems, began to appreciate these so-called pillars positively and intended to stress the uniqueness of Japanese development. In opposition to this view, however, Koike (1981) insists that such practices are not unique to Japan. He found similar phenomena in Western countries in his comprehensive investigation into employment and wages in Europe, the United States, and Japan.

Regarding this point, Magota (1978) indicates that such practices are contingent on certain historical conditions, including a remarkable increase of population and a national population structure of pyramid shape; and both economic and managerial indicators showing high growth rates. This view suggests that the existing institution and system of Japanese management are not fixed but changeable. This cannot be denied when we look at the formation and change of the Japanese employment system since industrialization. In other words, we need to examine what system can exist with what conditions.

It is generally believed that at present the above-mentioned conditions exist in the ASEAN countries, and some of this book's contributors have aimed to corroborate this view through surveys in such countries.

Most existing Japanese labor practices are acknowledged to have been formed in the postwar decades, even if their origins date back to earlier times. The practices themselves thus have not had such long lives and are not so well established in the history of the corporation. Moreover, we have already witnessed the changes in employment systems in big corporations during the early 1970s, which accelerated after the yen appreciation in 1985 resulted in the rapid increase of relative production cost. To cut labor costs, companies began to use more non-permanent workers outside of the lifetime employment system. The liquidity of the labor market was strengthened by the pressure exerted by the labor shortage. With such changes in mind, we must go on to examine the relationship between existing practices and their prerequisite conditions. Historically, lifetime employment is not a fixed practice, and it is not applied in the small businesses that account for 80% of the total workforce in Japan.

The Strategy-Structure-Performance Approach

The strategy-structure-performance approach focuses on the managerial aspects of companies, using more universal frameworks with the intention of implementing international comparative analyses. This approach differs from traditional ones in that its emphasis is on methodological universalism and empirical data. Most research which uses this approach has been done by strategy or organization theorists; this approach is based on, for example, contingency theory of organization or theory of strategy. The most thorough studies using this approach have been done by Kagono et al.(1983).

Kagono and his colleagues, using various methods, analyzed environment, strategy, structure, organization process, and performance of more than five hundred big firms in the United States and Japan. They concluded that each form of organization in the two countries has consistency, and they summarized the pattern of adaptation in companies of both countries, using the two dimensions of strategy and organization. Strategy is classified into two types: operation oriented or product oriented, and organization is classed into either group dynamics or bureaucratic dynamics categories. They discuss Japanese management within the framework of comparative analysis. The hypotheses that they have proposed may be summarized as follows: United States and Japanese management are characterized by strategic management and evolutionary management respectively; incremental, evolutionary adaptation is the main feature of Japanese management.

Kono (1984) believes that successful companies do have much in common in terms of strategy, structure, and other practices. He finds interesting patterns in the behavior of Japanese companies through several kinds of empirical investigations, concluding that successful Japanese corporations exhibit four characteristic management practices: they are innovative, they are competition oriented, they have centralized and "soft" organization, and they display respect for workers.

Itami (1982) compared the performance of Japanese and U.S. corporations quantitatively, though his number of samples is limited. He presented findings that are contrary to the common view of Japanese management. His research, which utilized several indicators for measurement of performance including return on assets, ROI, value added, labor productivity, and others, revealed rather low performance by

Japanese companies in comparison to their U.S. counterparts. His conclusion implies that it is necessary to base arguments on empirical evidence and to be more deliberate about the evaluation of Japanese management.

Strategy-structure-performance studies clarified the characteristics of corporate behavior quantitatively and contributed to the theoretical progress of the field, but they do not explain how we can integrate the different practices of the different countries, or how we can transfer Japanese management to overseas operations in the process of internationalization of companies. The next approach takes up these questions.

The International Approach

The international approach analyzes the international management of Japanese corporations. A number of studies have been done on such issues as development of foreign direct investment, ownership patterns, labor management, production management, technology transfer, and the applicability of Japanese-style management to foreign operations.

Basically, scholars in this category try to show the process of internationalization of Japanese businesses. For example, Yoshihara, Hayashi, and Yasumuro (1988) analyze the managerial problems, such as strategies, structures, and operations of multinational companies which are supposed to be different from those of companies which operate in one national economy. As a result, they deal with these problems: What characteristics do global production, sales, and procurement have compared with those in a national boundary? How are training and management of human resources, fund raising, and R&D different in multinational and national companies? How do overseas subsidiaries operate? They study these problems and try to clarify how and why Japanese companies develop different pattern of internationalization from that of American and European companies.

There are some empirical studies which demonstrate how Japanese companies apply their way of management in foreign countries. For example, Ichimura and others (1988) explain how the Japanese style of management is applied in Asian countries while Abo and others (1988) did the same type of study on the American market. Sakuma (1983) has developed studies comparing economic performance of particular Japanese companies in various countries including the United States, England, Malaysia, and Singapore. He emphasizes the relationship between economic performance and the degree of information sharing among organization members. The investigations presented in this book originated from such concerns.

Table 1. Historical Development of Japanese Management Studies.

Period	Researcher	Focus and Findings
1950s	Okouchi (1952)	Explained backwardness of industrial relations in Japan's capitalism
	Abegglen (1958)	Lifetime employment, seniority system, enterprise unions are positively related to economic development
1960s	Hazama (1963)	Management paternalism (later called welfare corporatism) brought high loyalty and work motivation
	Odaka (1965)	Illustrated modern as well as backward aspects of traditional management practices
	Yoshino (1968)	Explained historical development of Japanese management system
1970s	OECD (1972)	Lifetime employment, seniority system, and enterprise unions are three pillars of Japanese system
	Dore (1974)	Comparative analysis of the British and Japanese factory; Japanese practices are seen as products of rational development
	Hirschmeier and Yui (1975)	Historical development of management system from 1600 to 1973 is analyzed
	Iwata (1977)	Groupism is the underlying principle in Japanese organization
	Vogel (1979)	Analyzed reasons for Japan's economic "miracle" in terms of economic productivity, politics, company systems, education, welfare, and others
1980s	Koike (1981)	Denied uniqueness of Japanese employment and wage practices; data from Europe, United States, and Japan
	Ouchi (1981)	Proposed the theory Z model as a type similar to Japanese style but seen in U.S. organizations
	Pascale and Athos (1981)	Illustrated that Japanese style emphasizes soft management
	Itami (1982)	Performance analysis in United States and Japan; Japanese management does not lead to high performance
	Kagono et al. (1983)	Comparative analysis of United States (1983) and Japan on integrative contingency model; evolutionary management is essence of Japanese company (data from 518 samples)
	Aoki et al. (1984)	Economic analysis of Japanese firms. They explain the universal aspects of Japanese firms and try to demystify the myth of Japanese management

A brief summary of the development of Japanese management study is given in Table 1.

Future Perspectives

The study of Japanese management has obviously been affected by the evolution of the Japanese economy, which at present is entering a new phase in international relations. Japanese management is also facing new environmental conditions.

Lifetime employment and the seniority system, which have always been regarded as essential parts of Japanese management, now face difficulties. An intense labor shortage and a rapid increase in the aged population have put pressure on companies to reform those existing practices that lead to inflexible, higher labor costs.

Under such circumstances, views on the value of labor and loyalty to the organization are expected to change considerably, and the role of lifetime employment is apparently decreasing as a result. It cannot be denied that it may be possible to separate and change components without damaging the system as a whole: features once viewed as inherent in the Japanese management system should be reexamined in the context of new environmental conditions.

With regard to the theoretical and practical aspects of Japanese management, we consider several areas as important for future research. First, with the increase of foreign direct investment, Japanese manage-ment needs to build proper management systems in foreign operations, where elements from different cultures are mixed. Internationalization of operations at the same time requires the reformation of the domestic organization in order to meet new conditions. We need to search for a way of international management that includes both foreign and domestic organizations.

Second, the theory and hypotheses developed in most of the socio-cultural studies are not presently verifiable because socio-cultural factors are not presented as an operational concept. We need to make a concept operational that will make the testing of theories and hypotheses possible. Adequate data and evidence will lead to more productive study.

Third, the framework and key concepts of Japanese management study have not been well shared or agreed upon by researchers. As the dominant socio-cultural studies by Japanese as well as foreign research-ers, emphasizing the uniqueness of the Japanese management system, did not offer theory or hypotheses in an operational form, it was not possible to test them by subsequent research. Orientation toward general theory is necessary for further development of the theory, regardless of whether Japanese management is unique. In relation to the appraisal of Japanese management performance, thorough research is needed to clarify the relationship among the factors making up the Japanese management system.

Conclusions

The objective of this chapter was to give an overview of Japanese management studies in order to facilitate understanding of the subjects in the following chapters. Reflecting the different dimensions of analysis, a variety of concepts and theories have been proposed.

The traditional approach insisted on the uniqueness of management systems and tended to take the view that management systems are deeply rooted in the culture. Other approaches, however, indicate the similarity in practices among countries or emphasize the preconditions for certain types of management systems. They see, rather, universal aspects of the systems and compare the systems of different countries by using a common framework of analysis. Many believe that management systems are able to be learned and changed, even though differences in cultural and social conditions remain.

As the internationalization of Japanese corporations proceeds, recent approaches tend increasingly to implement empirical comparative analysis and to examine the applicability of Japanese practices in the context of international management. The subjects studied through the various approaches are likely to be reexamined and integrated in this context, which will provide good opportunities to develop the theory and research further.

6

Foundations of Human Resources Management Practice in Japanese Companies in Malaysia

Gregory T. S. Thong

Perceptions of Japanese Management

Since the late 1950s, tremendous interest has been generated in the study of Japanese management. The interested parties have initially been mainly such foreigners as academicians, politicians, and businessmen. The interest among academicians and politicians has been generated by admiration for the Japanese, who serve as a model for emulation for a number of reasons including their having achieved high economic growth and technological development and for their ability to overcome the difficulties caused by the increased oil prices in 1973 and 1979, the increase in the value of the yen beginning in the mid-1980s, and the trade restrictions introduced by the United States and the countries in the European Economic Community (EEC).

The interest of the businessmen has been spurred by the challenge to their survival that has resulted from the erosion and diminution of their market shares caused by the onslaught of Japanese competitors in their home and foreign markets. Those who have not been confronted by such competition are interested in preparing themselves for such an eventuality and in enhancing their prowess, vigor, and ability to operate against any other competitors.

In Malaysia, this interest has received wholehearted blessing, support, and encouragement at the highest level: the Prime Minister enunciated "The Look East Policy" in late 1981 with Japan specifically in mind. "Learning from the Japanese" has been in vogue for some time in Malaysia and still continues.

Information concerning Japanese management practices has been circulated by the mass media, through numerous articles in international journals, in books, and by Japanese scholars and management consultants, who have been invited to present papers at international conferences and to conduct seminars. In spite of the evidence found in this wealth of literature and knowledge, there is a small number of Japanese who deny that there is anything distinctive about Japanese management styles. One must take it that Japanese management practices are so commonplace to these individuals that they are unable to perceive the special characteristics that are associated with such practices. In this context, it is easier for a foreigner to make such distinctions.

Identified Areas of Japanese Management Practices

The major contributors to the literature on Japanese management practices include both foreigners and the Japanese themselves. Specific areas of Japanese management practices can be categorized under the headings of human resources management (HRM), production and operations management, marketing, and finance. This paper covers HRM only.

Foreign contributors include Abegglen (1958), Cole (1971), Dore (1974), Vogel (1979), Pascale and Athos (1981), Ouchi (1981), and others. Japanese writers include Tominomori (1982), who identified the special features of Japanese HRM practices that pertain to lifetime employment, the seniority wage system, enterprise welfare, enterprise unions, and "groupishness." He looks upon Japanese management as an interlinked organic system, emphasizing that each special feature does not exist in isolation or as a separate entity. All features must operate as an integrated whole in order to bring about overall effective results. The element that binds all the features together is "groupishness," which is the vital essence of the Japanese management system. It is the practice of group activities and egalitarianism in the workplace that has bred workers who are multi-skilled generalists, rather than narrow–scope specialists, with the inherent acumen and ability to introduce and to adapt to rapid technological change. "Groupishness" is enmeshed with the collective bottom-up decision making process known as the *ringi* system, and *nemawashi*, the application of broad consultation and consensus building (Tominori 1981–1982).

According to Mikami (1982), some of the representative characteristics inherent in the Japanese style of personnel and labor management are familism, lifetime employment, the seniority system, enterprise unions, annual employment of newly graduated students, concern for the employee's family welfare and private life, training and education for all levels of employees with funding from the company, compensation on the basis of the employee's academic qualifications, age and seniority, and others. Worker productivity gains have been enhanced through the application of suggestion programs and such small group activities as quality control circles (QCCs). It was reported that 93.9% of all the manufacturing companies in the 1980 Tokyo Stock Exchange listings have introduced the suggestion program (Ministry of International Trade and Industry, Industrial Policy Bureau, Business Activity Section, "New Management Indicators," 1981). Small group activities ranked next in popularity, with 75.4% of the companies applying them (Mikami 1982).

A book published by the Nippon Steel Company presented some of the characteristics of Japan's private enterprises. The characteristics referring to HRM were identified by Abegglen which include the collective decision making process, special employment features like direct hiring of new graduates, lifetime employment, seniority-pegged pay systems, and enterprise unions. The authors of this book sought to point out exceptions to these features. They noted that some of the blue-collar workers entered the organization not directly upon graduation but at a later time. Even with the practice of lifetime employment, the employees were given the freedom to leave the company at any time (Aoto, 1984).

Shimada (1980) provided an in-depth explanation concerning how and why the special features of Japanese human resources management practices evolved. In his opinion, the Japanese "employment system is probably one of the least properly understood Japanese social institutions among outside observers. Many foreigners are keenly impressed by the apparent peculiarities in some of the employment practices as well as behavioral patterns of workers and are inclined to attribute such impressive phenomena to the historical and cultural uniqueness of Japanese society. . ." (Shimada 1980).

Shimada felt that lifelong employment has been fostered by such environmental factors as high economic growth, intensified investment in human capital, freedom of job reallocation in large companies, the power of enterprise unions, and the guiding hand of the government. The period between the late 1950s and the early 1970s, prior to the first oil crisis, was a time of high economic growth, which generated increased demand for labor. During times of economic recession the large companies are adverse to laying off workers, due to the large investment in human capital formation through training, enterprise union pressure on management not to retrench worker numbers, and increased flexibility to reallocate work in other areas for workers found to be redundant.

The turbulence in the aftermath of the oil crises of 1973 and 1979 was dampened somewhat by the action taken by the Japanese government to furnish employment adjustment subsidies to employers in order to discourage the dismissal of workers. Thus the integrated, coordinated, and concerted policies of employers, trade unions, and the government contributed toward the maintenance of employment stability. Among small firms, however, due to the weakness of trade unions in such establishments, management was not faced with the same degree of trade union pressure to maintain employment as that found in large companies. Small companies may sometimes be able to provide alternative work to the redundant workers, but when times were hard the small companies were more vulnerable and often forced to lay off some of their workers.

The environment of rapid technological change is conducive to the employment practice of hiring young inexperienced workers who are more adaptable than older workers to new methods and techniques. The synchronized action, mostly by the large companies, to recruit new graduates from high schools, junior colleges, and universities has drawn lots of attention, as this exercise is practiced once a year in April. The companies also employ "halfway workers," who have gained work experience elsewhere prior to seeking employment in the current firm. Official statistics published by the Ministry of Labor for the years 1965 and 1970 indicate that halfway workers formed 47.5 and 57.1% of new entrants to job positions, whereas only 31.3 and 22.6% were represented by inexperienced new school graduates respectively (Ministry of Labor, *Survey on Employment Trends*). Large companies were often found to possess highly internalized labor market structures that support the recruitment of new graduates, but the smaller companies, with less rigid organizational structures, tend to recruit more halfway workers. It was found that, in general, during times of economic prosperity more halfway workers are recruited, but during times of recession their recruitment is reduced.

The recruitment of new graduates by large companies is inevitably accompanied by the increased stress on internalized on-the-job training (OJT) and job rotation for which Japanese companies are noted. Large amounts of money and resources are thus expended by the large companies in training employees. As for job rotation, Shimada reported that white collar workers who are deemed to have management potential are accorded a greater scope in experiencing job rotations. On the other hand, the opportunity for job rotation among the manual workers is limited by the constraints of technological factors and by the autonomy exercised by the team of workers on the workshop floor to allocate work among themselves.

Okubayashi (1989) discussed the factors contributing to the development of enterprise trade unions and why the concept of groupism has been practised in the industrial environment of Japan. He also noted that an enterprise union usually becomes a member of an industrial federation of labor unions, or "national center of labor unions." There are many national centers and industrial federations of labor unions. Each of them endeavors to coordinate the interests of their member labor unions. An example of the outcome of this coordination is the use of the "Spring Labor Offensive," commencing in 1956, which has enabled the enterprise unions to counter the power of the employers and bargain for increased wages and fringe benefits. Okubayashi found that, in addition to collective bargaining, the joint consultation system is an important vehicle in promoting the practice of industrial democracy on the Japanese industrial relations scene. According to the data obtained from a study undertaken by the Ministry of Labor in 1982, 71% of the big companies have introduced this system (Okubayashi 1989).

The emphasis of this literature review is on highlighting the contributions of some of the indigenous Japanese writers. It can be discerned that some common agreement exists among them regarding specific outstanding characteristics in Japanese HRM.

Some Research Findings

In collaboration with Hem C. Jain, University of New Brunswick, Canada, in early 1985 the writer conducted a comparative study of HRM practices among three sets of Japanese parent companies in Japan, Japanese subsidiary companies in Malaysia, and indigenous Malaysian counterpart companies (Thong and Jain 1988). Due to a lack of response from many of the companies that were invited to participate in the study, the sample was limited to only three sets of five companies each, with one company selected to represent each of the following five industries: airline services, banking, trading, electrical products, and bearings. The first three industries are involved in the provision of services, while the remaining two are in manufacturing.

The study, conducted through the use of a specially designed questionnaire, was undertaken first in Japan to collect data from the parent companies, and then continued in Malaysia. The following HRM characteristics that are associated with Japanese management were collected, on:

1. trade union representation
2. hiring practices
3. promotion practices
4. layoff practices
5. training practices
6. consensus decision making and consultation
7. conflict and grievance handling
8. quality control circles.

The research findings pertaining to each of these characteristics are now presented in greater detail.

1. Trade Union Representation

None of the five Japanese subsidiary companies in Malaysia have enterprise unions. Three companies, in airline services, banking, and electrical products manufacturing, have industry-wide trade unions, which is a significant characteristic among Malaysian companies that are unionized. The other two companies, in trading and bearings manufacturing, have no trade unions. These two companies are relatively small in size, employing about sixty and forty workers respectively. The practice of paternalistic management is also evident in these two companies.

Concerning the Japanese parent companies, the employees of four of them belong to enterprise unions. The employees of the fifth company, in the airline services industry, are members of occupational (or craft) trade unions.

2. Hiring Practices

Three subsidiary companies in the banking, trading, and electrical products industries followed the recruitment policies of their parent companies. The practice in the subsidiaries is not, however, as elaborate as in the parent companies, which make direct contact with educational institutions and conduct employment interviews on campus. In the other two subsidiary companies, a mixed preference was indicated. The airline services company hired experienced sales personnel and the bearings company hired some experienced clerical staff directly from the local job market. The other staff positions in these companies are filled by new graduates.

The airline services subsidiary's report that several experienced employees have been hired from the labor market contrasts with the five Japanese parent companies' practice of hiring new high school, college, and university graduates.

3. Promotion Practices

With some qualifications, all five subsidiary companies follow the practice of promoting from within. Four companies, in the banking, trading, electrical products, and bearings industries, indicated that they *almost always* promote from within. The respondent from the bearings company reported that if a person suitable for promotion could not be found within the company, then the search would be continued outside the company.

All the parent companies showed an unreserved preference for promoting from within the enterprise.

4. Layoff Practices

Only one subsidiary company, in the banking industry, has an explicitly defined policy of not laying off workers. The three companies in the airline services, trading, and electrical products industries do not possess such a policy, but so far they had not laid off any workers. There is no policy on layoffs in the bearings company. However, due to adverse economic circumstances in 1980, this company was forced to dismiss the factory operators when it closed its manufacturing division.

The parent company in the bearings industry has a definite policy of not laying off workers, but it has been shown that this policy does not cover the subsidiary company. In the other four parent companies the no-layoff policy is not stated but no workers have been laid off so far.

5. Training Practices

In-house on-the-job training (OJT) is practiced by all the subsidiary companies. Three companies, in the banking, electrical products, and bearings industries, provide formal classroom training. Some of the employees of the electrical products subsidiary are sent to the parent company in Japan for training. The practice of job rotation is less popular among the subsidiary companies—only the two in airline services and banking engaged in it.

All the parent companies practice in-house OJT, and the four companies in banking, trading, electrical products, and bearings provide formal classroom training as well. Job rotation also appears to be more popular among these four companies. The banking and trading companies have sent their employees to institutions of higher learning in the United States for training, but no subsidiary company has followed suit.

6. Consensus Decision Making and Consultation

Bottom-up communications in decision making is a practice followed by the three subsidiary companies in airline services, trading, and electrical products. The applications in the airline services and trading companies are not, however, as elaborate as those in their parent companies. Only major decisions are made through the use of consensus in the banking company. There is no practice of consensus decision making in the bearings company: all decisions are made solely by management. Regular management-labor consultation meetings are held only in the electrical products and bearings companies, the former with the trade union and the latter without. Among the remaining three companies, such meetings are held when the need arises.

All five parent companies apply bottom-up communications in decision making. Regular management-labor consultation meetings are held in the airline services, banking, trading, and electrical products companies. The bearings company holds such meetings on an ad hoc basis.

7. Conflicts and Grievance Handling

The four subsidiary companies in the airline services, trading, electrical products, and bearings industries settle conflicts and grievances through negotiations and discussions. The banking company settles its employee relations problems through the management-labor consultation machinery on an ad hoc basis. A permanent joint management-labor consultation system is established in the bearings company. No joint management-labor consultation meetings are applied in the trading company, which also has no trade union. Only the companies in airline services and banking have incorporated formal grievance resolving procedures in their collective bargaining agreements. The airline services company indicated, however, that such a procedure has not yet been exercised.

The settling of conflicts and grievances through negotiations and discussions is practiced in all five parent companies. Joint management-labor consultation is applied on a permanent basis in the airline services, banking, trading, and electrical products companies. The bearings company conducts such meetings on an ad hoc basis. The three companies in airline services, banking, and trading do not include the formal grievance procedures in their collective bargaining agreements.

8. Quality Control Circles (QCC)

Only the two subsidiary companies in the electrical products and bearings industries, which are undertaking manufacturing activities, show evidence of applying QCC. Participation of the employees is on a voluntary basis. The electrical products company operated 131 QCC in 1985, and even today it is acknowledged as one of the most prominent supporters of the application of QCC in Malaysia.

Among the parent companies, only the banking company had not introduced any QCC as of 1985. However, this company indicated that it plans to introduce the technique eventually. In the other four companies, the employees participate in QCC activities voluntarily.

Other Indications

Even though the research sample is small due to force of circumstances, the analysis of the data collected shows similarities and differences within each set of companies and among different sets of companies. Some indications of dissimilarities in HRM practices even among the parent companies in Japan were reported by Shimada (1980). In some instances a greater degree of variance in application between the parent companies and the subsidiary companies is apparent, which is a result of some modifications to such practices that were incorporated to suit the requirements of the local environment. The research findings of Sim (1978), Imaoka (1985), and Nakano (1985) show that the majority of the Japanese managers in Japanese companies in Malaysia hold the opinion that Japanese management techniques, with minor modifications, can be successfully introduced in Malaysia.

Putti (1984) conducted a study of the corporate culture and values of the employees in the Matsushita companies in Indonesia, Malaysia, the Philippines, Singapore, and Thailand, the five countries that formed the Association of Southeast Asian Nations (ASEAN) at that time. The operation of all the Matsushita companies are imbued with the late Konosuke Matsushita's philosophy. It is expounded through "The Basic Business Principle", and "The Basic Creed of Employees" and is anchored by "The Seven Objectives." The variables studied by Putti include pride in work, job involvement, and activity preference. These characteristics are considered to be associated with intrinsic work factors, attitude towards earnings, and social status, which in turn are tied to extrinsic factors, and to a scale of upward striving, which is reckoned to fall between the intrinsic and extrinsic categories. The research findings show a positive significant correlation among the intrinsic factors and the extrinsic factors, with the intrinsic factors ranking higher. It is demonstrated clearly that even though the employees in the five

Matsushita companies are influenced by the culture of the local environment, they exhibit work values that are more or less uniform. It must be remembered that such an achievement was not arrived at easily or quickly, but rather through the vision and enlightenment contributed by the founding father's personal philosophy and the untiring efforts of the companies' Japanese managers, who have striven over the years to make this philosophy a way of life among the employees. These findings provide a clear sign that Japanese management practices can be applied to the countries in this region.

Consideration should be given, however, to certain factors that counter the application of Japanese management practices in Malaysia. The comparative study using the three sets of companies in the five different industry groupings also shows that the majority of the Malaysian employees in the Japanese subsidiary companies feel that—even though they are loyal to the companies that they work for—if they had to choose between loyalty to the family and loyalty to the company, they would choose loyalty to family. The employees are not willing to sacrifice their family or private life for the company. Thus, unlike the Japanese workers, Malaysian employees are keen to stop work at 5 P.M. each day so that they can spend more time with their families. They are also unwilling to take on extended outstation work assignments during which they would be separated from their families.

The degree of loyalty among Malaysian workers towards the companies that employ them is also questionable in another respect. If the conditions are suitable—that is, when other jobs with higher remuneration and/or better promotion and career prospects are available, or sometimes even for the sake of decreased commuting time or of avoiding other inconveniences—many of these employees think nothing of resigning in order to work for other companies.

A few years ago, *The New Straits Times* newspaper in Malaysia published an article concerning a female production operator who was sent by a Japanese subsidiary company in Penang for six months of training in the parent company in Japan. This production operator was in her mid-twenties and had worked for the company for about five years. The company intended to reward her excellent work performance by sending her for training to Japan, but this strategy backfired because the production operator, after successful completion of the training, resigned from her job upon returning from Japan. She resigned because she was not given a promotion immediately upon her return. From her point of view she was better qualified after receiving the training in Japan and so deserved an *immediate* promotion. When such a promotion was not forthcoming, she felt justified in leaving the company. It may be possible that, from the management's viewpoint, this operator lacked seniority ranking and thus did not qualify for a promotion. In Japan, where the usual retirement age is sixty years, there is time for a worker to gain seniority prior to promotion. But in Malaysia the retirement age for female workers can be as early as 45 years, so workers look forward to receiving promotion opportunities even during their younger years.

At the height of the implementation of the "New Economic Policy" in Malaysia during the 1970s, the demand for Bumiputera* managers gravely exceeded the supply. There were stories of Bumiputera managers who changed jobs very often during this period in order to receive pay increases as well as promotions. Some of these managers might have been working for the Japanese companies in Malaysia. The environment has of course changed as a result of the increased number of Bumiputera graduates of local and foreign universities.

Evolutionary Changes in Japanese HRM

In any country the practice of management cannot remain static over time. Depending on the changes that occur in the external and internal environments, corresponding changes co-evolve in management practices in order to suit the times. Such evolution can be seen in Japanese management practices as the Japanese environment rapidly changes.

As recently as the end of July 1989, *The Sunday Times* (July 30, 1989) published a sixteen-page country report on Japan. Through such reports not only are readers kept up-to-date, but continued interest in Japan is maintained. One of the articles in this report discussed the cases of some Japanese employees who change jobs. Lifelong employment is one of the reported characteristics that has been entrenched in the literature concerning Japanese HRM practice. A qualification has been made that this characteristic is the norm only for the large Japanese companies— approximately thirty percent of the total workforce is provided with this privilege (Manasian 1985). Among the small and medium-sized companies, and especially among those in the service sector, the practice of lifelong employment is not prominent.

There are indications that the practice of lifelong employment is slowly being eroded even in the large companies that traditionally have practiced it. A number of evolving factors have contributed to this erosion. Among young Japanese employees job-hopping is not consid-

---

* A term referring to the Malays and other indigenous peoples in Malaysia.

ered to be a social stigma, and such employees "are not necessarily thinking of a life-time job with one company," according to the *Sunday Times* report. As a result of the practice of recruiting the best new graduates in large numbers over some years, many large companies now find that they have a surfeit of talented and relatively young staff and only a limited number of senior management positions to be filled. Many of these young employees are not willing to wait for approximately twenty years before "getting somewhere" in the company. At the same time, a bright, upcoming young manager may be given a notice of transfer to a foreign post. If the transfer demands that he be separated from his family, he may be reluctant to accept the post: in this situation a viable alternative is to resign and join another company.

The liberalization of financial markets in Japan and the effect of Tokyo's evolving role as a major world financial center has also contributed to this change. Many new foreign financial institutions have been established in Japan, increasing the job-market demand for experienced staff. Such jobs offer the attraction of more lucrative remuneration and better working conditions.

Companies in the high-technology industries are also responsible in part for the change. Due to the phenomenal rate of growth among companies that produce semiconductors and computers, the demand for expert and experienced staff in these fields has increased. At the same time, some companies in the smokestack industries have diversified into the manufacture of semiconductors and computers and caused a further increase in the demand for such staff already in short supply. Some companies have been forced to resort to the practice of poaching staff from other companies and/or making use of companies that provide headhunting services. According to the *Sunday Times* article, more than 150 companies in Japan currently provide executive search services, and the majority, about eighty percent, operate in Tokyo. It has also been reported that at least three weekly magazines in Japan provide information to people who are looking for opportunities to change their jobs.

Even though the practice of job-hopping has started to gain momentum in Japan, many Japanese companies that engage such mid–career employees insist on taking only those who are changing jobs for the first time. Those who have job-hopped more than once are often regarded with suspicion. Of course, experienced workers who job-hop "too often" may not be viewed in a negative light if they are applying for jobs with foreign companies operating in Japan.

Another factor that has brought about change in the practice of Japanese HRM is the increase in the value of the yen against other foreign currencies in 1985. This has caused Japanese manufactured goods to increase in price and to become less competitive internationally. In order to overcome the deleterious effects of this change, many Japanese have resorted to cutting back their manufacturing operations in Japan and transferring them to countries without export restrictions with regard to the United States and the EEC countries, and where labor and raw material costs are lower. Many Japanese companies have also set up factories in the United States and the EEC countries as a way to overcome restrictions by these countries on exports from Japan.

Such actions by the major companies with headquarters in Tokyo and Osaka often have a profound impact on the HRM practices of their branches and subsidiary companies located in other parts of Japan. During my four-and-a-half-month stay in Hokkaido in mid-1984, I was given the opportunity to visit a steel mill owned by a large Japanese company. I have since received information that the operations of the steel mill have been downsized, with the result that many employees have lost their jobs. As the steel mill is a major employer of people in the local community in particular, and in Hokkaido generally, the action has caused a lot of hardship for the local people because alternate avenues for new employment are lacking. This example may be seen as an isolated case of a big company that is not providing lifelong employment and is not following a no-layoffs policy.

To put this matter in correct perspective, Mroczkowski and Hanaoka (1989) showed that some Japanese companies take a lot of trouble to avoid layoffs. Such companies apply job rotation and employee reassignments, introduce hiring freezes, and do away with overtime. Extensive use of inter-company manpower leasing and transfer has been reported among company groups. These groups or centers are operated in a particular territory with the support of the local government bodies and Chambers of Commerce. A survey conducted in 1987 by NHK, the Japan Broadcasting Corporation, showed that 471 local manpower leasing and transfer centers involving 17,000 companies were established. It is reckoned that through the use of such strategies less than ten percent of the companies studied retrenched their full-time employees (although part-time workers are often laid off). Mroczkowski and Hanaoka concluded that "lay-offs of full-time employees will continue to be rare" (Mroczkowski and Hanaoka 1989).

Concluding Comments

This discussion of the characteristics of Japanese HRM practices has been divided into two parts, one concerning the commonly accepted practices and the other (which has been included in order to increase the study's current relevance) concerning the evolutionary changes that have taken place. The structural design of the comparative study of the three sets of companies in five different industrial groups (airline services, banking, trading, electrical products, and bearings) was based on the data available at differring times—this is why the findings have been sandwiched between the discussions of the commonly accepted practices and the evolutionary changes. This somewhat awkward arrangement was made not by choice but because of restrictions caused by the earlier date of the original data and the subsequent expansion of the study.

The study indicated that the unionized subsidiary companies are members of industry-wide trade unions unlike those in the parent companies that have enterprise trade unions. The structure and operations of the trade unions in these subsidiary companies are based on the British model, a legacy that is still perpetuating from the time that the country was a colony of the British for approximately eighty years prior to gaining its independence in 1957. Even though the trade union movement in Malaysia is different somewhat from that operating in Japan, the Japanese managers should not be affected adversely by this difference. This is substantiated by the reports of the Japanese companies, especially in the motor-car industry, that are operating successfully in Britain.

Another feature that may cause some disquietude among the Japanese managers in Malaysia is the prevalence of the Islamic way of life. Islam is the state religion in the country and the majority of the population profess this religious faith. However, where the companies employ predominantly Bumiputera workers, invariably the practice is to employ Bumiputeras as personnel managers. These local managers possess the knowledge and the skills that are necessary to solve problems that may arise with respect to the requirements of this religion. The presence of the Islamic way of life is also predominant in Indonesia, the countries of the Middle East, etc., where Japanese companies are operating. In Malaysia, an added advantage is that it is a multi-racial society where the various races are more tolerant to and sensitive of the requirements and practices of the different religious values and customs that are regarded as commonplace in their daily life. The Japanese managers can obtain an enhanced insight and sensitivity towards these values and customs by reading books such as "Managing in a Plural Society" (Hamzah, Madsen and Thong 1989).

The monoracial and monocultural nature of Japanese society and Japan's geographical environment have contributed to the emergence of the distinctive characteristics of the Japanese HRM practices that we see today. Studies have shown, however, that such practices can be applied, with modifications, in other environments where the workers possess different cultural values—for example, in Malaysia, a multiracial and multicultural country. The transference of Japanese HRM practices must be undertaken with patience and understanding, and in line with the mainstream of the basic cultural values of the local community. Transference is made easier due to the interest in Japanese HRM practices held by foreign academicians who are teaching such practices to their students in their own academic institutions. The local news media also play a role in disseminating such information to the general public. The groundwork for creating awareness and understanding of Japanese HRM practices has been started and still continues. This helps to ensure that when Japanese companies transfer manufacturing and service activities offshore, their presence and activities will not prove to be a cultural shock to the local populace.

Comment

Atsumu Hirano

Dr. Thong remarked that "learning from the Japanese" has been in vogue for some time in Malaysia and is still continuing. He also, however, cautioned that the transfer of Japanese HRM practices must be undertaken with patience and an understanding that is in line with the mainstream of the basic cultural values of the local community.

When we, as management staff of Japanese companies in Malaysia, try to introduce Japanese-style management there, we come across various standards or values. In my analysis, such standards are categorized as Malay local standards (Chinese and Indian standards to be added); Islamic standards (values)in Malay society; or British standards.

I am sure we would not be wrong in saying that executive members of a company tend to think and act according to British standards while workers who come from the Malay villages are inclined to think and act according to Malay standards, and in some instances, to follow Islamic values. In middle management, we find two categories of Chinese managers: those educated in English locally or abroad and who tend to adopt British standards (Western standards); and those educated in Chinese languages at local Chinese schools and who may adopt Chinese standards. Japanese management is therefore faced with two mainstreams of standards: British (Western) standards and local-Malay (Islamic), Chinese, or Indian values.

We can expect to find a positive and a negative side to the adaptation of Japanese-style management according to seniorities or ranks in a company. Executives and senior management staff (who follow British standards) give negative responses to the ideas of "egalitarianism," "shop floor priority," and "in-house union." For this reason I had great difficulty in explaining the concept of in-house union and how it works in a Japanese company during "dialog" between the Japanese Chamber of Trade and Industry in Malaysia and high officials of the Malaysian Ministry of Labour.

On the other hand, we can expect positive responses from the Malay staff and workers concerning the idea of "small group activities," "canteen facilities," and "company recreational activities."

According to the "Questionnaire Survey in Four ASEAN Countries" conducted by Professor Shoichi Yamashita and members of Hiroshima University, the concept of being "group oriented" is less welcomed by higher ranked staff (senior staff with high ranking), highly educated staff, and younger staff with the ability and potential to be promoted in a company.

In my opinion, those who may take a negative attitude toward the concept of being group oriented are the people who adopt the British standards, possibly because they were educated in English in a British (or Western) educational system and have been influenced by the cultural and moral standards of Britain (or Western countries).

I am inclined to think that the reason that the ideas of egalitarianism and group orientation are less popular in some groups of people in Malaysia is because they reflect the more deep-rooted "Japanese standards" (compared to other Japanese standards) and therefore will not be easy to introduce in a basically British (Westernized) environment.

At this point I refer to what Professor Nobuo Kawabe pointed out in his report; that the first problem for a Japanese company starting business in Malaysia is the confrontation with a management greatly influenced by the British style of management.

In Yamashita's Questionnaire Survey, "career development" received high marks while "life-time employment" got a negative evaluation. I would like to point out that career development is thought to be the most effective in a company which adopts a lifetime employment system. On the other hand, career development is *less* effective in a company which does *not* adopt a lifetime employment system. Career development is programmed for each staff member on the assumption that he or she will stay within a company until retirement. Therefore, both practices should be adopted if a company using Japanese style management is to expect good results.

Japanese companies starting businesses in Malaysia or other ASEAN countries have, in my opinion, two choices of management style: Japanese style management or British (Western) style management. A company of Japanese style management will need more time to enjoy good results. It is, therefore, encouraging for us to see that some Japanese companies that have operated for many years in Malaysia are successful and confident in pursuing Japanese style management and that some of them have even reached the stage in which they are establishing a "hybrid style of management," as Professor Kawabe calls it, by adding some Malaysian cultural elements to their management practices. They have been trying to establish their own corporate identity with consistency and patience. You will find in them good cooperation among Japanese and local executives and senior management, and you will also find able middle management staff who can understand Japanese, British, and local standards.

It seems that a company establishing the hybrid style of management has more chance of maintaining long-term stability in its management.

7

Localization and Performance of Japanese Operations in Malaysia and Singapore

Tatsuo Kimbara

Objectives of the Study

The spread of multinational companies was widely made known around 1970 through such studies as Harvard's Multinational Enterprise Project and the United Nations Report on Multinational Corporations.

Host countries, both developed and developing, responded to that spread in ambivalent ways. On the one hand, the strong power of multinational companies was often regarded as a threat to the national sovereignty of the host country. The host country was inclined to resist the foreign company's monopolistic powers, which were beyond the control of the host country's government. As a number of developing countries have past histories as colonies of Western powers they are especially suspicious of direct investment by multinational companies.

On the other hand, the capital, technology, and managerial skills owned by multinational companies are needed for the industrialization and economic development of the majority of developing countries. Without the introduction of technology and capital from developed countries, it seems difficult for most developing countries to attain economic development successfully. They thus seek to achieve industrialization with the aid of foreign capital.

The joint venture is one of the alternatives that a host country can choose in order to make compromises between the conflicting interests of the host country and the multinational company. And it is an effective measure by which the host country can reconcile its own ambivalent needs. The joint venture plays a role that becomes important in terms of function as well as numbers. In Thailand, for example, by regulation foreign capital cannot exceed 49% of a company's shares in manufacturing investment for the domestic market. This means that the local partner in principle holds the majority of shares. In Malaysia, foreign capital cannot hold more than 30% of shares in domestic market-oriented investment. Complete ownership by foreign capital is allowed only if the subsidiary company exports more than 80% of its products. It thus is common today for a developing country to demand the joint-venture form when it accepts foreign capital.

In the Thailand sample of our investigation in 1987, minority ownership by a Japanese parent company was the case in 72.3% of 47 instances. This pattern of ownership is also seen in Japanese foreign direct investment as a whole. In the Asian region, only 19.7% of the Japanese-affiliated companies in the manufacturing sector was wholly owned in 1983 while 49.1% was minority owned.

The joint venture is defined in terms of ownership; localization, on the other hand, is often treated as a matter of local content. Rarely do we find a model that encompasses analysis of joint-venture ownership and localization in the same framework. It is however clear that localization, in a broad sense, can occur in the various factors of corporate activities including ownership. It has to do with the relationship between the multinational company and the host country. From our point of view, the joint venture is one aspect of localization. We would therefore like to analyze joint venture ownership and localization in the same framework.

The purpose of this paper is thus twofold. First, we briefly examine the localization of Japanese affiliated companies in two ASEAN coun-tries, Singapore and Malaysia. To what extent does Japanese operation in these countries localize such factors as capital and position? Is any particular pattern found in its localization? Second, the relation of localization to corporate performance is examined. Performance is the most important criteria in evaluating corporate decision and behavior; the appropriateness of decision and behavior is finally assessed by outcome or performance. What level of localization is successful in joint ventures and subsidiary companies in ASEAN countries? We need to re-late localization to performance and identify the nature of this relation.

Survey of Preceding Studies

Localization as well as joint venture has not been well accepted by multinational companies, which wish to have complete control over foreign operations. Because localization and joint venture hold the potential to create conflict between partners or between host country and multinational company, they make the management of foreign operations more complicated. They constrain the management of multinational operations to negotiate the conflicting interests of joint-venture partners in order to achieve decision-making or to adapt to localization regulations. Some companies therefore deny joint venture as a means of direct investment in spite of the benefits it offers. Conflicts with local partners often occur over decisions regarding such matters as internal reserves or dividends, the price of parts and materials to be sold by the multinational company to the joint venture, factory expansion, and so on.

The host government's policy makers, who want to regulate the operation of multinational companies, commonly pay more attention to the regulation itself rather than to the performance of the operation concerned. They see the problem from the viewpoint of the total economy involving such issues as international balance of payment and development of domestic industry.

Reflecting the situation, only a limited amount of research on joint venture performance or localization has been done until now, although there are plenty of cases of both. Joint venture has aroused the interest of such researchers as W. G. Friedmann and G. Kalmanoff, L. G. Franko, J. W. C. Tomlinson, J. M. Stopford and L. T. Wells, P. J. Killing, and P. W. Beamish. In the early stages, analysis was mainly implemented from the viewpoint of the multinational company or the developed country. Later on it was often analyzed from that of the host country.

Based on the large sample data of the Harvard's Multinational Enterprise Project, Stopford and Wells analyzed ownership patterns of foreign subsidiaries of American-based multinational companies. They showed that the strategy chosen by the multinational company is closely connected to the design of the organization and to the ownership of the subsidiaries established to implement it.

The model proposed by L. G. Franko indicates that the decision regarding ownership of foreign operations depends on factors in the strategy of international management. Different strategic factors bring different choices of strategy, which then lead to the different kinds of operations ownership. Franko's model explains the choice of joint venture in relation to the multinational company's strategy, structure, and decision making.

Both the Stopford and Wells and the Franko studies, which were part of the Harvard Project, were outstanding analyses based on large empirical data bases, and they both proposed important hypotheses regarding strategy and ownership in international management. They did not, however, go into analysis of joint venture performance. Research on foreign subsidiary or joint venture performance was still rare even in the late 1970s, mainly due to the fact that performance depends on numerous factors internal and external to the organization. Such external factors as government regulation and the economy's developmental stage cannot be controlled by the organization. Because of the complex relations among diverse factors it was difficult to build valid models for performance analysis.

As we reviewed the studies on joint venture performance some common variables regarding performance analysis appeared. The most dominant variable is the nature of control held by the multinational company. T. T. Dang, P. J. Killing, P. W. Beamish, and A. Y. Al-Aali examined the relation between foreign control and joint venture success, and their conclusion is not affirmative. Beamish suggests that in addition to control, partner need and commitment are also main factors affecting joint venture performance. He excludes external factors as determinants of performance and treats profit as an indicator of performance. Al-Aali also insists that need, commitment, and control factors positively affect the joint venture performance and at the same time points out significant differences between manufacturing and service joint ventures. Thus, need, commitment, and control are often considered as main determinants in the analysis of joint venture success.

The definition of localization, which has a broader meaning than joint venture, is restricted in clarifying its impact on performance. But it is useful to refer to factors identified in the joint venture analysis in order to analyze localization. Both have to do with the relationship between the host country and the multinational company and depend on a successful mixing of resources.

Hayashi examines how Japanese affiliated companies in the United States and ASEAN countries transfer the management system and practices seen in the domestic operations and whether there is any specific relation between management system and performance. He finds that the existence of a strong Japanese-style management system correlates with high performance for certain types of organizations. A company with sophisticated interface management of systems and practices can successfully transplant the Japanese management system into different cultural environments, and the company can consequently attain high performance.

Hayashi hypothesizes that the foreign operation's performance depends on the interface management of different systems and people. He indicates a distinct comprehensive model for international management and contributes to clarification of the relation between localization and performance. His definition of localization, however, emphasizes the transplantation of Japanese systems and practices into the new environment, rather than the delegation of control so that the meaning of his references to the localization of capital and management systems is somewhat vague.

Analytical Framework and Research Methodology

The purpose of this study is to reveal the present situation regarding localization in the Japanese-affiliated company in ASEAN countries and to examine the relation between localization and performance there. We are concerned about how the joint venture and subsidiary company mix and balance the requirements of the host country and the multinational company and what results they get. Thus, two main factors to be analyzed here are localization and performance. But it will be helpful to define some concepts briefly before explaining the data gathered by the Yamashita project.

While localization indicates the mixture of various resources in the multinational company's foreign operations, performance reflects the consequences of the operation's activity. Localization is achieved through a mixture of managerial resources that come from both sides, the host country and the multinational company. We consequently define localization as the transfer of managerial resources from multinational company to local control. "Managerial resources" here implies a set of such resources within the company as human, physical, and financial resources, technology, and managerial skills. Because localization can take place in various elements of the foreign operation, the concept of localization is multidimensional. We regard localization as consisting of five main elements: technology, capital, local content or local procurement of raw material and parts, personnel, and managerial skills.

We examined the degree of localization of each element in the Japanese subsidiary or joint venture in Singapore and Malaysia. As the natures of these elements differ considerably it is difficult to use a common scale for their measurement. Furthermore, localization depends on a variety of factors in the host country and multinational company, and some of these factors—for instance, government regulations—are not controllable by the multinational company. It is beyond the purpose of this paper to argue in detail the reason for and process of localization in each element.

We then define performance as the outcome of corporate activity. Numerous external and internal factors of the organization have effects on performance. It is expected that localization has an important impact on the performance of the subsidiary company, but the causal relationship does not always move in one direction because the resulting performance can influence the degree of the localization the next time. We focus the analysis on the relation between localization and performance, and to that purpose it is helpful to examine the individual relation among factors rather than to attempt an unrealistic integration of factors.

Performance is measured by six indicators: return on investment, sales growth rate, profit growth rate, market share, morale, and employee turnover. The last two indicators are included because the localization of positions and managerial skills seems to have certain effects on the motivation and attitude of personnel. In other words, they represent behavioral consequences. Any organization's performance can be assessed from several different levels and perspectives, using different indicators. The evaluation of performance is not a simple matter. If we were interested only in financial consequences of localization, it would not be necessary to include the last two indicators. In the joint venture analysis conducted to date, such financial data as profit rate are normally used as indicators of performance, because the financial data have primary importance in the management of the company. We used six indicators and furthermore computed performance by both individual indicators and the aggregate.

In measuring performance we used the subjective evaluations given by the manager responsible for the operation. The evaluation is measured on a five-point scale, with "1" indicating quite unsatisfied and "5" quite satisfied. Though limitations exist in this method, it is sometimes the only way available to get financial figures from companies not listed on the stock exchange.

The investigation sample consists of Japanese-affiliated joint ventures or subsidiary companies based in Singapore and Malaysia. A subsidiary is considered to be majority owned by the multinational company, while from five to no more than fifty percent of the equity of a joint venture is owned by the multinational company. We investigated the firms through the use of a questionnaire and extensive interviews with the executives responsible for the operation. The questionnaire was completed during December 1987 and January 1988. The number of samples analyzed was 19 for Singapore and 24 for Malaysia. The electric and electronic industry constituted 33.3% of the sample for Malaysia and 73.7% of the sample for Singapore. No samples were taken from the automobile and related parts and textile industries in Singapore. We supplemented our data on localization with information from Thailand and Indonesia.

Research Findings

We chose five essential elements in localization in order to analyze the pattern of mixture of local and foreign resources in the process of localization. These elements—personnel, material and parts, capital, technology, and managerial skills—are analyzed in the first five sections that follow. In each case we questioned to what extent delegation to the local people is actually achieved.

Personnel

The localization of personnel means that positions and tasks held by expatriate employees are turned over to local people. It is, in other words, the appointment of local people to certain positions in the organization. Such transfer of positions to local personnel is strongly requested by the host country for several reasons, including the host country's expectation that the practice will promote the transfer of technology and managerial skills to the host country. In contrast the multinational company wants to hold the control of management in order to make decisions freely and to maintain the level of product quality or technology.

Organizational positions, excluding that of general worker, were classified into 12 ranks, which were then distributed into four groups according to level. Level I includes foreman, chief, and assistant manager. Level II includes section manager. Level III: factory manager, department manager, and division general manager. Level IV: director, vice-president, president, vice-chairman, and chairman. The proportions of local and Japanese staff were then calculated for each level.

The proportion of Japanese staff at levels III and IV is substantial (Fig. 1). At level IV they hold almost half of the positions. Thus the degree of localization in terms of positions transferred is relatively low in Japanese foreign operations. This is due partly to the Japanese management's heavy reliance on human relations in decision making and productivity improvement. More Japanese staff are usually required for the overseas operations compared to the case of a Western multinational company. We found that about half of the Japanese in foreign operations are in production departments as engineers; as a result, the proportion of Japanese staff at level III is very high.

In comparing the four countries investigated, the degree of transfer is found to be higher in Thailand and Malaysia than in Singapore. Foreign capital in Singapore is free to set up wholly-owned subsidiaries in the manufacturing sector, while strong regulations on capital owner-

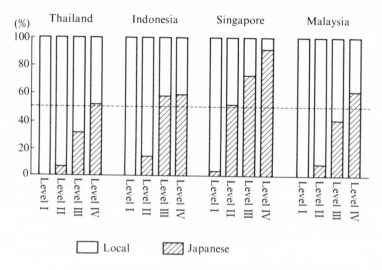

Fig. 1.   Ratio of Local to Japanese Staff by Rank Level.
Source: Yamashita 1988.

ship are exerted in the other countries. We therefore hypothesize that when there exists stronger regulation on ownership, the proportion of local personnel at the top level increases. Ownership is reflected by the make up of the board of directors. In a similar way, the interdependent relation between the average ratio of ownership and the ratio of local/Japanese personnel can be seen at the top level.

Material and Parts

The localization of material, including parts, implies purchase from suppliers in the host country. It is measured by the percentage that local procurement represents in the manufacturing cost of the company's main products. Purchasing of local material by foreign-based companies is a matter of primary concern for the host country government. First of all, it is related to the international balance of payment. It can offer additional employment opportunities and can contribute to the growth of domestic industry, which leads to technology improvement. For such reasons, regulation of the import of material is commonly seen in developing countries. Our data (see Table 1) show that the ratio of average local procurement of all industry in Thailand was 47.3% in 1970 and 62.3% in 1986, an increase of 15% over fifteen years. In Singapore and Malaysia it was 28.8% and 54.5%, respectively, in 1975, then 59.9% and 50.5%, respectively, in 1987. In Indonesia it was 13.7% in 1975 and

Table 1.   Ratio of Local Procurement to Manufacturing Cost.

(%)

	Malaysia	Singapore	Thailand	Indonesia
1970	80.0		47.3	15.0
1975	54.5	28.8	42.5	13.7
1980	51.8	43.2	47.9	28.5
1985	51.9	55.8	57.0	40.5
1986	49.9	55.8	62.3	42.4
1987	50.5	59.9		

Source: Yamashita 1988.

42.4% in 1986. In both developing and developed countries, in general, it can be seen that regulations aimed at increasing the local materials content have been strengthened over the years.

The main difficulty however, in achieving high local content in the developing country is that the development of the economy may be disturbed when local content is introduced too hastily and in disregard of surrounding conditions. The host country faces a trade-off between local content and economic development. To overcome such a dilemma, the developing country often creates such specific areas as the Free Trade Zone in Malaysia; in this export processing zone, the company can import raw materials and parts regardless of local content regulation. It is also possible for foreign capital to increase its ownership, depending on the export contribution.

Such zones and other treatments accordingly bring down the level of localization in raw material and parts, ownership, and personnel. The extent of local content in Indonesia is the lowest among the countries investigated despite its regulations on local content, which suggests that such fundamental economic conditions as supporting industry are crucial constraints on the achievement of local content in the countries investigated. Regarding the differences by industry, the food industry has a high degree of localization when plentiful supplies of the raw materials needed are available in the host country. In the automobile industry, however, where more than ten thousand parts are used for one complete car, the rate of localization is relatively low.

Capital

The localization of capital means that foreign ownership of equity is replaced by local capital. It is measured by the ratio of locally owned capital in the total equity of the company. According to our 1987 data, the average Japanese-owned proportion in the total equity of a company is 52.6% in Thailand, 58.9% in Indonesia, 85.5% in Singapore, and 60.1% in Malaysia.

Singapore allows foreign companies to have 100%-owned subsidiaries in the manufacturing sector if the company so desires. Figures from Malaysia, which emphasizes export-oriented industrialization, indicate that the proportion of foreign capital is relatively high even though the government regulates capital ownership by foreign capital under the New Economic Policy. In Thailand, Japanese ownership is between 40–50% in 53.2% of the firms—that is, more than half of the companies hold minority shares. We therefore consider Thailand's regulation of capital ownership to be substantial, which also implies the existence of favorable conditions making possible the execution of such regulation.

In spite of strong demand for localization of capital from the host country, there exist some prerequisites to the fulfillment of this demand. First, capital accumulation in the host country is necessary to replace the foreign capital. Second, technology, capital, and managerial capability will be in short supply if the multinational company does not want to provide such necessary operational resources when it loses ownership control. In other words, less foreign ownership leads to less commitment on the part of the multinational company, and the host country will therefore need to supply more resources in the place of the multinational company. If the localization choice is not reasonable the competitive position of the joint venture or subsidiary company will be weakened. In the arguments for localization the viewpoint of business competitiveness is often forgotten.

Technology

The objective of technology transfer for the host country is to obtain advanced technology and to improve the level of existing technology, which leads to the strengthening of economic competitiveness. To what extent do Japanese-based companies in ASEAN countries transfer technology to local operations? We classified the technology involved in a range of activities from operations to design of manufacturing equipment into nine groups: operation technology of the existing production process, maintenance, quality control, improvement of production technology and introduction of new technology, production management, modification of existing products, design and development of new products, mold development, and development of manufacturing equipment and facilities. The degree of localization was measured by the number of companies that transferred technology to local control for each type of technology.

Several interesting points were discovered. First, Japanese companies transfer technology that is necessary mainly for routine operations. In Thailand, operation and maintenance technology are transferred by 78.7% and 57.4% respectively, but the other kinds of technology are transferred in less than half of the companies. In Malaysia, operation and maintenance technology are transferred by 75.0% and 54.2% respectively. Second, measuring by industry, the electric industry generally shows a high degree of transfer of technology, which contrasts with the automobile industry's low rates of transfer for most technology types. This accords with the conclusions gained by looking at the company's entry year. The automobile industry technology transfer rate in Malaysia is high, however, because a government-owned joint venture gets the biggest role. Third, companies that started operations before 1974 show higher rates of transfer in all types of technology when compared to companies that started after that year. Fourth, if the president of the joint venture is a local person then the transfer of technology is further accelerated, but questions arise about the role played by a president who is a local person. It is often said that a local-person president does not promote the distribution of technology within organizations because such a person, especially a partner in family-owned capital, is reluctant to disclose technology to lower-level organization members who expect to change jobs for better opportunities. We cannot confirm this view by our data.

Maintenance and quality control are transferred more effectively when a Japanese rather than local person holds the position of president, which may indicate that maintenance and quality control are well implemented under Japanese supervision.

Why does the transfer of technology in Japanese companies tend to stay at the level of operation and maintenance technology rather than expanding to other technologies as well? The principal reason arises within the context of the Japanese management system: there are obvious differences between Japanese and local staff in the perception of technology. Japanese companies, for example, adopt OJT in order to continually improve technology at the shop floor level. Technology cannot be written into the manual thoroughly because technology always progresses to a higher level; there is no end to technology development. Technological progress is seen as dynamic and incremental, and it must be pursued by all members of the organization—it is not a job only for engineers but for everyone. Thus Japanese workers on the shopfloor are deeply involved in the activity of technological improvement and development. This view is realized in the QC activity that is by now a synonym for Japanese production management. The effect of such incremental innovation is quite large when the product or technology is standardized.

A different reaction by the two sides to technology transfer thus exists. Consequently we often see conflicting views regarding evaluations of technology level and competitiveness, product quality, and positions to be transferred.

Managerial Skills

The localization of managerial skills here means the transfer of such functions as marketing, finance, and so on. The proportion of companies that transferred such functions to the local people was measured. The transfer of these functions is strongly related to the transfer of the first element mentioned: personnel. The elements of personnel and managerial skills are in fact interrelated; neither one can exist by itself, and therefore a certain consistency in the localization of these elements exists.

Some Evidence on Performance

The extent of localization in terms of personnel, material, capital, technology, and managerial skills has been explained; now the relation of localization to performance will be examined. We need to consider the economic outcome of localization as well as its present extent if we are interested in the effective transfer of management systems from one country to another.

When a company can achieve an adequate mixture of company requirements and local conditions the localization will be effective. But if it cannot the company gets into trouble. What criteria will lead to rational choices? And why? Performance offers one standard for evaluating localization. It is obvious that the performance of domestic operation depends on a variety of such factors as economic environment, market strategy, attributes of members, leadership, and so on. The performance of a joint venture is more complicated because it is influenced by both the foreign company and the host country.

In our study, performance was measured by six indicators: sales growth rate, profit growth rate, return on investment, market share of main products, motivation, and employee turnover. Each indicator was measured on a five-point scale, and overall performance was measured by the average of the indicators' scores. Each indicator was related to the elements of localization.

We initially hypothesized that multinational companies are likely to hold a competitive advantage over local companies or there would be no proper reason to make foreign investments. The competitive advantage derives from advantages in price, quality, reliable supply, and so on, and is based on such factors as technology and human resources.

When a company invests overseas the combination of resources it uses will change. It needs to use more local resources, which may be lower in cost but less skilled or of lower quality. Until the company well integrates its resources and workers become accustomed to tasks in the new situation, the company will be faced with a decline in managerial effectiveness. When the company becomes experienced in the operation, however, it is possible to improve effectiveness and performance.

Localization and Performance in Malaysia

First, when the organization has a high proportion of Japanese staff at level II, III, and IV, a high level of performance is seen. This pattern is clearly seen at level III, which holds substantial control over the production activity. At this level, a high-performance company has a 52.5% proportion of local staff, while a low-performance company has 70.0%. That is, the company that is slow in the localization of personnel shows high operation performance and vice versa. This is partly because a low-performance company puts localization above economic rationality. Consequently it does not attain adequate integration of resources. Regarding the six performance indicators, only employee turnover shows the opposite tendency—that is, employees seem to be more satisfied with local managers and tend to stay longer in a organization because of higher localization.

Second, local procurement indicates a conclusion similar to that indicated by personnel. When a company buys less material and parts from local suppliers, including multinational company subsidiaries, a high performance is seen. In contrast, high localization leads to low performance (Fig. 2). Why does this occur in a company which is supposed to be seeking better performance? Due to constraints imposed by inside and outside organizations, the company's choice seems to result in unfavorable consequences. Activity since 1980 should be studied, however, because the above relation seems to be weakening in Malaysia. Also we cannot estimate the exact role of the foreign-based company with regard to local content.

Third, the company that shows a high degree of technology transfer is low in performance in terms of the level of the operation and maintenance technology of the existing production process.

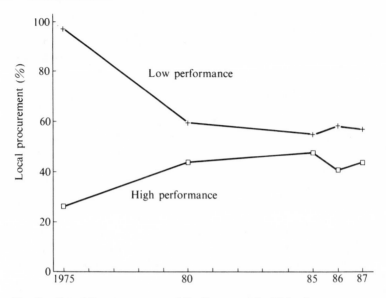

Fig. 2.   Local Procurement and Performance in Malaysia.

In summary, in Malaysia, the company that shows a high degree of localization has a low performance level. But this trend is now gradually weakening, which may be due to fundamental improvements in the Malaysian economy during the past decade. The government policy for developing small businesses and investments into a supporting industry for multinational companies has had a considerable effect on this point.

Localization and Performance in Singapore

Our data for Singapore, the most developed of the ASEAN countries, contrast strongly with that for Malaysia. First, when the proportion of Japanese staff is high at the top (level IV), performance is high. But at levels II and III a low proportion of Japanese staff interrelates with high performance, which is different from the case in Malaysia. In Singapore, more delegation is seen at levels II and III, which are responsible for operative decision-making, and high performance is measured.

Second, the degree of local procurement is high in the high-performance company, and vice versa (Fig. 3). Therefore the progress of localization is interrelated to high performance, which suggests that supporting industries in Singapore are well developed to supply material and parts to companies in the existing production process. As for the individual performance indicators, four out of six fall into the same pattern. This pattern, which contrasts substantially with the Malaysian

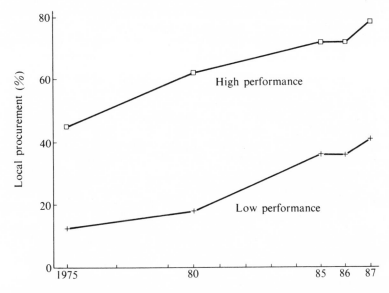

Fig. 3.   Local Procurement and Performance in Singapore.

case, was already evident by 1975.

Third, a high degree of technology transfer is related to a high performance level, and this holds for seven of the nine types of technology. On the other hand, the low-performance company is slow even in transferring operation and maintenance technology. In the high-performance company, transfer of production management function is obvious, with 70% of companies having already transferred it.

In summary, our data show contrasting results regarding localization and performance in Singapore and Malaysia. The results indicate a certain direction of change—that is, from the Malaysian type to the Singaporean type. Concerning Singapore, we recognize that increase of local content and technology transfer leads to high performance, as does the localization of personnel at levels II and III, which are responsible for daily operation (Table 2). While the extent of localization in capital ownership as well as in top personnel at level IV is revealed to be quite low, we believe the level of localization at Level IV will increase in the long run. The contrasting relation between localization and performance reflects the underlying conditions of the two countries; different conditions influence performance. Therefore, in order to advance the process of localization, it is necessary for the company to choose the proper level of localization based on the underlying

Table 2.   Ratio of Local Personnel by Rank Level.

(%)

	Malaysia		Singapore	
	performance		performance	
	low	high	low	high
Level I	99.1	100.0	96.5	96.7
Level II	93.8	90.3	38.1	57.0
Level III	70.0	52.5	8.3	44.2
Level IV	42.3	35.0	11.1	8.1

conditions. And the improvement of underlying conditions is the main task for the host country in achieving localization.

Conclusion

A foreign operation depends on numerous local and foreign conditions. Every multinational company needs to find a better mixture of human and other resources, otherwise it cannot continue its foreign operations for long. Our model is intended to identify such a successful resource mix in the subsidiary company or joint venture. Our research findings, though still tentative, are quite suggestive.

It is evident that there are several limitations in our model. It does not explain the causal relationship between localization and performance. The impact of localization on the economy is also excluded from our analysis. Policymakers usually have strong interests in these points. Our focus is rather on the internal factors of the organization that is in the process of localization.

Through this investigation we found contrasting moves taken by Malaysia and Singapore with respect to performance, and it is suggested that the performance of localization depends heavily on the conditions in the country concerned. The same level of localization does not result in the same outcome in countries with differing conditions. Through recognition of the importance of this fact and confirmation of the current relation between localization and performance, it will be possible for both multinational companies and host countries to achieve localization more successfully.

8
Technology Transfer in Thailand's Electronics Industry

Prayoon Shiowattana

Evolution of Thailand's Electronic Industry

The history of Thailand's electronic industry began in the early 1960s with the establishment of Tanin Industrial Co., Ltd., a wholly Thai-owned firm producing radios and televisions. The industry has since gone through many stages of evolution and the number of firms in operation has increased to over one hundred in 1987. Starting from the end of 1986, the number of firms applying for the Board of Investment's promotion has soared remarkably. The consequences of this are becoming clear since the end of 1988, as many of these firms start their operations. The status of Thailand's electronic industry and its evolution, especially the changes that have occurred in recent years, will be briefly described in this section.

Status of Thailand's Electronic Industry

There presently exist about one hundred electronic products manufacturers in Thailand (Table 1). We may classify the development of this industry into five major phases, each exhibiting specific characteristics, as discussed in the following.

(1) The Consumer Electronic Phase (1960–1970). This period is characterized by the establishment of Tanin Industrial and five Japanese joint ventures producing consumer electronic and electrical products, including radios, televisions, electric fans, refrigerators, and so on. Of all the electronic firms established in this period, seven were consumer electronic producers and comprised over 60% of the total. These firms employed more than 6,000 workers, which amounted to over 90% of total employment in the industry.

The reason behind these investments was the establishment of the Board of Investment (BOI) in 1962 in order to promote foreign

169

Table 1.   Electronics Producing Firms, by Start-up Period and Product
Group, 1960–1988.

Product Group	Consumer Electronics		Industrial Electronics		Electronics Components		Total Electronics	
Period	No. of Firms	Total Employees	No. of Firms	Total Employees	No. of Firms	Total Employees	No. of Firms	Total Employees
1960–1970	7	6,066	2	185	2	164	11	6,415
(% share)	63.6	94.6	18.2	2.8	18.2	2.6	100.0	100.0
1971–1974	4	836	2	126	4	5,932	10	6,894
(% share)	40.0	12.1	20.0	1.8	40.0	86.0	100.0	100.0
1975–1981	12	1,084	7	781	12	1,568	31	3,433
(% share)	38.7	31.6	22.6	22.7	38.7	45.7	100.0	100.0
1982–1986	11	1,414	10	1,205	16	19,050	37	21,669
(% share)	29.7	6.5	27.0	5.6	43.2	87.9	100.0	100.0
1987–June 1988 (% share)	1	700	4	1,240	8	1,277	13	3,217
	7.7	21.8	30.8	38.5	61.5	39.7	100.0	100.0
Total	35	10,100	25	3,537	42	27,991	102	41,628
(% of Total)	34.3	24.3	24.5	8.5	41.2	67.2	100.0	100.0

Source: Compilation from BOI's investment statistics and the author's survey.
Note: Firms with and without BOI promotion are included.

investment,* with the objective being to substitute for imported industrial products.

(2) The Integrated Circuit Phase (1971–1974). The conspicuous
event of the period was the establishment of three IC assembly factories
by the major U.S. producers National Semiconductor, Signetics, and
Data General. The BOI's promotion policy began to shift from emphasis
on import substitution to the promotion of more export-oriented
projects. The number of firms (accumulated) promoted by the BOI,
classified by nature of investment, is summarized in Table 2. It is evident
from the table that number of export oriented firms has increased
steadily since 1975.

---

* Some important incentives provided by the BOI include: (a) an import ban on
competitive products, (b) exemption from import duties and business taxes on imported
machinery, and (c) exemption from corporate income taxes for 3 to 8 years.

Table 2. Changes in Number of Electronic Projects Receiving BOI
Promotion, by Nature of Investment, 1970–1988.

Year	Import Substitution		Export Oriented		Total	
	No. of Projects	Total Investment (mil. baht)	No. of Projects	Total Investment (mil. baht)	No. of Projects	Total Investment (mil. baht)
1970	7	1,640 (100.0)	—	—	7	1,640
1975	11	1,973 (50.2)	5	1,957 (49.8)	16	3,930
1980	11	1,973 (48.1)	10	2,130 (51.9)	21	4,103
1985	14	2,052 (14.4)	27	12,181 (85.6)	41	14,233
1986	14	2,052 (12.8)	36	13,952 (87.2)	50	16,004
1987	17	4,842 (18.1)	82	21,951 (81.9)	99	26,793
1988 (up to end of June 1988)	18	4,949 (14.0)	112	30,492 (86.0)	130	35,441

Note: All figures are accumulated. Figures in parentheses show percentage share of
each item at the end of the year.

(3) The Consolidation Phase (1975–1981). This period is characterized by investments of 12 predominantly Thai companies in consumer
electronic products catering to domestic demand and by the establishment an equal number of Thai and joint-venture companies producing
a wider range of electronic components primarily for export. The
former covered two major products, televisions and radios, while the
latter produced mainly new electronic components such as electrolytic
condensers, loudspeakers, crystal oscillators, ferrite devices, and so on.

(4) The Component Expansion Phase (1982–1986). A rapid expansion and diversification of firms in the electronic component industry
occurred during this phase. Of the 37 firms that started operation at this

time, 16 were electronic component manufacturers employing more than 19,000 workers, which amounted to almost 90% of total workers being newly employed in the period. The period was also marked by a gradual shift by two major electronic component producers from their production bases in Singapore to Thailand. The first firm is a Japanese ball bearing producer, and the second is an American hard disk producer.

(5) The Post-Yen Appreciation Phase (1987–). Development in this period resulted from a series of international trade and economic changes, including rapidly increasing labor costs in most industrialized countries, a rapid appreciation of yen, and a growing protectionist trend. The surge in foreign direct investments has been phenomenal, as can be seen from the number of projects receiving promotion from the BOI in Table 3.

Table 3.   Electronics Projects Promoted by BOI, by Promotion Period and Product Group, 1960–1988.

Product Group	Consumer Electronics		Industrial Electronics		Electronics Components		Total Electronics	
Period	No. of Firms	Total Investment (mil. baht)	No. of Firms	Total Investment (mil. baht)	No. of Firms	Total Investment (mil. baht)	No. of Firms	Total Investment (mil. baht)
1960–1970	5	1,611	2	29	—	—	7	1,640
(% share)	71.4	98.2	28.6	1.8			100.0	100.0
1971–1974	3	410	—	—	5	1,878	8	2,288
(% share)	37.5	17.9			62.5	82.1	100.0	100.0
1975–1981	—	—	—	—	6	175	6	175
(% share)					100.0	100.0	100.0	100.0
1982–1986	1	639	6	413	22	10,849	29	11,901
(% share)	3.4	5.4	20.7	3.5	75.9	91.2	100.0	100.0
1987–June 1988	9	4,468	13	3,159	58	11,810	80	19,437
(% share)	11.38	23.0	16.3	16.3	72.5	60.8	100.0	100.0
Total	18	7,128	21	3,601	91	24,712	130	35,441
(% of Total)	13.8	20.1	16.2	10.2	70.0	69.7	100.0	100.0

Source: Compilation from BOI's investment statistics and the author's survey.

Japanese Involvement in Thailand's Electronic Industry

Until 1985, about 13 Japanese projects in the electronic industry, in joint venture or wholly-owned forms, had received promotion privileges from the BOI. In recent years, however, over 40 electronic projects with Japanese involvement, of which about half are wholly Japanese-owned, have already been approved by the BOI (Table 4). In terms of investment value, Japanese involvement in the electronic industry is exceptionally high. Until June 1988, Japanese investors have been involved in 61 of the total 130 electronic projects being promoted by the BOI. Their investment value is about 25.3 billion baht, which comprises over 70% of the total 35.4 billion baht investment in the industry. Aside from the investment value, the following conspicuous changes could also be observed.

Product Groups. Japanese investment until the early 1980s had been concentrated on consumer electronics both in terms of number of projects and in value of investment. The shift by a Japanese ball bearings

Table 4. Japanese Electronics Projects Receiving BOI Promotion, by Type of Ownership, 1965–1988.

Ownership	Japan-owned		Joint Venture			
			Japanese Minority		Japanese Majority	
Year	No. of Projects	Total Investment (mil. baht)	No. of Projects	Total Investment (mil. baht)	No. of Projects	Total Investment (mil. baht)
1965			2	694		
1970			4	1,608		
1975			6	1,924	1	3
1980			7	1,983	1	3
1981			7	1,983	1	3
1982	1	592	8	2,005	1	3
1983	1	592 (22.8)	8	2,005 (77.1)	1	3 (0.1)
1984	4	6,570 (76.6)	8	2,005 (23.4)	1	3 (0.0)
1985	4	6,570 (76.6)	8	2,005 (23.4)	1	3 (0.0)
1986	6	7,423 (73.0)	10	2,749 (27.0)	1	3 (0.0)
1987	18	9,375 (50.1)	16	5,795 (31.0)	6	3,544 (18.9)
1988	25	11,113 (44.0)	24	6,650 (26.3)	12	7,521 (29.7)

Source: Compilation from BOI's investment statistics and the author's survey.
Note: All figures are accumulated. Figures in parentheses show percentage share of each item at the end of the year.

manufacturer from its production base in Singapore to Thailand was an early sign of the new trend. The impacts of the rapid yen appreciation greatly enhanced the change, and a surge of Japanese investments was seen in this area. As of June 1988, of all 61 electronic projects with Japanese involvement, 45 are in electronic components. Only 11 and 5 projects are in consumer electronics and industrial electronics, respectively. In terms of investment value, electronic component projects comprise up to 70% of total Japanese investment in the industry.

Nature of Investment. Another remarkable change is the high concentration of Japanese investment for export. In the early 1980s there existed only one Japanese export-oriented firm in this industry, but during the last two years a surge of such projects occurred—from 10 in 1986 to 31 and 51 in 1987 and mid-1988 respectively. The total value of investment will be 20.5 billion baht, which comprises over 80% of total Japanese investment.

Types of Ownership. In terms of value, share of investment in wholly-Japanese-owned projects has declined remarkably from its peak of 77% in 1984 to about 44% in 1988. This, however, has been compensated for by an increase in projects with Japanese majority, which jumped to 30% in 1988 from a formerly negligible figure. As for projects with Japanese minority, there are cases, comprising a total investment of over 1.0 billion baht, of joint ventures between Japanese firms and Singapore-based Japanese firms. If these projects are deducted, the real share of Japanese minority projects is only about 21%. So it can be concluded that though wholly-Japanese-owned investment declined relatively, it was compensated for by the increase in joint venture investments with Japanese majority.

Technology Transfer: Its Definition and Roles

Technology is one of the most important factors determining the outcome of the industrialization process of developing countries. As technology has evolved rapidly, the technological gap between the developed and developing countries is said to be increasing. The developing countries have weak technological bases and, on top of that, their capacities for research and development activities are limited. Such a situation allows these countries no choice but to rely on foreign investment as a major mechanism for technological acquisition. However, the introduction of new technology, though a very important step, does not necessarily lead to successful industrialization. The capability to absorb and master the acquired technology proves to be much more important in ensuring healthy industrial development. The successful cases of Japan, Korea, Taiwan, and others are the outcome of conscious effort and striving for effective and rapid absorption and mastery of imported technologies.

From the first introduction of technology to its mastery a long and continual learning process, generally known as the technology transfer process, is necessary. In Thailand, the attention of people from many walks of life has been focused on this topic during the last few years because it is generally perceived that Thailand's future will be greatly influenced by the outcome of this learning process.

Before engaging in a detailed discussion of the situation and problems of technology transfer, it is first necessary to define "technology transfer" and its framework. This is the heart of the discussion. The definition of technology transfer used here is "a learning process wherein technological knowledge is continually accumulated into human resources that are engaged in production activities; a successful technology transfer will eventually lead to a deeper and wider accumulation of knowledge."

Thus defined, the technology transfer process is comprised of two distinct characteristics. First, the learning process is a dynamic and continual one that eventually leads to an accumulation of knowledge in human resources. This implies that the process does not mean merely a physical transfer of production machinery or the setting up of a manufacturing plant, but rather a human capital formation through the accumulation of technological knowledge. In order that this learning process result in technological mastery, it has to expand in both "depth" and "width."

In a proper learning process, engineers, operators, or workers will continually gain a deeper understanding of the technology they are dealing with. This is termed a "deepening" effect. We will divide such levels of understanding into four interrelated stages—acquisitive capability, operative capability, adaptive capability, and innovative capability—as described in the following.

Acquisitive Capability. This capability involves the ability of the firm to search for process or product technology, to assess the suitability of various possible choices, to conduct a feasibility analysis, to negotiate with the foreign supplier and procure the technology, to install the technology or production process in the factory, and to carry out the necessary test runs prior to start-up.

Operative Capability. This capability deals with the efficiency with which the firm is able to use and operate the technology once it has been acquired, and it may itself depend crucially on the understanding of the technology process that the firm acquired during the initial acquisition of the technology. The types of activities that characterize operative capability include process operation and control; quality control of both products and inputs; manpower development programs to enhance human capital and employee involvement; service, maintenance, and calibration procedures relating to machinery and equipment; inventory control of products, inputs, and spare parts; and subcontracting and input sourcing arrangements.

Adaptive Capability. This capability is reflected in the ability of the firm to carry out incremental modifications and improvements to existing plant and processes as well as minor product design changes. It generally requires the development of an in-depth knowledge of the product or process technology and is likely to involve the establishment of either a basic R&D facility, a product design facility, or both.

Innovative Capability. This capability is present when the firm can make radical or major modifications and improvements to products or processes or invent completely new products or processes.

Foreign investment helps to bring in new production technologies that generally do not exist previously in the country. In most cases, however, these technologies are fragmented and usually produce low value-added results, which indicates that the deepening effect alone will not help in the mastery of technology in the practical sense. The learning process must be extended to cover related and necessary areas. Such a learning process will be called a "widening effect." Developing countries would first have to master technology at the periphery, which is the part that most foreign investment would bring in, and gradually extend its learning process to cover the core technology.

In the specific case of television production, the widening effect would mean that a country starts the production by introducing the "low end" process of product assembly (Fig. 1). After the mastery of necessary technologies in such a process, the learning process would gradually be shifted to the more "high end" processes of components manufacturing, material processing, and so on.

The second distinct characteristic of the technology transfer process is the cardinal role of the human resources who stand at the core of the process. On the one hand, they function as accumulators of technological knowledge, without which the deepening and widening effects of the learning process would never be realized. On the other hand, they function in a more active role as conscious actors striving for deeper and wider knowledge.

The first characteristic of the technology transfer process (as described earlier) can be used as a basic indicator for measuring the degree of success (or failure) of the learning process. Suppose we have a firm that started as a mere assembly line of end products. Later on it gradually accumulated technological knowledge deep enough to adapt and even to develop its own end product. In such a case this firm could be evaluated as successful in deepening the technological knowledge considered to be an element of the technology transfer process. Similarly, a firm that extended its production activities from mere assembling to manufacturing of important parts and electronic components should be rated highly in its widening capability. If, contrarily, the learning process is limited only to the repetition of similar operations with no further deepening or widening effects, then the technology transfer process is said to be stagnant.

The second characteristic, which puts great emphasis on the role of

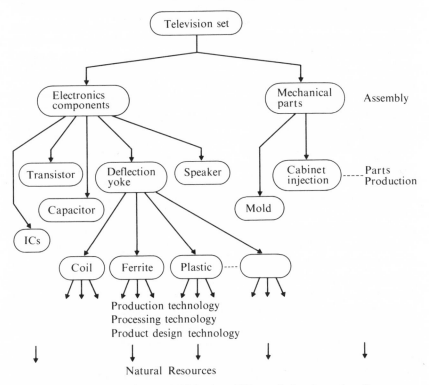

Fig. 1. Diagram Showing Widening Effect of the Learning Process which Eventually Leads to Upstream Integration.

human resources, serves as a basic framework for understanding the dynamism of the process. The learning process, as may be clear, comprises three major elements: teacher(or donor), learner (or recipient), and an environment conducive to a good learning process. The outcome of the technology transfer process will, therefore, depend largely on these elements. Understanding the different roles of each element will help us in identifying policy measures that could stimulate active and effective transfer of technology.

Technology Transfer in the Electronics Industry

As mentioned earlier, characteristics of Japanese investments in the electronic industry have been significantly affected by the rapid yen appreciation. In elaborating on the technology transfer process, therefore, it is most suitable to consider the process in terms of pre- and post-yen appreciation periods. Accordingly, outcomes of the technology transfer in the pre-yen appreciation period will first be discussed and analyzed; then, developing trends in technology transfer in the post-yen appreciation period will be examined.

Pre-Yen Appreciation Period

Japanese investments in the electronic industry during this period were characterized by their high concentration in consumer electronic products, particularly the television set. Joint ventures were established with local investors as a mechanism for penetration into the protected market of Thailand. In the early days, the government rigidly pursued the policy of import substitution without any long-term consideration for the development of the industry. As a result, most Japanese major makers and other MNCs from Europe were allowed to invest and compete in the merely budding market. Most developed into inefficient firms, being unable to reach economies of scale and operating only under heavy protection. They had to rely heavily on imported electronic components. Only the assembly process, which benefited highly from available low cost labor, was set up in the country.

The introduced technologies were characteristically labor intensive, stagnant, fragmented, and dependent. Such were the starting conditions for most firms in the early days of the industry.

The labor intensiveness of introduced technologies was due mainly to the massive cheap labor forces available in the country. In addition, the attitude on the part of the Japanese joint-venture partners, who looked at investment in Thailand merely as a mechanism for penetration into the protected market, made their marketing strategy passive. Most of these firms restricted their production activities to the minimum necessary level of product assembly, relying solely on imported parts and components from the mother companies. As a result, the learning process was concentrated mainly on assembly and related technologies, thereby fragmenting the transferred technology. On top of that, technological development was stagnant as a result of low competition due to the protected market. Because the learning process had been limited, dependency on imported technologies was unnecessarily prolonged.

The learning process in Japanese joint ventures was concentrated on assembly technology, production, and quality controls. It barely widened to other related areas, except for one Japanese joint venture. Most of

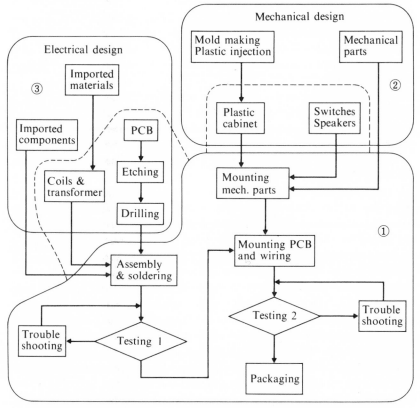

Fig. 2.   Typical Production Process in the Manufacturing of Television Sets.

the electronic and other mechanical parts still had to be imported. For most firms, even after over two decades of operation, localization of parts had been achieved only in such items as carton boxes, packaging materials, wooden television cabinets, packaging foams, and so on.

A typical production process in the television industry may be sketched as shown in Fig. 2. Most firms concentrated their production activities in area 1, with some elements in area 2 being localized. Only one Japanese joint venture had endeavored to invest in the production of components in area 3.

As for deepening of the learning process, achievement could occur only at the level of minor adaptation of electronic circuits to suit local conditions. Most firms could not develop even the capability of electrical/ electronic and mechanical designs. After more than two decades of operation, such a learning process could be evaluated as static or stagnant.

Two firms, however, succeeded remarkably in transferring technology to local human resources, both in width and depth. One is a Japanese joint venture (we shall call it "M") which due to its emphasis and effort in strengthening its technological capability has gained control of the largest local market share. The other is the only local Thai firm that is still operating in this industry. We shall discuss the process of technology transfer and the elements that helped facilitate such achievements in these two cases in the following sections.

The Case of a Japanese Joint Venture. The firm is a joint venture between a major Japanese home appliance producer, M, and an importer of their products. Established in 1961 to produce electrical appliances, its television factory started operation in 1967 with a production quantity of some hundreds of black and white television sets per month. Presently the firm's production quantity for color televisions has soared to over 20,000 sets, with control over one-fourth of the market share.

An important difference between M and other Japanese joint ventures is its marketing philosophy. Most Japanese joint ventures considered the market size in Thailand too small to facilitate the local manufacture of electrical/electronic and mechanical components. They had therefore been relying wholly on imported parts. M's approach, however, is quite different: According to its Japanese executive, M's marketing strategy is to build a "production stronghold" within the marketplace. Through gradual and continual strengthening of this production stronghold, the market shares will eventually be increased.

Such different strategies have resulted in starkly different approaches and actions, which subsequently have led to different outcomes. Japanese executives in M have been determined in trying to localize as many parts and components as possible, provided such schemes are economically feasible in either the short or long term.

The firm set up its Manufacturing Equipment Section in 1971 in order to provide the whole company with such production facilities as plastic and metal molds, production jigs and fixtures, and so on. Such equipment was among the first to be introduced in the country.

Some years later, an engineer was dispatched to Japan to receive training on design and production of molds and to participate in on-the-job training. Similar training was given to other engineers and technicians a year later, after which the firm began to design and manufacture its own production molds and dies for use in the manufacturing of electronic and mechanical parts. Through such localization, the cost of molds and dies was reduced to just about half that of imported ones. Recently, the firm has succeeded in upgrading the accuracy of such tools to within .01mm. The quality and cost of its products have been so remarkably improved that they have already been exported to such countries as Australia, Brazil, and others.

Since 1971 the firm has started its electronic component factory, producing such components as mechanical and electronic tuners, speakers, coils, variable resistors, flyback transformers, and printed circuit boards. Teams of engineers and technicians were sent to Japan to be trained in both the production and design processes of these components. One engineer, for example, participated in the electronic tuner design process with the Japanese team for six months. The model was later produced in Thailand. Such training proved to be very valuable both in the start-up of production and in the diagnosis for quality assurance later on. The firm's tuners and printed circuit boards were exported to many countries, including Japan, the United States, Singapore, Malaysia, Egypt, China, and others. As many of the markets mentioned have very stringent regulations and specifications, the success of export indicates the firm's high capability in terms of quality control.

After having firmly established its operating capability, the firm did not limit its learning process to such levels as found in the cases of most other joint ventures. Development works were later started with an aim to modify electronic circuits to suit the local geographical conditions. Some modifications of appearance through redesign of plastic parts were also done. The learning process has gradually moved into deeper levels, with a larger part of the printed circuit boards and other mechanical parts being modified locally. One model of color television set with major modifications carried out locally was launched in 1985. The model proved to be quite successful in terms of both technicality—appearance and performance—and sales. Two years later another model was turned out, and a new model was planned for 1989.

Another important milestone was reached in 1987 when a Research and Development Center was founded as a separate section within the firm. The Center has been allotted its own budget and personnel, with a total of eleven engineers assigned to work. The major aims of the Center are to "grasp the new technology trends" and to "design and develop new features and new models of television."

The R&D Center does not only engage in development and design of new products but also deals with improvement of the production process. Redesign and improvement of the line system have been continually implemented through careful analysis of the system since 1987. Remarkable successes have been achieved, leading to impressive productivity improvement.

All the above activities have gained the firm fame as an innovator and quality manufacturer. Productivity improvements have additionally brought about a continual reduction in production costs. All these factors combine to work as a driving force behind the strong position of the firm in the local market. The firm presently controls a share of about 25% in television sales.

The Case of a Thai Firm. Another firm that succeeded in transferring technology in terms of both width and depth is a Thai local producer. The firm was first established in 1962 as a family business under the leadership of an entrepreneur who has immense interest in electronic technology. This man has been the sole pioneer that steered the company from nothing into one of the country's major electronic appliances manufacturers. He is also a strong advocate of the rapid and effective mastery of imported technology in order to develop technological self-reliance.

The firm began producing black and white television sets in 1965 by importing components from Japan. The production of some electronic components, however, had been initiated from the very early days of operation. The firm had already gained some knowhow in manufacturing IF transformers and other coils from its experience as the first radio assembler in the country. The technology was initially introduced through machinery imported from Japan combined with self-studies by the owner. Valuable advice was also sought from Japanese technical personnel who came to install the machinery. In addition to electronic components, many metal parts had also been· produced from the beginning.

After gaining more confidence, the firm started in 1968 to produce television sets using its own Thai brand name. The products proved to be competitive and were famous for their high receiving sensitivity particularly in remote areas. This was because the circuits were modified in-house and therefore considerations were given to particulars of local geographical conditions—something that joint ventures could not afford to do in the early days.

As the business grew, the firm decided to set up a separate factory to produce electronic components for in-house use. The factory started operation in 1973, producing coils, transformers, resistors, capacitors, and so on. One year later it launched a Thai brand-name color television with technical assistance in circuit designs from Japanese consultants. And a couple of years earlier the firm had begun the design and manufacture of such production tools as molds for plastic injection, punching dies for drilling holes in printed circuit boards, and so on.

The firm also has pushed hard to deepen its understanding of technology. It set up a small R&D section to do design work. The section contains about ten engineers and technicians who work on the adaptation and improvement of electronic circuits designed by Japanese consulting engineers. All design related to television appearance, from sketching to mock-up production, is done here. Design of molds, dies, and speakers are also carried out in-house. The firm claims that it was the first in the country to set up an acoustic laboratory for use in testing loudspeaker characteristics. (A similar laboratory was set up a few years ago in a public university.)

Human resource development has been carried out primarily through in-house training by technical persons dispatched by machinery makers. Through such mechanisms many engineers and technicians were able to absorb knowhow in mold design and manufacturing, coil production, and circuit adaptation and development.

The major mechanism for technology acquisition is the importation of production machinery accompanied by technical advice from the makers' sales engineers. The owner seems to be the principal person who knows what technologies are needed and where to get them economically. There are also cases of licensing agreements with Japanese makers and consultants for designs of electronic circuits and coil production. Given the limitations of size of capital and information resources, the firm's achievements so far may be evaluated as remarkably successful.

Analysis

The cases of these two firms help to illuminate some critical factors that greatly influence outcomes of the technology transfer process. We will now summarize three important points derived from the cases.

(1) Role of the Government. The lack of an active learning process in technology transfer can be attributed to a large extent to improper policies and in many cases absence of policy on the part of the government. Through overly rigid implementation of an import substitution policy, the government allowed too many firms to produce and coexist in a small market that had been highly protected too long. As a result, economies of scales could hardly be reached; this subsequently led to a delay in or absence of the development of the many crucial supportive industries that are essential for the healthy growth of the industry. The government moreover has periodically changed the tax structure in hope of gaining more revenues. Such changes have been detrimental to the development of component industries. In many cases, taxes levied on raw materials for use in components manufacturing proved to be far higher than those on finished products.

In recent years the BOI has been the most important government mechanism helping to shape policy toward the electronic industry and pulling the television industry into better shape. The BOI set up a Subcommittee for Development of Electronic Industry in 1985 in order to formulate policy that would help to put the industry on more healthy ground. The first task of the Subcommittee was to find effective measures to develop the more-than-twenty-years-old television industry. The Subcommittee commissioned university academicians to survey the status of the industry and to submit recommendations for its restructuring. One of many important recommendations was to promote and strengthen the supportive industries. The products that were recommended for promotion ranged from color picture tubes, tuners, coils, transformers, and PCBs to molds for plastic injection and so on. The first result of such actions was the promotion of color picture tube manufacturing. As the investment is on the scale of billions of baht, the BOI has to coordinate the joint investment of all major television producing firms in this important endeavor. Similar moves are subsequently underway for other joint efforts in the production of electronic tuners, deflection yokes, flyback transformers, and PCB mainboards. Such BOI policy measures function positively in widening the learning process to cover related technologies and thus increase the effect of the technology transfer.

(2) Role of the Technology Donor. The government's policy has significantly affected an environment within which the firms have to develop. Similarly, the firm's attitude or strategy determines to a large extent the attainable limit within which technology transfer can take place.

In the case of joint ventures, it is clear that differences in marketing strategy have brought about distinct outcomes in the technology transfer process. The case of the joint venture M indicates that active localization of components benefits both local industrialization and the joint venture itself. Strong policy to localize components manufacturing created a favorable environment for the widening of the learning process. Such development will in turn contribute positively to local industrialization. Strengthening of a firm's technological capability has similarly led to products with higher performances and lower costs.

Technology transfer in other Japanese joint ventures has been stagnant, with repetition of the learning process in assembly technology. Widening and deepening effects can barely be detected. The main reason is probably the MNCs' policy to keep these firms as assembly lines rather than to develop them into self-contained industries as in the case of M.

In the case of the local Thai firm, the extent of its learning process depends largely on its capability to acquire. As mentioned earlier, the owner of the firm has a profound interest in electronic technology and a strong dedication to strengthening the firm's own technological capability. Such a personality has been very helpful for the firm in getting access to appropriate information sources in order to acquire necessary technology.

(3) Role of Technology Recipient. The attitude and capability of technology recipients determine the degree and effectiveness of the learning process. The supportive roles played by technical manpower can never be overlooked. Technological capability and a nationalistic consciousness on the part of recipients has proved to have strongly affected the course of technical improvement in firms. In the case of M, we found that a Thai engineer has played an important role in facilitating the successful transfer of essential technologies. The engineer engaged in feasibility studies, negotiations, assessments, and so on in order to push for localization of many important electronic components. Working with the firm from the beginning, he has accumulated the technological knowledge that allows him to understood which technologies and components are crucial for the development of the television industry in particular and the electronic industry in general.

Besides having a good university background, he has a nationalistic mind that moves him to strive for a deeper and wider learning process. On the other hand, we witnessed cases in many other joint venture firms where recruitment of incompetent technical manpower had later badly affected the technology transfer process. In one case a vocational diploma student was recruited to work under a Japanese manager. His absorption capability for technological knowhow proved to be sufficient, but his limitations were soon approached when managerial and decision-making powers were gradually to be transferred to him. In addition, the owner of the firm had little interest in human resources development, and as this attitide was quite common among most Thai managers and owners up to the early 1980s, the employee's limitations could not be overcome.

Human resource development in the successful firm M has been systematic and intensive. Prior to the introduction of new machinery or a production process, a team of technical personnels will be dispatched for training. The period sometimes lasts as long as six months. Such well-planned on-the-job training has proved to be very fruitful in strengthening the firm's technological capability.

In the case of the Thai local firm, development of its human resources has been concentrated principally on two mechanisms. The first is the

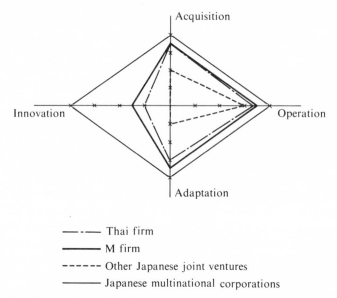

Fig. 3.   Comparison of the Learning Processes in Four Types of Firm.

negotiation for a package deal with machinery makers in order to obtain training for its technical staff. The second is the sending of staff to participate in training, both technical and management, available locally. Compared with M, the training of the Thai firm's technical staff is not that intensive and systematic; however, given the relatively small size of capital and the limited information resources (as is evident when compared with M), such shortcomings are understandable. In fact, the situation also reflects the different approaches of the two firms. While M looks at human resource development as a long-term investment essential for the firm's advancement, the Thai firm still considers it as a cost and puts more emphasis on immediate outcome.

A comparative picture of the learning processes in the Thai firm, the M firm, and other Japanese joint ventures is shown in Fig. 3. The technological capabilities of the Japanese multinationals in four inter-related stages are given full marks. M has the best performance, though it is still some distance from full marks. Its innovative capability, although very advanced among local television producers, is nonetheless in an infant stage as compared to the world standard. The Thai firm has similar technological capabilities, but still falls a bit behind M. Other Japanese joint ventures fall behind these two firms in all areas.

Post-Yen Appreciation Period

Since the post-yen-appreciation period started just a few years ago, the outcomes of technology transfer in the newer companies are not yet clear. Judging from cases of investment in the pre-yen-appreciation period and recent development in international trade, however, we may anticipate two broad patterns of firms' behavior. We will briefly discuss the differences between these patterns and their subsequent outcomes, particularly those in connection with technology transfer, in the following section.

The Somewhat Self-contained Type of Investment

The yen appreciation has brought about far-reaching effects upon Japanese industrial structure. Growing production costs coupled with protectionist trends have forced many Japanese electronic firms to establish their new manufacturing bases abroad. Such investments are no longer confined to firms that assemble end products and that rely heavily on imported components from Japan because such a structure can no longer withstand pressure from the rapidly increasing cost of production in Japan.

In the case of older electronic firms that invested before the yen appreciation, Japanese executives in such joint ventures have begun to encourage their Thai partners to diversify their sources of components supply. Instead of relying heavily on Japanese suppliers as before, Japanese counterparts have become more willing to use cheaper components from Korea and Taiwan. Some firms have actively engaged in the localization of such production tools as molds for plastic injection and pressing dies. Although it seems that since the yen appreciation many joint ventures have begun to evolve toward the form of self-contained types of industry, it should be stated that such a trend has only just started, and no one can yet say how far it will go and how long it will last.

We witnessed many cases of new investments into increasingly self-contained projects since the yen appreciation. One such case is that of consumer products manufacturer S, with 100% Japanese shareholders, which invested in the production of microwave ovens and electrical rice cookers for export. The investing firm brought along some tens of its subcontractors from Japan and set up a complex of factories to manufacture supplies for its assembly lines. The firm also set up within the factory much equipment for the production of metal parts that are not available in the host country. Such a practice of in-house manufacturing is extraordinary, as the firm has always relied solely on subcontractors in its Japanese operations.

Another case, electronic component manufacturer M, had set up a group of factories in provincial areas. An assembly factory for miniature ball bearings was established in 1982, followed later by huge investments to install manufacturing equipment for the in-house production of necessary metal and plastic parts. The firm's machine center is probably one of the best in the country. The firm has recently applied for BOI promotion of another project, the production of the steel balls that are the most crucial part used in bearings production. Such a move indicates further attempts to integrate upstream to materials production at higher levels.

Moreover, the group's record of manpower development is exceptionally conspicuous. By the end of 1987 a total of over 2,000 engineers, technicians, and workers had already been dispatched to participate in on-the-job training in various countries. As the length of a period of training varies from several months to two years, the firm's commitment probably reflects its urgent need to upgrade and strengthen its operative capability. The group has indisputably succeeded in transferring production technology to local technical staffs. Huge amounts of resources that have been poured into equipment and human resource development prove the group's dedication. Production value figures have abruptly increased at rates of more than over 30% to as high as more than 200%. Such rapid increases of production with no evidence of adverse effects on product quality indicate high operative capability on the part of workers, technicians, and engineers.

Similar development can be seen in the group's motors and speakers production operation. Assembly lines for motors and speakers were started in 1985, with all necessary parts imported. The group later began to produce most metal parts in-house. A new factory was constructed in 1987 to produce ferrite magnets, a crucial production part.

The firm's plans include not only the extension of the scopes and areas of the learning process but also its deepenning. Top executives have disclosed their intention to set up an R&D center in Thailand with the primary objective of putting Japan-based research findings into product development. The center will also serve as a prototype plant, performing test runs of production processes before a factory for a full-scale manufacture is set up. Groups of engineers and scientists have been recruited and already dispatched to participate in production design and on-the-job training in the group's R&D center.

The Division of Labor Type of Investment

This type is also a result of rapid yen appreciation, but the MNCs' strategy is to distribute production facilities in different countries according to their comparative advantages. Investment(s) in each country, therefore, will constitute a part of the global production system. As a result, technologies introduced into each country will be highly fragmented. Among the many cases we came across of such investments are some conspicuous ones for the assembly of heads for disk drives, assembly of ceramic capacitors, assembly of cords and connectors, and others.

One manufacturing group visited, F, is very dynamic. Because the firm's strategy is weighted toward the division of labor type, its plants are essentially assembly lines using mostly imported parts and raw materials. Some important products are computer cords, copper wires and connectors, and so on. Upstream integration is relatively slow in comparison with the earlier mentioned components manufacturer M.

The division of labor type of firm concentrates its efforts toward upgrading its operative capability. In the case of group F, production technologies have evidently been successfully transferred to local staffs. IBM in 1986 named a firm in this group as "Vendor of the Year" for its zero defect performance—no defects had been found in a total of 1.5 million sets of keyboard cords supplied to IBM. In areas other than operative capability, transfer of other technological capabilities has been very limited in F. Decision making in design and purchase of production equipment and other raw materials is done at the headquarters. Minor product design is allowed at the local level, but most research and design is carried out in Japan.

Analysis

The two types of firms possess distinctive behaviors in regard to technologies according to the differences in their strategies. Some important variations will be discussed as follows.

(1) Labor Intensiveness of Technology. As both types of firms are producing for export, quality and productivity become the most important goals. Technologies used in these firms would therefore not be as labor intensive as those in the pre-yen appreciation period. We came across cases of a mix between capital-intensive and labor-intensive types of technologies, but in long-term development, capital-intensive technologies will come to prevail because the cost of labor in Thailand is increasing continually.

(2) Dynamic of Technological Changes. Electronic technologies are continually and rapidly evolving. In order that a firm be able to compete in the international market, its production technologies must adapt quickly to such development. As both types of firms are export oriented, the tempo of technological changes in the work place should be rather fast. The learning process, therefore, is expected to be dynamic, which differs starkly from the case of consumer electronic producers in the pre-yen appreciation period wherein the learning process has been stagnant.

(3) Technological Self-containment. Technologies introduced through the investments of division of labor type firms will be highly fragmented. In most cases, the technologies introduced will be peripheral and fragmented. The situation is similar to the case of assembly line industry in the pre-yen appreciation period wherein learning had been centered around assembly and quality-control technologies. Learning processes in this type of firm will be limited.

In firms with more self-contained types of technologies, learning processes could be more easily extended to related areas. There exists, however, a strong trend within Japanese investors to formulate a "closed system," which is represented in two major patterns. One is an attempt to bring in all important subcontractors and set up a closed production network. The other is an attempt to manufacture everything in-house.

These practices prevent the emergence and growth of local supporting industries and obstruct the diffusion of modern technologies to such industries.

(4) Technological Dependency. As most recent Japanese investments are in whole or major part Japanese-owned, the width and depth of technology to be transferred will be determined by and for the interest of the MNCs. In comparison to joint venture cases, the role of the technology recipient in the learning process will become trivial. Decisions regarding the breadth and depth of the technologies to be transferred will rest solely with the MNCs. Factors influencing such decisions will depend largely on the MNCs' global strategy and changes in international trade and economics. In this sense, it seems that Thailand has partly entrusted the MNC decision makers with the future of its technological independence.

By Way of Conclusion

In the previous sections we presented a comparative discussion of the technology transfer process in two successful firms. We also looked at some reasons for the stagnant learning process in other Japanese joint ventures that produce televisions. We furthermore attempted to anticipate the behavior of firms that have recently invested in the host country, particularly in connection with technologies. The following summarizes our findings and our analysis of the future trends.

Marginal differences existed between the two successful firms in their learning processes (Table 5). Both firms, Japanese joint venture M and a local Thai maker, could progress at similar paces, which indicates that in the case of the transfer of conventional technologies there is no conspicuous difference between the use of foreign investment and the use of licensing and importation of machinery.

More differences in the learning process have been observed among Japanese joint ventures. It is obvious that variations in firms' market strategies have brought about such outcomes. Japanese counterparts in the stagnant firms are likely to consider a joint venture only as a mechanism to penetrate into the protected market of Thailand. The joint venture's main function therefore is assembly, using imported parts and components and local, low-cost labor. Such a policy greatly limits the width and depth of the learning process.

The case of the successful firm M shows that the self-contained network of factories provides a major reason for its achievements in transferring technology. Furthermore, resolute efforts to deepen and

Table 5. Comparison of Technological Development in Two Successful
Television Set Producers, 1961–1981.

Year	Firm 1	Firm 2
1961		Establishment of the company
1962	Establishment of the company	
1965	Started assembly of B/W television under foreign brand name; started production of coils and transformers for in-house use	
1968		Establishment of B/W television factory under foreign brand name
1968	Launched television set under Thai brand name	
1969	Started production of printed circuit board; started development of B/W television circuit	
1970	Started production of hybrid-type television (combining vacuum tubes and transistors)	Started production of color television under foreign brand name
1971		Establishment of electronic components factory; set up manufacturing equipment section within the firm
1973	Establishment of electronic components factory	
1974	Started production of Thai brand name color television	
1979	Started export to Great Britain	Started production of plastic and metal components
1981		Opened new television factory

widen the learning process serve the mutual interests of both local industrialization and the M firm.

Firm dynamism is generally a key factor in fostering effective transfer of technology. Many elements help to bring about firm dynamism—the most important one is perhaps pressure from competition. We have previously seen that most of the dynamic firms are either export-oriented firms or firms that are competing for larger market share. Pressing need to be competitive has forced the firms into improving product quality and productivity. One powerful means to achieve such ends is to upgrade firms' technological capability, which will lead further to wider and deeper understanding of production knowledge.

As most of the recent Japanese investments are export-oriented projects, it is likely that the learning process in these firms will be dynamic. Dynamism alone, however, does not necessarily lead to deepening and widening of knowledge. Given the dynamism, firms with differing strategies would experience differing outcomes. Three possible developments in recent Japanese investments follow.

The Best Scenario. This is a case of investment by self-contained type firms. The firms will try to establish links with local producers as their subcontractors in a systematic and well-planned manner. Research and development work in local subsidiaries will be promoted gradually in order to deepen the learning process. Some firms presently are following this scenario, and others are likely to follow.

The Second-best Scenario. This is also a case of investment by self-contained type firms. Some of these firms, however, will not or will be reluctant to establish links with local producers. Some would continue using their Japanese sub-contractors, others would turn to in-house production. Adaptation and some modification work would be allowed in these firms, but research and product development will be carried out in Japan. A large portion of Japanese investors will follow this path.

The Worst Scenario. This is mostly a case of division of labor type of investments. Such firms would view their production facility in Thailand merely as a sub-unit in a worldwide network of production facilities. Though changes in production technologies in these sub-units are likely to be dynamic, such technologies are extremely fragmented. Widening and deepening effects in the learning process would be quite limited. Though no firm will come to such extremes, many firms will follow a somewhat similar path.

Comment

Ichiro Sato

Technology Transfer

ASEAN countries often make the criticism that Japan and/or Japanese firms are reluctant to provide technology transfer—but the definition of "technology transfer" is always vague. It is my view that four types of technology transfer, defined as follows, exist.

The first type of technology transfer, and the one regarding which ASEAN governments expect Japanese cooperation, is direct investment from Japan aimed at contributing to the development of the host country's economy and society; specific actions include invitations for the establishment of labor-intensive, export-oriented, and high-technological industry according to the policy of each country, as well as the localization of management and increased training and education provided by the Japanese government or public organizations. Sometimes the host countries expect the transfer of high-technology research and development.

The second type, and the one that local private firms in ASEAN countries expect from Japanese firms, is the new technology and/or knowhow aimed at expanding business and increasing profits.

The third, and the one that local employees expect from Japanese firms, is the promotion of local employees to top and middle management and participation in the business administration of the company. Some local employees expect to gain increased knowledge of high and deep technology and knowhow for the benefit of their own careers.

The fourth is the type of technology transfer that is required to operate manufacturing businesses. Professor Takeuchi has made a detailed survey and report on this type in his paper (Yamashita 1988). He classifies it into two groups, production management and business management, in order to make a value assessment. Production management covers daily operation skills, maintenance, quality control, technical improvement, engineering, and research and development while business management covers labor, production, and procurement

194

management, as well as stock control, marketing, and financial and general business management. Professor Takeuchi points out that the transfer of technology and knowhow relating to engineering, research and development, and some business management in particular is rather delayed.

When referring to "technology transfer" one person may be thinking of direct investment, another may be pointing to research and development, and yet another may be speaking of promotion—thus giving rise to confusion and misunderstanding among the parties concerned. Accordingly I would like to clarify the present situation of Japanese firms in Thailand from my point of view as a businessman.

Regarding the first type of technology transfer, Japanese firms have been contributing remarkably to the development of the Thai economy and society in terms of technology transfer, increase in employment, expansion of export, human resources development, development of supporting industries, and so on. I must point out, however, that private Japanese firms are enterprises aimed at long-term prosperity with reasonable profits, and they are not charitable organizations, so that such firms may not show any interest if no feasible or favorable conditions exist in the host country. This may be seen clearly in the trend of Japanese firms to rush to Thailand but not to India, China, and certain other countries.

As for the second type, the just-mentioned rationale applies equally to technology transfer proposed by ASEAN business partners to introduce new products for expansion of their businesses. Japanese partners may not be agreeable if they find such transfers to be unfeasible particularly from the cost point of view. Japanese firms might also hesitate to transfer research and development technology if conditions in the host country make production costs, period of manpower development and technical requirements unfeasible.

Regarding the third and fourth types, the most important factor is not feasibility but the period of time needed for human resources development based on Japanese-style management. Japanese firms have been making all possible efforts to transfer the technical and management knowhow required for manufacturing and business operations mentioned by Professor Takeuchi to local employees through on-the-job training, education and training in Japan, QC circle activities, and so on because it benefits the firms to do so. Consistent production of high-quality products would not otherwise be possible under the supervision of the very limited number of Japanese engineers, and any firms lazy in technology transfer would lose the business game due to inferior product quality and high costs.

It is, however, necessary for Japanese firms to modify such parts of Japanese-style management as the seniority system and vagueness in decision-making processes and job descriptions and to adapt a bit of American-style management in analyzing the social customs of individual countries. In this sense I generally agree with Professor Takeuchi's study because he considers the subject of production and business management in terms of technology transfer as an issue for discussion.

Finally, I suggest that when we take up technology transfer as a subject for discussion among the parties concerned we make it clear which types of technology transfer we plan to discuss, in order to avoid misunderstandings by the party not satisfied with the Japanese responses.

On an earlier point I would like to stress that although private Japanese firms are not charitable organizations and are always sensitive to cost analysis in whatever they do, such firms operating businesses in ASEAN countries are well aware of the necessity as good corporate citizens to contribute to the local society.

Regarding Professor Prayoon's observations, my view is slightly different. Japanese joint-venture firms that started the assembly of consumer electric products in Thailand as a form of import-substitution industry in the beginning of the 1960s were, as Professor Prayoon points out, simply assembling parts imported from Japan. During the first half of the 1970s, however, they started to manufacture the component parts in-house or to patronize local parts manufacturers while providing, particularly to the local manufacturers, such technology transfer as technical know-how, quality control, and productivity improvement for many years. The local content ratio for television sets is still around 30%, as Professor Prayoon remarked, but we must also look at the local content ratios for other products: for instance, 100% for electric fans, 80% for electric refrigerators and electric rice cookers, 60% for automobiles, and 75% for motorcycles.

The achievement of such high local content ratios is not possible without technology transfer. In this sense the early Japanese joint ventures made a big contribution to the development of the supporting industry with whom Japanese newcomers (after the yen appreciation) are very eager to link. Now we see a scrambling on the part of joint ventures for securing production capacity in local parts manufacturers.

The expected contribution to technology transfer by Japanese firms following the yen appreciation is evaluated very highly by Professor Prayoon. I believe that such firms will surely make a big contribution in terms of employment, increase in exports earning more hard currency, local industrialization, and so on in five to ten years' time. Because they are mostly export-oriented industries and should export their products immediately upon opening their factories, there is not in any case enough time for them to develop the linked parts by way of procurement from Japanese parts manufacturers.

In sum, we should not ignore the big contributions in all fields including technology transfer made by Japanese firms that have been operating businesses in Thailand for many years.

9
"Technology Transfer" and Japan-Thai Relations

Johzen Takeuchi

Industrialization and Technology Transfer

"Technology Transfer"

"Technology transfer" is a misleading concept. It gives the impression of a whole set of "technology" that is complete and transferable like a piece of baggage accompanied by a bundle of handbook manuals. As I noted in an earlier report, there has been a serious information gap between the Thai and Japanese people regarding the understanding of this concept (Yamashita 1988, Part 3).

Most Japanese manufacturers consider the concept of technology as implying accumulative and dynamic processes. They regard the process of technology transfer, including manufacturing technology transfer, as a step-by-step promotion beginning with the stage of ordinary factory operation and maintenance and moving on to more sophisticated operations like adaptation, modification, research and development (R&D), and so on. They usually believe that the possibility of improvements or innovation depends on the prior achievement of sufficient efficiency in ordinary operations and adjustments. Japanese manufacturers have valued highly the performance of Korean industrialization since the 1970s in catching up to advanced countries in industrial operations and maintenance because the Korean pace was much faster than they, in the 1960s, had imagined to be possible.

In south and southeast Asia, where the historical background for maintaining traditional craftsmanship, as found in advanced countries, is lacking, manual labor is traditionally generally despised. This historical factor is partly responsible for the lack of sufficient productivity in some industrial sectors where the accumulation of various skills is required, while productivity is sufficient in those sectors where only simple manual or limited skilled labor is required. Japanese manufacturers, on the

199

other hand, had been extraordinarily concerned even in ordinary operations to achieve higher quality and productivity in order to be able to catch up to the countries that had led in these areas for more than a century. This is one of the reasons that Japanese firms have lots of complaints about the contrasting conditions of "technology transfer" in developing countries. Managerial class people in most developing countries are inclined to believe that it is the individual responsibility of each working class person to achieve sufficient production efficiency. Most managers seem to think that the final stage of technology transfer is the establishment of R&D sections in the recipient country; they also believe that advanced countries' multinational corporations (MNCs) do not intend to complete their technology transfer.

The concept of technology transfer (TT) is defined in this paper as 1) the production of a new commodity or adoption of a new manufacturing technology in the recipient country, and 2) such production or technology made possible, or realized, through import or direct investment from abroad instead of through invention in the recipient country. Thus even the manufacture of traditional commodities like Japanese rice cakes or bamboo goods can be called a technology transfer according to this definition if the commodity has been produced in the country and if its manufacture is realized through input of direct investment from abroad. Compared to the famous concept "innovation" defined by Schumpeter (1930), TT is a limited concept having narrow implications. While the former has a wide range of such implications as new products, new materials, new technologies, and new markets, the latter has an overly limited range of implications. TT is, however, one of the important key steps to industrial innovation in each developing country.

This paper furthermore stresses three points as follows in order to clarify some characteristics of the industrialization of Thailand.

1. TT is classified into two types: government-to-government based (GG based) and non-government based (NGO). NGO is further classified into a type promoted by voluntary groups and a type promoted by private companies. This study concentrates on the case of the private sector.

2. There are many discussions about the international relations of industrial development, most of which depend on the theory of comparative costs.[1] This study, however, will concentrate on the empirical analysis of the process of each TT rather than on utilizing

---

1. For a view based on the theory of comparative costs, refer to Chapter 3 of (Saito, 1970).

commonplace theory without regard to the differences in the historical backgrounds of each national economy.

3. Country-to-country changes in value systems and social structure are
considered in this study, even if the given data are limited. When the
TT is related to changes in those factors, it may be concluded that
the transfer is in an advanced stage of development in the recipient
country.

Technology Transfer from Japan and Repercussions from Thailand

Thai people have generally regarded Japanese people and companies
as not eager to promote TT in Thailand, especially before 1986. The
major reasons given by the Thai people for this are:

1. The scale of Japanese firms is smaller than that of European and
American firms, especially in terms of employment. Japanese business
activity therefore does not have sufficient beneficial effects on employment creation (Chinwanno et al. 1983).

2. Japanese firms are indifferent to adopting local materials and/or
intermediate goods, and their business activity does not have enough
beneficial repercussions on domestic industrial sectors (Chinwanno
et al. 1983).

3. Japanese firms do not export their products, which shows that they
favor transferring out-of-date production systems that lack the potential
to generate enough productivity to gain competitiveness in international markets.[2]

4. Japanese firms do not take care to complete handbook manuals for
operation and management, which makes the understanding of
knowhow and principles of production and management difficult for
Thai people to obtain.[3]

Before investigating these matters, the image of technology generally
held by Thai people should be noted. In a variety of discussions with
Thai partners, I found that most considered semiconductor production
to be highly technological and rice cooker production to be "low-tech."
In the Thai electrical industry sector, most American firms have concentrated on manufacturing semiconductors for export only while all of
the Japanese joint ventures have produced electrical appliances mostly

---

2. From my interviews at Thammasat University and Chulalongkorn University during the
latter half of the 1980s.
3. Bankokku Nihonjin Shokokaigisho (Bangkok Japanese Chamber of Commerce; BJC),
Nihonkigyo no Taijinjyugyoin ni taisuru Anketo (Questionaire Survey of Thai Employees
in Japanese Joint Ventures) (Bangkok, 1987), pp. 21, 22.

for domestic use. This contrast seems to have given the impression to the Thais that Americans have been eager to transfer their technology and Japanese have not. But actually there are various kinds of production processes even in the manufacture of semiconductors, including development and refining of such materials as gallium, arsenic, and so on; research and development of such production equipment as synchrotron radiographic equipment, photographic hole burning systems, and so on; design and development of production processes from the layout of manufacturing lines to so-called clean technology; design of integrated circuits (IC), large scale integrated circuits (LSI), super-LSI (SLI) and so on; printing of circuits for the IC boards, and so on; and assembly of such memory goods as RAM, ROM, and so on. Lots of unskilled and/or semiskilled manual laborers are needed on the assembly lines, and actually most American firms have only this type of processing line in Thailand. Still most local people and mass media regard the industry as "high-tech," while they do not always regard the accumulation of design ability related to changing the specifications and design of rice cookers for export to be an R&D activity. Most Japanese manufacturers, in contrast, do not consider the semiconductor assembly line to be highly technological but merely regard it as the simple and final part of the overall production process. Here, then, is another information gap.

Business conditions in Thailand have changed radically since 1986–87, and local criticism of Japanese business activities seems to be changing during recent years. However, it is noteworthy that the managerial strategies of Japanese joint ventures have also changed at the same time. Before investigating present business conditions, some managerial problems which were seen before 1985 will be discussed.

Compared to Japanese firms, Euro-American firms have long historical backgrounds to the development of their business activities in Thailand since before World War II. They have developed such activities based on their world market strategy. Before the war, they concentrated on developing the food industry, wood industry, and mining. They characteristically did not pay attention to the development of the local market and concentrated on exporting most of their commodities, such as teak, rubber, tin, jewelry, and so on. It is quite natural for them now to utilize the Thai labor market to assemble semiconductors only to export all of their products to their home countries and to import most of the raw materials needed from their parent companies. During the latter half of the 1980s, about two thirds of American direct investment in Thailand was shared by the semiconductor industrial sector.

Japanese joint ventures naturally lacked sufficient business background in sectors where Euro-American companies had already established their business networks, so they had to concentrate in sectors where they were able to develop some competitiveness in the domestic market. These included such industrial sectors as motorcycles, electrical appliances, and some others. Their local products, however, did not have any international competitiveness due to wage cost shares only within 10% of total cost and heavy import duties and business taxes. Only after 1986 did a number of Japanese firms begin to export their products, largely because at the end of 1986 the Board of Investment (BOI) changed its policy and eased conditions on direct investment from abroad, deciding to cut the import duty for raw materials and intermediate products on the condition that they would be processed in Thailand only for export.[4] It should be noted that political decisions are one of the decisive explanatory variables for economic conditions in most developing countries.

It has been a long-time criticism that Japanese joint ventures do not take care to arrange handbook manuals for each kind of job in the factory. It should be noted, though, that it is easy to introduce manuals in some industry sectors but difficult in others. Operation handbooks may easily be introduced in such sectors as semiconductor manufacturing, where numerous unskilled and/or semiskilled female workers of the same type are needed, and the petrochemical industry where a type of watchman to checks meters in a standard way, and where the total system of equipment cannot easily be changed once it begins to function. However, Japanese manufacturers did not care to transfer these sectors because they could achieve enough competitiveness in the semiconductor manufacturing industry without going abroad, and because they are not good at strategic development in some process industries like the petrochemical sector. They tried to transfer those sectors in which Euro-American firms did not have a strong intention to transfer their manufacturing systems, including the motorcycle, automobile, electrical appliances, and other sectors, which needed not only capital but also skilled workers. In addition, Japanese manufacturers needed to be able to change product models quickly, which meant that they had to pay large maintenance and modification costs frequently, and so it became more and more difficult to create completed handbook manuals. There is one more reason for their reluctance to utilize completed manuals. In Japanese car manufacturing, firms have had to produce a minimum

4. *Nation*, Bangkok, Dec. 18 and 22, 1986.

of 100,000 of one model of car in order to achieve sufficiently profitable commercial conditions. But until recently, the total market size of Thailand was less than 100,000. In addition, eleven Japanese car makers and a number or European makers have saturated this small market with supplies of various kinds of cars. Market competition has been so severe that they have had to make model changes often, which has made the adoption of shape-up manuals more and more difficult.

Characteristics of Japanese Technology Transfer

Japanese manufacturers have a historical reason for not being eager to arrange handbook manuals for operation and management. Japanese firms have characteristically been anxious to achieve higher productivity not only through technology transfer from advanced countries but also

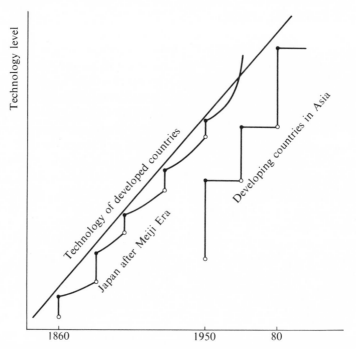

Fig. 1.   Technological Catch-up Patterns of Japan and Developing Asian
Countries as Compared to Developed Countries.

Source: Institute of Developing Economies, *Study on Technology and Trade
Frictions between Japan and Developing Nations* (Tokyo: IDE, 1985),
p.22.

through their own daily endeavor to promote new adaptations and/or modifications of the production process. Such an endeavor, or the will to change the way of production day by day, became one of the decisive factors in the development of these firms' competitiveness in their hard global market. A report published by the Institute of Developing Economies (IDE) distinguished the Japanese technological catch-up pattern from the conventional patterns that we can see in most developing Asian countries (Fig. 1).

This difference can also be explained otherwise. In the ordinary patterns of achieving higher productivity, labor-intensive modes of production were substituted for capital-intensive modes. This path, taken by all national economies, is shown as path I in Fig. 2. Since the 16th century, however, there have been a great many cases in which a

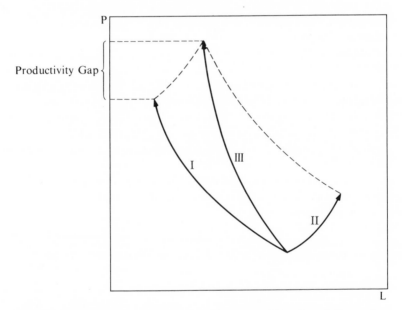

Fig. 2. Technological Development Patterns of Developed Countries and Japan.

Source: J. Takeuchi, "Some Aspects of Technology Transfer by Japanese Management in Thailand," mimeograph (Hiroshima, 1989), p.11.

Note: P, Productivity; L, Labor Intensity; I, Path of Modern Developed Countries; II, Japanese Path under Traditional Restriction; III, Path of Modern Japan.

country managed to improve productivity by intensifying manual labor; this is path II (Fig. 2), which we see more often than not in Japanese historical experience. Labor intensity is strengthened through certain channels as follows: expansion of working hours (Ishikawa, S., 1978); higher working efficiency without improvement of production system; individual worker's accumulation of manufacturing skill and sensitivity to the quality of intermediate goods and final products; and promotion of adaptation or modification of each production process (Takeuchi 1989); and so on.

It is curious and interesting that Japanese people were obliged to intensify their work in these ways without extra reward partly because of severe natural conditions and partly because of the strict socio-political conditions rooted in the feudal ages. With this historical background it is quite natural that the Japanese have tried to combine the two paths whenever they got a chance for technology transfer during the process of their modern industrialization, thus creating path III (Fig. 2). Certain social conditions were essential to this kind of industrial intensification: high social mobility among people; development of the commercial economy to a certain extent in rural communities; tradition and social respect for craftsmanship; and high diffusion of and demand for education; and so on. Such conditions show that much emphasis was placed on the dimension of "humanware" as differentiated from the "hardware" and/or "software" of economy (Shimada 1987).

Japanese experience and historical background is of course not always relevant to other nations with their own different kinds of historical experiences, and this is the very reason why we need socio-economic and econo-historical perspectives for the analysis of modern international economic relations.

Japanese Business Activity and the Industrialization of Thailand

Japanese Direct Investment and Supporting Industry

Japanese manufacturing firms started their business activities in Thailand in the 1960s. The annual economic growth rate surpassed 7% in the latter half of the 1960s, utilizing military procurement caused by the Vietnam War. Those were the days of military government, led by General Thanom and General Prapert. Japanese joint ventures were given some incentives when they began their activity, and they also benefited from the political stability that existed under the pressure of military rule. They managed to develop the domestic market for their products, even though the scale of management and market was small and limited.

The Thai economy in the 1970s lost the special procurements and suffered from the so-called oil shock. The economic growth rate, however, increased to 8–9 % owing to the economic boom in primary products. The military government was forced to retreat by the student revolution in 1973, and from around that time the formation and development of a real business class was noticeable. The 1970s proved to be difficult days for Japanese joint venture business activity. Severe restrictions were placed on the use of local contents and other policies changed from time to time. The ventures also experienced the anti-Japan movement during the middle years of the 1970s. Even under such circumstances they managed to expand their production and market year after year and succeeded in arranging business conditions for the big spurt that took place during the latter half of the 1980s.

It is in such industrial sectors as electrical appliance and automobile manufacturing, together with their supporting sectors, that the activity of Japanese joint ventures is much more positive and takes advantage of Euro-American competitors. Joint ventures in these sectors simultaneously started manufacturing in Thailand in the 1960s. In the automobile industry almost all Japanese car makers established joint ventures in Thailand (Table 1). In 1962 the Thai government improved the Investment Promotion Act, making it easier for foreign capital to make direct investments, and many car makers began to supply by way of complete knock down (CKD) instead of by importing completely built-up cars (CBU) (Adachi 1980, 150).

The establishment of Japanese joint ventures in the electrical appliance industry was not as active in the 1960s as the automobile industry (Shiowattana 1990: 130). Exceptionally, Thai National Corporation (TNC) started the production of dry batteries in 1962 and consecutively increased its line of products. It established a radio manufacturing plant in 1965, a black and white television set plant in 1967, and electric fan and storage battery plants in 1968.

The business activity of Japanese joint ventures in the electrical appliance sector has been positive since the latter half of the 1970s. It is noteworthy that TNC began to produce partswares after 1970 and started to supply jigs and molding patterns first for itself and later for the domestic market. Until about 1980 TNC was able to produce tuners, speakers, coils, and printed wiring boards, which it supplied also for the local market. At the same time it achieved 100% localization in the production of electric fans and received promotional support from BOI

Table 1.   Car Assemblies in Thailand, 1961–1977.

Company in Thailand	Parent Company	Thai Equity (%)	Foreign Equity (%)	Start of Operations	Products
Ford Motors (Thailand) Co., Ltd.	Ford Motors	—	100 (US)	1961	C, P, A
Thonburi Automotive	Mercedes-Benz	100	—	1961	C
Karnasutra General Assembly	Fiat	100	—	1962	C, P, S
Siam Motors and Nissan Co., Ltd.	Nissan	100	—	1962	C, P
Prince Motors (Thailand) Co., Ltd.	Prince Motors	60	40 (JPN)	1965	P
Toyota (Thailand) Co., Ltd.	Toyota Motors	—	100 (JPN)	1964	C, P
United Development Industry Co., Ltd.	Mitsubishi	40	60 (JPN)	1966	C
Isuzu Motors Co., Ltd.	Mitsubishi and Isuzu	—	100 (JPN)	1966	C
Thai Hino Industry Co., Ltd.	Hino Motors	—	100 (JPN)	1966	C
Thai Pardith Assembly Plant Co., Ltd.	Harser	80	20 (RC)	1968	S
Amalgamated Engineering Co., Ltd.	Magirus-Deuts	—	—	1968	—
Bangchan General Assembly Co., Ltd.	General Motors	50	50 (US)	1968	—
YMC Co., Ltd.	B.M.W.	100	—	1972	—
Sukosol and Mazda Motor Ind. Co., Ltd.	Mazda	30	70 (JPN)	1974	P, C
Toyota (Thailand) II Co., Ltd.	Toyota Motor	—	100 (JPN)	1975	P, C
Asoke Motor	G.M.	100	—	1976	C
Thai-Swedish Assembly Co., Ltd.	Volvo	N.A.	N.A.	1976	P
Yontrapan Co., Ltd.	International Harvester	N.A.	N.A.	N.A.	C
Nai-Lerd Co., Ltd.	—	100	—	N.A.	C
Siam Automobiles Co., Ltd.	Nissan	100	—	1977	P, C

Source: T. Adachi, "Tonan Azia Jidoshakogyo ni okeru Shuhenkigyo no Hatten," *Academia* 67 (Tokyo: Hitotsubashi University, 1980), pp. 150–151.

Note: RC, Republic of China; C, commercial car; P, passenger car; A, agricultural machine; S, cars for special use.

to begin the production of electric components for export.[5] Around 1985 most Japanese joint ventures achieved 100% localization for electric pots, nearly 90% for refrigerators and rice cookers, but only 35% for televisions.

The automobile industry had started earlier, but it could not promote localization as smoothly as the electrical appliance industry had. The difference is understandable when the amount of annual production is taken into account. In the case of TNC, for example, the manufacture of electric fans began in 1980, with the 500,000th unit off of the line in 1985 and the 1,000,000th in 1988. The 500,000th black and white television set was lined off in 1984 and the 1,000,000th in 1987.[6] These huge amounts show the expansion of the domestic market and the diffusion of mass consumption. Such market potentiality has been the fundamental factor motivating Japanese joint ventures to promote higher localization, but the expansion of the automobile market was not as easy as that of electrical appliances.

Slightly more than 110,000 cars were supplied in 1983 and 1984, but the market shrank to 70,000 in 1986 and various kinds of cars had to be produced as well. Fourteen car makers supplied 120 kinds of cars in 1985,[7] and it was impossible for them to depend upon mass production effects. The automobile manufacturing sector is a scale-merit-oriented industry except for the manufacture of some luxury cars that are famous in the world market. This sector could not rely on sufficient industrial and market conditions to develop quickly and to promote its localization in Thailand, especially before 1986 when there was no chance to gain access to foreign markets.

The Thai government changed its localization policy regarding products other than just small products more often than not. It adopted the so-called given percent method in the localization program declared in 1978 and 1979. Under this scheme, each local-made partsware was given its own point value, and the total sum of those points for a product was 100. In the case of the passenger car the total was 107.7 points. Car makers could freely select partswares of local make so that they could get higher points than those given in the guidelines. The first year's

---

5. From an interview with Mr. Kiyoshi Sakai of Thai National Corporation on Dec. 11, 1987. On the manufacturing of parts, refer to page 11 of the *Corporation Outline* published by the company in 1987.

6. Thai National Corp., *Kaisha Gaikyou*, Bangkok, 1989, p.6.

7. The Thai government restricted the number to 80 in 1986. On these restrictions, refer to BJC, *Taikoku Keizai Gaikyo 1984–85* (General Economic Conditions of Thailand), Bangkok, 1985, p.283.

guideline for passenger cars was 30%, and the government regulated point increases by 5% each year in order to arrive at the final guideline of 50% in 1987.[8]

The cost price increased rapidly, however, and pushed up the price of the final product. At the level of 40% localization, car makers needed to raise the price about 1,000 baht in order to increase one point. They needed to raise 2,500 baht to get one more point at the guideline of 45%.[9] They sold more than 100,000 cars in 1979, but the market shrank to 90,000 in 1981 and 1982. The government was obliged to hold the localization guideline at 45% in 1982, even though it had succeeded in localizing 74 items up until that time.

The Thai government in 1984 declared its goal of localizing the manufacture of automobile engines and requested car makers to promote localization again and rapidly. The government announced a localization timetable that started at 50% in 1985 and rose for engines; it was planned that manufacturers should start at 20% in 1989 and reach 80% in 1993. It was also stipulated that the majority ownership of the joint ventures should be Thai and that the companies should export engines after 1993.[10] Certainly these conditions are severe for joint ventures, but business activities in foreign countries, whether a Japanese joint venture in Thailand or a Thai capital project in some other country, always face such conditions.

Japanese joint ventures have tried to increase the ratio of local contents. In the case of Toyota Motors Thailand (TMT), the localization ratio is 54% for passenger cars and 60% for commercial vehicles without regard to the value added of press works, so the total ratio is estimated to be 70% in 1988.[11]

The localization of partswares is a kind of technology transfer, but it should be noted that the localization has some ripple effects: accumulation of skill and ability for adaptation; accumulation of human resources; development of supporting industry; cultivation of entrepreneurship; and so on.

In the electrical appliance sector 250 small and medium firms were supplying partswares in 1985, and 350 firms in 1988.[12] In the automobile industry about 120 partsware manufacturers employing 35,000 persons

8. BJC, *Tai no Sangyou* (Industries of Thailand), Bangkok, 1985, 5.
9. Naka, T., Tai no Jidoshasangyo (Automobile Industry in Thailand), BJC, *Shohou* (Chamber Monthly Forum), Nov. 1982, p.41.
10. BJC, *Taikoku Keizai Gaikyo 1988–89*, p.364.
11. From interviews with Mr. Ichiro Sato during 1985–89.
12. BJC, *Taikoku Keizai Gaikyo 1984–85*, 282, and *1988–89*, p.262.

existed. About 20 firms developed into large-scale operations during the 1980s, though most of them were Japanese joint ventures. TMT, for example, ordered partswares from 13 Japanese joint ventures and 34 Thai companies in 1988.[13]

Each partsware manufacturer has some subcontractors and also transacts business with some manufacturers from each supporting sector. More than 300 firms now produce molding patterns for the metal manufacturing industry and the plastic processing industry,[14] and both of those industries have close relations with the automobile industry and the electrical appliances industry. The development of new businesses has created new industrial relations and transactions within themselves as this study will show in the following section.

Japanese joint ventures have concentrated in the sectors where lots of supporting industries are needed because, in brief, Japanese firms initially had to introduce their TT into complicated sectors or at random since they were facing the Euro-American companies which had already staked out the mining, petrochemical, semiconductor, and certain other sectors. But there is one exceptional case among the Japanese companies: NMB (Nippon Miniature Bearing).

NMB has manufactured precise electrical machines and partswares in the north of Bangkok since 1982. It adopted an American-like system of production. Importing all kinds of raw materials and intermediate goods from abroad, the company has exported all of its products to advanced countries where it has its own market. The company developed rapidly and became one of the most aggressive Japanese multinational corporations. Its main factory is now in Thailand rather than Japan. NMB is evaluated highly by the Thais: some intellectuals have even gone so far as to say that NMB's business activity is a typical case of effective TT, and that other Japanese joint ventures have been too fainthearted in transferring their technology in comparison (Nawadhinsukh 1983).

NMB started as a manufacturer of steel balls after World War II. Though it was not a top company supplying this item, its quick subsequent development was based on the following factors.

1. It had a leader named Takami Takahashi, who, as he was not a man who favored collective decision making, was unique among Japanese managerial-class people. Further, his company has preferred to proceed with mergers and acquisitions, which most Japanese firms

---

13. Interviews with Mr. I. Sato.
14. BJC, *Taikoku Keizai Gaikyo 1988–89*, p.277.

would not like to do, especially in Japan.

2. It concentrated on supplying a special kind of item that other manufacturers of steel balls and bearings would not produce.

3. It succeeded in establishing its major plant outside of Japan, first in Singapore and then in Thailand. So far as its business performance is concerned, NMB is one of the most successful cases of Japanese TT, even though it did not need to develop supporting industries and though none of its manufacturing activities remained in Singapore after its shift to Thailand.

New Wave of Technology Transfer from Japan

Japanese investment in Thailand increased radically after 1986 (Table 2). BOI policy began to promote foreign investment in 1960, and Japanese companies invested 44.6 billion baht for 178 projects during the next 24 years. For 1988 alone Japanese investment reached 77 billion baht for 265 projects. The high valuation of Japanese currency after the Plaza Agreement among advanced countries in September 1985 is commonly taken as the cause for this boom in investment, but there were some more reasons for Japanese firms to shift to Thailand.

First, business conditions in Thailand had been improving since the end of 1986 (Suehiro 1989: 191). The price index of primary goods showed a recovery. The export of textiles, garments, canned foods, jewelry, and so on was increasing and actually showed a big spurt after 1987.

Second, the business climate was turning better not only in regard

Table 2. Firms Applying for BOI Agreement, 1983–1988.

No. of Applications	1983	1984	1985	1986	1987	1988
Japan	27	32	30	53	199	389
Other Foreign	N.A.	N.A.	N.A.	207	629	1,271
Total	341	376	325	431	1,058	2,125
Total Amount of Investment Applied for (billion baht)	56	55	60	60	209	530

Source: P. Shiowattana, "Japanese Technology Transfer in Thailand," in *Japan in Thailand*, K. Yoshihara, ed. (Kuala Lumpur: Falcon Press, 1990), p.192. (Original Source: BOI and NESDB data.)

to its macro-base but also to the manufacturing sectors, which had closer industrial relations with business activities of Japanese joint ventures. Production of automobiles and electrical appliances stepped up briskly and supporting industries rose strongly, all of which arranged favorable conditions for Japanese firms to shift to Thailand. This point will be further examined in Part III.

Third, the Thai government intended to ease regulations on foreign business activity and to arrange additional incentives for foreign investment after December 1986.[15]

The response by Japanese firms was so quick and aggressive after the end of 1986 because they were eager to claim the privilege of establishing wholly owned companies on the condition that they export all of the products. Small and medium firms especially rushed to Thailand because BOI's new policy allowing full ownership removed their anxiety about getting trustworthy counterparts in developing countries. Two hundred fifty-six new Japanese companies obtained BOI agreement in 1988, and it became clear that 85% of them intended to export more than 70% of their products. Until this change in economic policy, most Japanese joint ventures had concentrated on developing the Thai domestic market. The new wave changed the characteristics of Japanese investment and most of the newcomers preferred to be export oriented.

Some Japanese manufacturers in the new wave started projects to produce semiconductors in Thailand. Before the wave they hadn't given much thought to shifting to Thailand because they had sufficiently competitive conditions through their manufacturing in their home country. Sony commenced to construct a new plant in Thailand for the manufacture of semiconductors in 1989, and Oki Electric and Toshiba also successively made public their projects.[16] Japanese joint ventures have been criticized for being bad at preparing operations handbook manuals in the electric industry, but they will be able to complete them more successfully in the semiconductor sector.

It is noteworthy that the Japanese firms are not going to follow the same kind of managerial policy as American semiconductor makers do. The latter has utilized Thailand as a simple production base, while the former has developed the local market within ASEAN countries. Japanese joint ventures have increased the production of electrical appliances within the area. The ASEAN market shared 30% of the total export by Toshiba Company of Japan, which started to supply semiconductors

---

15. See note 4.
16. *Nikkei Sangyo Shinbun*, Feb. 2, 1990. *Nikkei Shinbun*, Dec. 9, 1989.

from its own ancillary in Malaysia and then planned to establish another one in Thailand. Malaysian production of video tape recorders has increased so rapidly that the country will be the fourth biggest supplier of VTRs to the world market in 1990. The demand for semiconductors is also swelling. Thailand succeeded in manufacturing picture tubes in 1989, and the domestic demand is experiencing a strong expansionary phase. The ASEAN countries are now a big market for semiconductors.

Until recently Japanese firms in foreign countries were criticized for not exporting their products, having small-scale management, supplying out-of-date models to the local market, using out-of-date technology, and so on. I do not agree with these criticisms at all because they are too simplistic and have not reckoned with the host countries' historical and present background in domestic demands, industrial relations, labor markets, social stratification, international trading conditions, technological development, and most important, global management strategies of Japanese firms.

It must, however, be recognized that strict regulation by the Thai government has succeeded in promoting the industrialization of Thailand, despite the fact that it was a tough job for Japanese firms to follow the frequent changes of policy. It was also difficult for Japanese firms to put up with the various criticisms mentioned above and such well-known jeers as "Japanese know what to do but not what to say," and "Americans are good at thinking, Japanese are good at manufacturing, Thais are good at consuming," and so on. It should be noted that most Thais keep the above criticisms to themselves, and so it is not fully known how they take their socio-economic backgrounds into account.

Another important point has become more and more distinct these days: a new wave of the so-called ASEAN Complementary Scheme (ACS), which is aimed at establishing a kind of social division of labor in key industries among ASEAN countries. Governments of ASEAN countries had earlier tried to complete the scheme but could not do so. The new wave is quite different: now, instead of governments, some corporations are promoting their own style of ACS.

In relation to the new ACS, the case of the automobile industry in Thailand will be examined by the example of MMC Sithiporn (MMCS), a joint venture of Mitsubishi Motor Company (MMC), which succeeded in exporting automobiles from Thailand. At the time of the high valuation of Japanese currency, MMC invested in the new company. MMC needed to arrange for a new production base in Asia because, first, it had lost its power to have a direct affect on the Korean automobile industry owing to the development of its Korean counterpart Hyundai and, second, MMC still finds assistance to Proton Saga in Malaysia indispensable. MMCS went into regular operation in 1987 and succeeded in exporting its products. Its success has depended upon the following factors.

1. MMCS received a tax incentive on the condition that it maintain the high export ratio guideline.
2. MMCS can receive a supply of partswares from MMC, which still has sufficient international competitiveness even though it is supplying goods from Japan, excluding some low-price goods.
3. MMCS can utilize newly developed partsware manufacturers even though its growth depended heavily upon business activities of preceding car makers and also upon political regulations.
4. It became possible for MMCS to use partswares made at lower prices in other ASEAN countries through the "grant tax cut" (GTC) guaranteed by the ASEAN Committee on Industry, Minerals, and Energy (COIME).
5. Mitsubishi is a huge business group and has a global network of marine transportation, through which MMCS can export its completed cars to Canada at a lower transportation cost.

MMCS was the first company to get the COIME grant, followed by Mercedes-Benz, Volvo, and Toyota (Table 3). In Toyota's case, the grant was obtained after Toyota offered to supply small Diesel engines from Thailand to the Philippines and Malaysia; to supply transmissions from the Philippines to Thailand and Malaysia; and to supply steering systems from Malaysia to the Philippines and Thailand.

TMT started to produce its diesel engine in July 1989, and the group intends for its three ancillaries to specialize in one item each and to transact business with each other. None of the ancillaries will have to pay the import duty, enjoying the GTC benefit that the three governments agreed to give. Toyota estimates that the value of import from two

Table 3. Firms Benefiting from COIME Agreement.

Firm	Countries Issuing Agreement
Mitsubishi	Thailand, Philippines, Malaysia
Mercedes-Benz	Thailand, Philippines
Volvo	Thailand, Malaysia
Toyota	Thailand, Philippines, Malaysia

Source: Bankgkok Post, Nov. 28, 1989.

of the countries is expected to be $19 million and that the value of export to two of the countries will reach $8.2 million. TMT explained that the imbalance could be offset by the export of Thai-assembled cars with Malaysian and Philippine components to such non-ASEAN countries as Portugal, where Toyota estimates the market at about $22 million a year.[17]

ASEAN countries seem to complete ACS partly by the political cabalization of the governments concerned and partly by the economic potentiality of some business groups. These kinds of groups may increase year by year. Not only complete car makers but also partsware manufacturers are planning to obtain GTC or to complete their private ACS. Some companies seem to promote a kind of international complementary scheme which is far wider than ACS.

Tsuchiya Manufacturing Corporation, for example, is going to replace its Japanese suppliers with Thai suppliers for such automobile components as air cleaners and oil filters. The company has its own markets in Thailand, the Philippines, and Indonesia, not counting its markets in advanced countries.[18] The Hino group is said to have a plan to exchange its own partswares among its ancillaries in Indonesia, Malaysia, and New Zealand.[19] Toyota plans to supply small diesel engines to Japan from Thailand and also to have 20–30,000 transmissions sent per annum from the Philippines to Japan.[20]

A number of people, however, criticize the shift of manufacturing by small and medium Japanese firms into Thailand. They charge that small Japanese firms deprive Thai firms of the chance to develop supporting industries.

It is certain that big Japanese firms began to have their subcontractors shift to developing countries in order to bypass the local contents regulation guidelines. Sharp Appliances Corporation (SAC) concentrates on television set production in Malaysia, and at the same time has its Thai ancillary specialize in the production of refrigerators, electric ovens, and air conditioning apparatus. Given the tax incentive, SAC is going to export most of its products. SAC actually had ten subcontractors establish joint ventures or ancillaries in Thailand. They supply most of their products to SAC, but it should be noted that SAC also needs to have contact with 47 local manufacturers according to its new manage-

17. *Bangkok Post,* Nov. 28, 1989. *Nikkei Shinbun,* Jan. 24, 1990.
18. *Nikkei Sangyo Shinbun,* Feb. 27, 1990.
19. *Nikkei Sangyo Shinbun,* Feb. 8, 1990.
20. *Nikkei Sangyo Shinbun,* Feb. 19, 1990.

rial strategy.[21] It is true that a technology gap exists between small Japanese firms and local firms, but the latter benefited from the new demand that resulted when SAC came to their country.

The small and medium firms (SMF) enabled big firms to develop the Japanese subcontracting system during the past several decades (Takeuchi 1989). Owner-managers of Japanese SMF in host countries have not maintained the so-called lifetime employment or seniority systems but rather encouraged their employees to be independent or self-employed when they became highly skilled workers. In a report by the Osaka prefectural government, it is noted that most Japanese SMF still maintain characteristic behavioral patterns that will also be transferred when they shift operations to developing countries.[22] When intellectuals discuss so-called Japanese-style management, they are mostly referring to the situation found at the famous big firms. The way of management at small-scale firms is quite different. We, as well as the Thai people, should pay attention to this fact.

Technology Transfer by Thais

Some Cases of Spin-off

It is impossible to collect data on all those who once worked for a Japanese joint venture and then retired. This writer is sure that there are a number of Thais who later became independent or self-employed, and it is their cases which this paper calls "spin-off." Of course, there also are many cases of employees spinning off Thai firms and Euro-American joint ventures. However, it is difficult for employees in the semiconductor or petrochemical sector to spin off and become independent in the same sector. As we know from the experience of Japanese industrialization, it has been easier for workers to be independent in the sectors like metal manufacturing and various kinds of machine industries; and, as is well known, Japanese "capitalism" is good at manufacturing in these sectors.

It was interesting that most Thai intellectuals in the mid-1980s did not believe it possible for Thai workers to be independent after retiring from Japanese joint ventures and to succeed in managing their own factories. However, from 1986 to 1988, this writer talked with 12 persons who had

---

21. Interview with Mr. Isao Tsuta, in March 1988.
22. Osaka Prefectural Government, *Osaka Keizai Hakusho 1987* (Osaka Economic White Paper 1987), Osaka, 1988, p.249.

succeeded in spinning off from Japanese joint ventures. He obtained their names through the Japanese Embassy in Bangkok, the Faculty of Commerce and Accountancy at Thammasat University, and through the others he interviewed.

Among the 12, two were university graduates and two were graduates of the institute of technology. Five of them had high school or middle class vocational school training, while three of them did not have secondary educational training. The interviews were held during 1986, 1987 and 1988.[23] Nine of them are dealing in the same manufacturing sector; the others perform services which are related to the former—for example, a consultant to Japanese joint ventures or a self-employed piano tuner.

Among those who are in manufacturing, only two employ more than 200 persons. On the other hand, three firms employ fewer than five persons; the rest of them employ 20 to 50 persons. This paper introduces three of these enterprises to show the level of Thai industrialization and social reformation at the time in question.

Press Manufacturing

Kh. Firm is located in Samrongtai Phapradaeng, Samutprakan. The firm mostly specializes in press manufacturing but has also small lines of lathe manufacturing and bolling. It employs 200–210 persons and is equipped with about 100 press machines, 30 lathes, 20 bolling machines, and others. The factory site covers an area of about 2 lai (about 3200 square meters). Mr. K., the owner-manager, was 47 years old in January 1990. He is from northeastern Thailand. According to him, he has no educational background. He came to Bangkok in his teens and changed his workplace five times before being employed by a Japanese joint venture manufacturing electric appliances.

He paid about 10,000 baht to purchase three hammer press machines in 1980. Adjusting those secondhand Bangkok-produced machines by himself, he became independent and started a small family enterprise. Supplying spare parts for motorcycles, electric appliances, and automobiles, his firm developed until it employed about 200 persons in 1987. He concentrated on supplying spare parts for the first two years; then one of the Japanese joint ventures contracted with him to supply parts

---

23. It is reported in one of the publications of IDE that there were many entrepreneurs without any educational background in the ASEAN countries in those days. This trend is one of the criteria showing the dynamism of social changes in these countries. For the sample survey, refer to (IDE 1986).

for the manufacture of electric appliances. He says that he was surprised that his first client introduced him to other joint ventures, from whom he got more orders. Even now he cannot understand why they did not mind introducing their competitors to him and enabling him to open new markets. These companies sometimes even send staff members to give him technical advice, which he can then use in manufacturing for other companies.

He obtained raw materials and machines at the local market, and with the approval of his joint venture clients. This is quite different from the subcontracting system in Japan, where parent companies are usually too nervous to allow subcontractors to obtain production means independently and sometimes go so far as to supply raw material and equipment themselves. Mr. K. added to his stock of machines, which were second-hand and made in Thailand, Taiwan, and China, until 1987, when he could purchase new machines for the first time. Those machines were made in Taiwan.

Mr. K. first trained his workers on the job by himself, but now he employs five foremen who train newly employed workers. He considers that press work is not so difficult as to require highly skilled workers. Most of the manufacturers in Thailand regard press manufacturing as easy, unlike their Japanese press counterparts, who know that there is a wide range of press manufacturing, from precise moulding pattern processing to simple punch press work for cheap toys.

Kh. Firm has a section for the production of moulding patterns, but there seems to be little interest in improving it. The workers don't worry about the maintenance of the products, and sometimes a pattern is left on the floor after a press head is changed[24]—something that can hardly be imagined in Japanese small firms because it can cause distortions or scratches on the surface of the moulding pattern. Under these conditions, it is difficult for this company to supply precision press wares. The operating gears of press machines are almost always driven by foot. Most machines made in developing countries are designed for foot operation, but those made in developed countries are operated by hand to minimize the chance of accident. Skilled workers are needed to produce moulding patterns, but Mr. K. does not spend time on training

---

24. We can find the same kind of trouble reported in the following: Kaigai Konsarutingu Kigyou Kyoukai (Overseas Consulting Companies' Association), *Chuushou Kigyou Tekisei Gijyutsu Fukyu Shido Jigyou ni kakawaru Tekisei Gijyutsu Kaihatsu Kyoryoku Chosa Kokunai Hakkutsu Chosa Hokokusho* (Appropriate Technologies Related to Japanese Overseas Technological Cooperation for Small- and Medium-scale Firms), JETRO, Tokyo, 1983, pp .59–65.

because he can employ those who were already trained at other companies. His workshop has five foremen, three of whom had experience working at Japanese joint ventures and were trained as skilled workers arranging moulding patterns. He would not give details about wage levels.

He takes pride in employing a young diploma holder who takes charge of the accounting and of arrangements for subcontracting, and prepares projected statements, cost analyses and so on. She is not a relative of his but worked at his firm part time for five years and then, after becoming thoroughly accustomed to her job, she became a manager of Kh. Firm. This is quite noteworthy because Thai society is a blood relation-oriented society in which management, especially in small or medium scale-enterprises, is open only to family members.

Mr. K. has five younger brothers, and two of them now have their own firms in the same line of business. Each has about 10 machines, including press machines and sharing machines, and employs from 20 to 30 persons. When he has too much work, Mr.K. asks for help from his brother firms. He believes that the other three brothers, who now work for him, can also be independent in future. They are all sure of that.

They don't have any complaint about the business activity of Japanese joint ventures (JJVs), but they think it funny that Japanese always prefer to stay on the workshop floor rather than in the office, whenever they come to his firm. Also, after giving technical advice, they usually depend upon Thai staff members to conduct business negotiations. Though these behaviors are not unusual in Japanese society, they are regarded as fresh or extraordinary among Thai people. When Mr. K. worked at a JJV, he never had a chance to speak with Japanese staff members because there were only one or two Japanese on his floor; but now he has many chances, and he likes it. He appreciates Japanese introducions to other JJVs that result in new business relations, and he says that it is also unusual for Thais to introduce their competitors to their business partners. He had some experience with quality control (QC) movements when he was at a JJV, but he says that the QC movement is not needed in his factory as his line and products are too simple to adopt them. He started to construct a new factory in 1988, and he stressed that he would select about 50 workers for the new factory and try to organize his own QC movement.

He has two sons and two daughters. The elder son attends a technical college, and the elder daughter studies accounting at a commercial college. He hopes that his children can have a chance to study in Japan and they can take over his business, but he says that children's lives are their own and they should decide for themselves. Here, we can see evidence that the traditional value system of the Thai family is changing.

Plastic Parts Manufacturing

Klongtoi is a famous slum in Bangkok. When Prasert Yamklingfang conducted a survey at Klongtoi at the beginning of the 1970s (Yamklingfung 1973), there were no manufacturing enterprises there; jobless people or those dealing in small miscellaneous services occupied the area. However, in the latter half of the 1980s, we noticed numerous manufacturing enterprises emerging and growing year after year in this district. Plastic manufacturing is one of those sectors; almost all of the manufacturers are small and clustered in neighboring areas. This writer found seven firms in the small apartment houses located on the same alley stretching about 40 meters. P. Firm is one of them.

Mr. V., the owner-manager of the firm, was 40 years old in 1990. He was the sixth child of a Chinese medical practitioner in Bangkok, and has nine brothers and sisters. One of his younger brothers also has a small plastic processing firm, and one of his elder brothers is a manufacturer of textile products. Two elder sisters are guides for foreign tourists. Three are merchants and two are students. Their father allowed his children to make their own decisions about their occupations. After leaving commercial school, V. was employed by a small Thai manufacturer, which became a joint venture with a Japanese company, a famous producer of electric appliances. He worked on the partsware manufacturing line and soon became a leader of the line. He noticed that the JJV was interested in developing its subcontracting system, and he decided to be independent. He says that at least 10 persons spun off from the company to become independent small manufacturers.[25] He purchased two plastic injection machines and started his own firm in 1983. The JJV was very severe in checking the quality of his products, and would not accept them at first. However, once they decided to purchase his products, they did not mind introducing him to other competing joint ventures. Demand for his products increased after 1985, and now he has four injection machines, supplying partswares for electric appliances and also such items as clothes hangers for the textile industry.

In 1989, he employed 20 persons, of whom two were foremen. He hired those two when they were jobless in the business decline of 1985,

---

25. He was unwilling to introduce me to those firms.

because they had experience in operating injection machines. He arranged operation manuals for his workers by himself, but the variety of products obliged him to change those manuals frequently. Processing the moulding patterns requires highly skilled workers. Since it is difficult for small enterprises to employ such workers on the local labor market, he has trained them since the establishment of his firm. Sometimes one of the other manufacturers living in his neighborhood, who is specialized in the processing of patterns for plastic injection, helps him to arrange new moulding patterns for his factory.

It is one of the characteristics of this factory that it is clean. Until the beginning of the 1980s, manufacturing factories were usually very dirty in developing countries, except those of joint ventures with firms from developed countries, but it should be noted that the domestic industrial atmosphere is steadily changing in the ASEAN countries. Workers are trained to keep patterns neat, and injection machines are well maintained as workers become accustomed to taking care of them after daily operations. In addition to secondhand machines, this firm purchased new machines made in Taiwan. The importing agent sends its staff to maintain and repair the machines, but Mr. V. sometimes repairs them himself to save time. However, there still are some technological problems. For example, he is not interested in the quality of raw materials so he does not check the materials he purchases. He does not have enough information about modern plastic materials or special patterns.

In some developed countries, "maintenance" means repairing parts which are out of order; in Japan, it means to repair beforehand or improve partly to get higher productivity. Mr. V. understands the concept of the Japanese way to some extent, but he is not experienced in the improvement of his machines. He has spent about 10 million baht in all on equipment and machines for his factory. He used his own savings and borrowed from his brothers. At the time of his establishment, he spent about 3 million baht, 40% of which he paid himself; two of his brothers contributed the rest in equal shares.

There are numerous poor and miserable areas in Klongtoi even now, but many small shops and factories are developing in the area. Actually, we might call it a "downtown" area instead of a "slum." A number of Japanese regard Thailand as poor and think that its slum areas must be tremendously indigent and dirty, but this is not correct at all. Thailand is poor in terms of GDP, or if poverty is estimated only by the means of modern economic statistics, but the word does not always reflect the quality of people's lives.

Mr. V. does not live in Klongtoi but in the outskirts of Bangkok. This writer met a number of people like him, and not a few of them did live in this town at the beginning of their business lives. He has two children, one 11 years old and the other 8. He says that they should decide on their way of life by themselves. He is rather optimistic about their future and also about the development of his business. His neighbors share his optimism: they are confident of the brightness of the business climate in Thailand for the next couple of decades. Mr. V. is going to concentrate on his present business for five more years, and after that he intends to depend on others for the management of this factory and to start a new business. He doesn't have detailed ideas about his next business, but he would prefer to work in the area of trading. On this point, his way of thinking is quite different from those of Japanese small manufacturers.

Integrated Circuit Manufacturer

G. Company, located in Pathum Thani, might be one of the most impressive and successful companies among those which spun off from Japanese joint ventures and developed successfully. The mainstay of the company's business is integrated circuits (IC), but they actually are assembled print boards or control panels utilizing some ICs, which are used for the control of engines especially for aquatic sports equipment. As they supply special-order items, they do not produce their commodities in a mass production line, and local people are inclined to view the company as one of the "high-tech" companies. This may look like labor-intensive manufacturing from the point of view of Japanese technical specialists. However, we should appreciate that they have succeeded in developing their ability to design appropriate circuits for customers. The world market is growing closer and closer connected, and the demand for special use is increasing together with the demand for mass production commodities. It is sure this kind of company will have its own raison d'être and many chances for further development from now on.

Mr. S. was the key person in the establishment of this company. When this writer met him in January 1990, he was 38 years old. After graduating from Chulalongkorn University, he got a job at an electric generating company. He worked there for half a year; then he shifted to a Japanese joint venture company producing electric appliances. He was employed as an engineer and then promoted to production manager and then to vice plant manager of the company's electronics factory. He played an important role in the negotiations with the BOI office and in the setting up of a cost reduction plan, and he was selected and sent to Japan to study "quality control" for about 4 months. His monthly income was 30,000 baht in 1984, which he says was not so high as that of his Thai colleagues working at famous Thai firms or European companies. He did not mind the salary differential, he says, but he was eager to do more difficult and sophisticated tasks. He thought that the Japanese joint venture did not transfer its latest technology to Thailand, and he explains that this was the most decisive reason for his leaving the company.

He considers that there are numerous people who are eager to be independent manufacturers but that none of them has set up a factory with as high a level of technology as his. He investigated so-called "venture businesses" in the United States, looked for an investor in Bangkok, and succeeded in establishing G. Company in 1984. However, he is not satisfied with his present situation because he does not have the majority ownership of the company even if he is sure of his ability in management and technology. Compared to managers in Japan, where the majority of the shareholders are frequently corporations or public organizations, he is far more nervous about the ownership of the company. He did not identify the total amount of investment but the company had about 250 employees, and annual sales were five million dollars in 1988. He succeeded in obtaining tax-free privileges for eight years from the BOI on the condition that the company will export its whole output to the United States.

A walk around the floor of the factory reveals that most of the important materials and parts are imported from abroad, but the number of domestic products has been increasing since the end of the 1980s. Mr. S. purchased both new machines and secondhand ones and he himself has been involved in adjusting them. There is an R&D section, and its staff members are specialists in designing whole circuits, or control panel components, whose specifications differ in response to the requests of customers. The market for these special products may expand as the demand for highly luxurious consumer durables increases. The advanced countries and the oil producing countries have a number of rich people who are not satisfied with mass-produced goods. Japan, which supplies these countries with automobiles and cruisers, is not particularly good at filling special orders.

Mr. S. is not interested in "Japanese-style management" at all. More often, he talks about "scientific management" or "situational manage-ment." His understanding of these concepts is much more related to American-style management. However, he frequently walks around the shop floors to (1) promote more efficient operation, (2) maintain the cleanliness of the lines, and (3) adjust equipment. This kind of behavior is normally more typical of Japanese managers than of Americans or Europeans. He explained that the rationale for the layout of the factory line is based on "scientific management," but this writer wonders whether there are any factory managers who are not nervous about the rational layout of their production lines. It can be said that Japanese are inclined to have their lines laid out rationally in smaller spaces than managers in other developed countries. The site of G. Company is not spacious, but Mr. S. has a keen interest in expanding it to have space for a more refined layout.

He was born one of six sons of a Thai Christian merchant who has his business in Ratchaburi. His brothers are all medical doctors except one who was a university student in December 1989 and intended to go into business in the future. Their father did not dictate his sons' lives and occupations. Mr. S. has five children and he also considers that they should select their lives' courses by themselves. He does not intend to ask any of them to live with him.

Mr. S. expects engineers to be more highly esteemed in the future. Engineers are regarded as lower-middle class people in present Thailand, but he is rather optimistic about this social problem and thinks that they will be appreciated more highly in the near future. On this point, his way of thinking is closely related to that of many Japanese[26] and some Americans.

A Case of Fade-Out

Those who consider that "fade-out" is the final stage of technology transfer are a minority among Japanese (Shishido 1981), but we can see some typical cases of fade-out in ASEAN countries. This writer believes that there are several types of the final stage of technology transfer, and fade-out should be one of them. In this section, only one case is introduced, but it is certain that we will have many cases like this even in manufacturing sectors from now on, such as that of the famous Bangkok silk dealer Jim Thompson.

Sw[27] is a manufacturing company specializing in dyeing and weaving of synthetic fibers for men's suits. It was established in 1970 by two

---

26. As Akio Morita (Chairman of Sony Corp.) has frequently emphasized, most Japanese business people are proud of their way of management and appreciate highly skilled workers and engineers.
27. This writer visited the company on Dec. 11, 1987, and Feb. 1, 1990.

Japanese general trading companies and a Thai textile merchant. All of the equipment was imported from Japan by these trading companies. At the first stage of its manufacturing, TR X TR accounted for 80% of their total products and TW X TW[28] shared the rest. They needed more than 10 Japanese engineers, who were sent by textile manufacturers and machine dealers in Japan to install and adjust the imported equipment and train Thai workers. They still required six Japanese engineers and highly skilled workers in 1976. Business conditions were not favorable until then.

One Japanese, Mr. Ym., was sent to this company as one of its executives from the time of its establishment. He noted that the greatest expense for this company was the wage cost for the Japanese staff, and determined in 1976 to run the business without Japanese technical assistance. He suggested that one of the Thai staff members, Mr. Dg., draft a plan for the operation and maintenance of the factory without Japanese technical assistance. Mr. Ym. intended to train this Thai as an engineer in the style of Japanese management. He is a diploma holder of a commercial college and had no experience or academic background in engineering, but was sent to Japan in 1973 for on-the-job training (OJT) in a textile factory in Niigata for a year. Besides him, six other workers were sent to Japan for OJT for six months. All of them utilized the program of the Association for Overseas Technical Scholarship (AOTS) and received funds from it.

The behavior which Mr. Dg. displayed at this time of management crisis was quite interesting, because it was similar to that of Japanese in a similar situation. He began to hold meetings with the chief foreman and other foremen, rather than making decisions by himself. He was sure that the productivity would go down without Japanese assistance. However, he and his foremen made up their mind to keep their productivity within 95%. On hearing of their determination, Mr.Ym. cancelled the contract with Japanese personnel. After the Japanese went back to their country, Mr. Dg. started to meet with the two chief foremen[29] and 22 foremen every week, preferring to decide everything collectively. Top executives including Mr. Ym. depended completely upon the foremen to solve technical and/or manufacturing problems. Mr. Dg. looked around each production line every day to give technical

---

28. The former shows the warp and the latter shows the woof. TR is thread made of 65% tetron (polyester) and 35% rayon. TW is made of 65% tetron and 35% woolly nylon.
29. The one was a production manager and the other was an assistant production manager in 1990.

suggestions and mechanical assistance, as the Japanese staff members had done before, and he did not mind instructing workers directly and speaking with them. Close human interactions became one of the characteristics of this company.

Productivity did not decline so severely as they had feared. It went down about 3 to 6%, but they were unsure of the quality of their product, so they concentrated on checking final products. They found that 5 or 6% of their products were defective and suggested that the sales managers not sell them at the normal price. In most developing countries, marketing managers are independent of and/or superior to manufacturing sections. We know that there are close and competitive relations between them in Japanese factories, and this company shows a similar pattern. It was said that Thai wholesale merchants paid 20% more for commodities made by manufacturers with Japanese staffs than for those produced without direct assistance by Japanese. Sw. Company could sell its products at the same price as before, even if there still was just one Japanese man among the top executives. They would not mix defective goods among normal ones in their transactions, which was an exceptional attitude among Thai merchants in those days.

Since 1976, when it cancelled Japanese technical assistance, Sw. has tried to increase the production ratio of high-value-added commodities. TW X TW products are more expensive than TR X TR, so they have managed to increase the former to 80% of their product mix. In addition, they began to dye TC X TC products.[30] They purchased second-hand Taiwan-made machines and readjusted them for their own use. They promoted an OJT program for the workers of the weaving section so that they could operate two weaving machines at the same time. They succeeded in reducing the number of workers from a little over 700 to 430 in 1987 without decreasing the total amount of production. The turnover rate among Thai workers is high, especially in and around Bangkok, even if it is not so high as in other ASEAN countries. So, they were able to reduce the number of workers easily just by not filling vacancies. Through this reduction by attrition, they could increase the wages of workers to a level about 20% higher than those of neighboring factories.[31]

Mr. Dg. is now the factory manager of this company. Factory managers do not have such a high status in Thailand as in Japan, but he is fairly

---

30. TC is thread made of 65% tetron and 35% cotton.
31. This company is located in Rangsit near Bangkok. The average daily payment for workers was 85 baht around this area in 1987, while this company paid 105 baht.

proud of his status and is satisfied with his production manager, assistant production managers, and chief foremen. What worries him now is that the ability and potentiality of his foremen are not so high as he requires. He sometimes complains that foremen will not take leadership in their lines and prefer to maintain conservative human relations and the stereotyped system of production. His workers have higher incomes than those at neighboring factories, and he considers that the top executives can and should increase wages for their workers. However, at the same time, he thinks that both workers and foremen should work harder at daily improvement and development.

Sw. Company is appreciated highly by some Japanese who know about this company and its type of human relations. Social stratification is too severe in most developing countries to allow the growth of a middle class, and in manufacturing, the tradition of family enterprise is another bottleneck preventing the promotion of lower class people in business organizations. Owner-managers of family enterprises do not give any incentives to their employees. Under these circumstances, this company looks exceptional. It succeeded in promoting key persons from among the floor workers. Mr. Ym. also appreciates this point; he was the last Japanese to stay in this company, until in 1986 he decided to sell all of the Japanese shares to the Thai partner and he himself faded out of this company. After that, he went back to the Japanese trading company in which he worked before. The trading company doesn't have any business relations with Sw. Company except for occasional transactions, while the latter has formed a sort of business group including cotton spinning, yarn manufacture, and so on. It sold about 40% of its products through Japanese trading companies to foreign market in the 1970s. It expanded its own exports, and now transactions through Japanese companies are less than 10% of its business. This is a good example of "fade-out."

We can see some more cases of fade-out especially in the textile industry. The development of the Sukree group must be one of the most prominent cases of fade-out. Sukree, which started to develop as a Thai-Japanese cotton spinning joint venture, is now one of the leading business groups in the Thai textile industry and it doesn't need any Japanese assistance. The Japanese spinning company which organized the joint venture at first is now a very small share holder, and top executives are all Thais (Suehiro 1989: 237–239).

Transfer by Thais

The development of Thai business groups is prominent in recent years, and we have some noteworthy studies on big groups (Prasartset 1975; Suehiro 1989a, 1990). However, we do not have sufficient analyses about their empirical process of technology transfer. This writer studied a manufacturer employing 600 persons in 1989, and located in Samutsakorn. The case of this company shows the progress of technology transfer by Thais without foreign technical assistance.

Tc. Company was established in 1970 to supply sanitary wares.[32] The founder was a Chinese Thai, a merchant and importer of bicycle tires. He introduced Japanese technology through a Taiwan trading company with which he had business contacts. However, the Japanese staff members sent to the company were not specialists in the manufacturing of sanitary wares, and the goods they produced were more than 50% defective. It was the policy of the Thai government to protect local products through high import duties, and local distributors would not complain about defective goods in the interest of expansion of the local market.

It was Mr. Bd. who established the technological base of this company. He was a graduate of a Japanese university and one of the relatives of the owner-founder. He agreed to be a plant manager in 1972, and wanted to concentrate on improving the total manufacturing system to the level he experienced in some Japanese factories during his university student days. His family was reluctant to allow him to work in the factory, and suggested to him many times that those coming back from foreign countries should remain in office work and not go into production. Even the factory workers were critical of his going around the factory floor checking machines and systems. He persuaded them that it was essential for him to do this if the company was to improve the production system by itself. He succeeded in changing the production system and achieving higher productivity after cancelling the contract with Japanese engineers for technical assistance.

Mr. Bd. says that Thai people can do everything if they are instructed with kindness, and explains that workers soon neglect troublesome jobs whenever they do not receive any daily instruction from those in positions of authority. His explanation is quite similar to what we hear from Japanese staff members in numerous joint ventures in Thailand. However, Mr. Bd. considers that Thai workers are too optimistic and

---

32. I visited this company and had many interviews and discussions in August 1985, October 1986, and February 1990.

generous to remember what they were told earlier, while Japanese local managers, with a few exceptions, are inclined to regard them to be idle by nature. There is a delicate perception gap here.

According to the common understanding of Thai business people, factory managers belong to the lower middle class, and they should not concentrate on management but only on production. Mr. Bd paid no attention to this, but devoted himself to higher efficiency in both manufacturing and management. In the latter half of the 1980s, he managed to achieve sufficient productivity, though it was not so high as that of Japanese firms, but the local market was protected by the government policy, and the demand was increasing year by year. He designed a tile factory and imported a whole set of equipment from Japan in 1980; the factory was quite successful, and achieved a level of efficiency as high as that in Japan. There were two more serious problems he needed to solve in those days: (1) a lack of lower middle class persons and (2) the sense of severe social stratification which obliged Thai managers to organize their business system in accordance with the educational and academic backgrounds of employees.

Like many other factories in Bangkok, Tc. company suffered high rates of both turnover and absenteeism; the rates were highest among middle-level men. He proposed that the directors adopt a new wage system which would enable mid-level workers to accumulate extra base-up points for low levels of absence and for continuous service. With this new wage system, the company had to pay much more to highly skilled workers and leaders than neighboring factories, but they became key persons in increasing the productivity of the company.

When he introduced a new production line for wall tiles in 1980, Mr. Bd. made up his mind to establish an R&D section in the factory for the first time. At the same time, he determined to recruit as staff for this section not only college graduates and high school leavers but also floor workers who showed high motivation for production. He considers that academic background is one of the criteria for appreciating human potentiality, but not a decisive and perfect factor. He says that human capabilities should be empirically valued by managers—a philosophy which is similar to that which we saw frequently among tremendously successful Japanese manufacturers in the 1950s and 1960s. The R&D section showed itself to be very useful in the development of the company. It succeeded in developing new designs for wall tiles and new intermediate colors, which most of the developing countries are not good at exploiting.

The Thai economy has been active and aggressive since the latter half of the 1980s, and Mr. Bd. has concentrated on improving the productivity of old production systems and introducing new lines of manufacturing. It is commonly said that the average depreciation term of a hearthstone is about 15 years, but he started a plan to increase the productivity of the hearth in 1985, just 15 years after its installation. He was planning to develop a new line of sanitary products in 1990, but what he needed was information on modern hearths and hearthstones which were introduced from Japan. He made minor improvement in small parts of the hearth and, without substituting stones, succeeded in attaining productivity levels about three times as high as before. He is now promoting the construction of a new plant in the neighborhood of the present factory, and he is sure of attaining even higher efficiency in the new plant. He is going to import some major pieces of equipment from Japan, but, at the same time, he intends to introduce a number of supplementary parts made in Thailand and Taiwan. He stressed that the Thai people should be proud of their own products and regard them as equal to imported goods. He says that there are many local items now which can be used in production as well as materials imported from advanced countries.

He obtained the agreement of the directors to purchase a whole set of production lines for large wall tiles in 1988, and decided to get them from Italy and Germany. He traveled to Europe and Japan, and found that Japanese manufacturers have no tradition of supplying large wall tiles even if they are good at manufacturing small tiles. He designed the lay-out of the new factory and offered to purchase equipment from European companies. The factory was completed in 1989 and went into full operation quickly; it proved to be a keystone for the business management of this company. Mr. Bd. is not satisfied with the productivity of the new plant yet. He sometimes neglects the specifications and operation manuals of imported equipment in order to get higher efficiency. He intends to improve the system by himself; again, his attitude is reminiscent of that of famous manufacturers in Japan in the course of rapid economic development.

Concluding Remarks

It is easy to criticize the Thai economy as immature. Even in the case of G. company, we can say it can only design and assemble components in response to the specifications of customers, and is unable to develop new materials or highly technological parts, relying on imported high-tech parts. Workers at Sw. Company, for example, could dye only with several dozen colors in 1987 and with 200–300 colors in 1990, while it is the minimum qualification for the highly skilled dyeing workers in Japan to be able to identify about 3,000 colors in a moment. However, the skill of workers as well as the variety of products may improve with increased affluence and the development of a sophisticated market. The Thai people are so good at consuming modern goods that they have the potential to increase their consumption of goods in the short term. What we need now is not a static definition of the stage of economic development but a dynamic understanding of the process of development.

Not being affluent in natural resources and geographical conditions, the Japanese economy has been said to be dependent upon overseas markets. However, Japan has actually depended mainly on the domestic market, and the value of exports has not usually exceeded 15% of GDP. We should note that the local market is the decisive factor in economic development, even if international economic conditions have been changing since the 1970s. Thailand has plenty of natural resources and favorable weather conditions, and these factors may make it possible to expand its domestic market in the near future, if they are combined with proper economic policies and political stability. One of the severe factors retarding the growth may be the intensification of social stratification which we see commonly in developing countries, even though it is not so striking in Asia as in Latin America. This problem is related to the wage system and the possibility of incentives for lower-class people. This paper will not expand on this point,[33] except to note that a new trend seems to be emerging in Thai society, as we saw in a few examples.

We also found various new trends leading to the social reformation of traditional Thai society. The number of children per family is decreasing. Parents can no longer prescribe the life style of their children in many families. The traditional value system is changing gradually. Military personnel were esteemed far more highly than business people until the 1970s. The latter have increased in status during the 1980s, and now we see a new trend toward the appreciation of engineers.

The estimation of so-called Japanese-style management is changing bit by bit among Thai people, and some local people are now inclined to value it more highly. It has been said that Japanese management is informal relations-oriented, but some Thai businessmen suggest that

33. Refer to the following comment by Yasuda.

Japanese management is closely related to the personal characters of each local resident and it can only be thought of as informally oriented in this sense. Mr.V. reminds us that turnover rates declined when quality Japanese staff was sent from parent companies. Most of the Thais whom this writer met highly valued Japanese joint ventures and knew well that those joint ventures used their surplus not for rewarding personnel but for investment. At the same time, some of them said that Japanese staff members should utilize their stocks not only for innovation but also for the replenishing of human resources, commenting that they know very well the restrictions of parent companies and the lack of free decision making power of Japanese staff members stationed in Bangkok.

We noticed in our early report that the Thai people complained about Japanese reluctance to transfer the latest technology or R&D sections (Yamashita 1988, Part 3). We can see in this paper that the operation and maintenance are directly related to R&D, and this is the reason why the author is so nervous about Japanese partners' following through with sufficient support of overseas operations. It is noteworthy that most of the local partners are conscious of this meaning, even though most of the high-ranking people do not express concern about it. We need to collect far more information and case studies to increase understanding and minimize the perception gap. However, this writer must thank our partners and the local people for their kindness and zeal, through which we increased our own understanding and obtained some clues for further surveys.

Comment

Osamu Yasuda

Many information gaps exist between parties on the Japanese and Thai sides regarding technology transfer. The Japanese insist that they have transferred their basic technologies while the Thais usually criticize the transfers as insufficient because Japanese joint ventures neither export their products nor develop new models in Thailand, preferring to produce the old models that they produced in Japan. Some changes are, however, noticable based on the evidence that a number of companies have begun to export their products and that QC movements have recently become popular in Thailand.

Both sides share the view that the final level of technology transfer is the establishment of the R&D section, but they differ in evaluating the possibility of transferring that section. Most business people and scholars in developing countries seem to believe that they will be able to promote the development of new products and technologies without regard to the decision making of their parent companies if R&D sections can be transferred separately or independently. Officials of Japanese companies, in contrast, believe that R&D activities should be promoted only after a sufficient foundation of effective operations, tough maintenance abilities, modification capabilities, and so on has been established. They can hardly imagine that R&D can be accomplished without the accumulation of sufficient and trustworthy resources.

It should be noted that, among various points explained by Professor Takeuchi, wage structures in ASEAN countries are closely related to social stratifications and especially to the academic background of individuals. Those with a poor educational background can never get higher wage rates than those with a higher academic background, even if the former have far better experiences and/or skills. The characteristics of wage structures in four ASEAN countries are shown in Fig. 1.

It is often claimed that Thais do not highly value technologies and, especially, skills; the data shown in Fig. 2 clearly indicate that their value system does not provide incentives to working-class people to develop new skills and technologies. Some Japanese have insisted that business

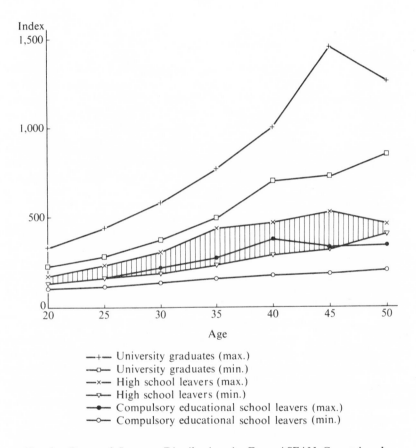

Fig. 1.   Personal Income Distribution in Four ASEAN Countries, by
           Academic Background and Age.
Source: Yamashita, S., et al., 1989, p.50.
Note: Minimum wage rate for middle-school leavers is indexed as 100.

leaders should pay attention to giving incentives to their workers if they
are interested in achieving a higher economic growth rate, but such
suggestions are often met with offensive responses.

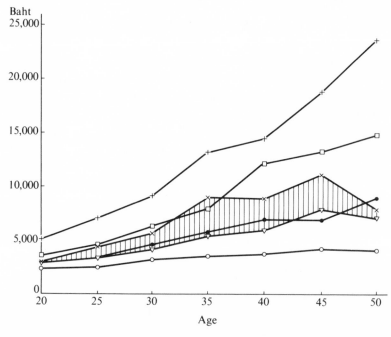

Fig. 2.   Personal Income Distribution in Thailand, by Academic Background and Age.

Note: Minimum wage rate for middle-school leavers is indexed as 100.
The symbols are the same as in Fig. 1.

The atmosphere of this conference was quite different from that of
others I have attended during this decade: ASEAN partners agreed with
the idea of giving incentives. Even if the rearrangement of the social
value system to guarantee such incentives is not at all easy, the partners
seem to be following that track in order to achieve further economic
development.

Comment

Ichiro Sato

I would like to express my great esteem especially for Professors Prayoon, Takeuchi, and Takehana, whose efforts have been so great. This section is not a comment on their papers but an attempt to define from a different angle the framework of technology transfer. ASEAN countries often criticize Japanese firms as being reluctant to promote technology transfer. The definition of "technology transfer," however, is not always clear. During the past two decades I have had the opportunity to have several meetings with Thai business representatives in Bangkok; when I would ask them what kind of technology they would like to have, there was never an answer to my question. They are always anxious to have modern technologies transferred to their country, but they neglect to appreciate what technology transfer concretely and specifically comprises.

Technology transfer may be divided into four categories. The first is the direct investment that ASEAN governments generally expect. Some governments expect investment in labor-intensive and export-oriented industries, others in high-technology industries. The governments believe that direct investments will foster the development of their economies and societies as well as the localization of management and the technologies relating to research and development.

The second category is the type of technology transfer that is generally desired by private or local partners. They appreciate new technologies and knowhow for expanding their businesses and increasing profits.

The third category is the type of transfer desired by local employees, who see in technology transfer another chance to win promotions to top and middle management or to participate in the business administration of the company. Some local engineers would like to learn about higher technologies in order to benefit their career formation.

Finally, the fourth category is the technology transfer that is required to develop the manufacturing sectors, and this is the type of technology transfer discussed in the papers of this conference.

I appreciate the studies of my colleagues and most of their points, but it must be stressed that private enterprises have to promote their long prosperity with reasonable profits. Private firms are not welfare organizations, and they cannot promote technology transfer without regard to cost-profit analysis. Japanese or any other foreign firms will not show interest if feasibility is nonexistent. It is clear from the recent rush of Japanese firms to Thailand that the Thai economy has achieved the economic conditions for further development. Japanese joint ventures in Thailand have made various contributions, including the supporting of industries, to build up and level industrial conditions, which is why so many manufacturers are now scrambling to Thailand.

The case of Toyota Motors Thailand, which established a branch office in 1957 and began assembly of vehicles in 1965, will make this point clearer. In 1989 the firm assembled 3,000 automobiles every month with 1,305 employees, only 15 of whom were Japanese. Sales are made all over Thailand through 70 dealers. For passenger cars 54% of component parts are manufactured in Thailand and for commercial vehicles 60%. Body press works are not counted in the local content ratio. In total about 70% local content is achieved for a one-ton pick-up truck. These local content ratios are the highest among ASEAN countries. Toyota Thailand now purchases 990 items in the domestic market, amounting to about 950 million baht per year from 47 parts manufacturers, of which only 13 are Japanese joint ventures. In the Thai automobile industry Japanese firms have already transferred the technical knowhow of such daily operations as welding, painting, and assembling. In a plant where, say, 700 Thai employees fulfill their responsibilities every day with only three Japanese engineers present, it obviously would be impossible to maintain daily operations if the transfer of technical knowhow to the Thai employees were not achieved. The main issue in technology transfer today is organization reform and managerial development in such areas as quality control, production control, and purchasing control not only at the engineer level but also at the level of foremen, supervisors, workers, and parts manufacturers employees.

10
Problems of and Perspectives on Japanese Management in Malaysia

Nobuo Kawabe

Introduction

Malaysia, located between Thailand and Singapore, is not so familiar to many Japanese people. Particularly for the last couple of years it has been hidden in the shadow of Thailand, where numerous Japanese companies have rushed to invest. Because of limited infrastructure, human resources, land, and other factors, however, it has become difficult for Thailand to accept more Japanese investment. As a result Japanese companies have started looking toward Malaysia and their investment there has been increasing rapidly.

Malaysia has a plural society—of the total population of 16 million, Malays account for 51%, Chinese 35%, and Indians 11%. This multi-racial society has given rise to a variety of religions, cultures, and languages. Moreover, as Malaysia was a British colony it has been influenced by British standards.

Because of the plural nature of Malaysian society, Japanese companies with investments there seem to have various problems that they do not experience in other countries. In this paper, therefore, the present situation of Japanese investment in Malaysia; the evaluation of technology transfer and management by Japanese companies; and the character-istics and problems of Japanese businesses will be analyzed.

Profile of Japanese Business in Malaysia

Trend of Japanese Investment in Malaysia

Japanese investment in Malaysia after World War II started in November 1959 when Nozawa Asbestos Cement Company established Marex In-dustries as a joint venture with a local partner. Japanese investment during the 1960s did not exceed that of 26 investing companies.

The first big wave of Japanese investment took place from 1973 to 1976 when about 80 companies, mainly in the integrated circuit industry, were established. During a second wave, from 1982 to 1985, many Japanese construction companies established joint ventures engaged in the construction of buildings, dams, electric power plants, and highways. Following a a severe recession in the Malaysian economy, investment by Japanese companies decreased.

Following the yen appreciation of autumn 1985, however, a third wave of Japanese investment in Malaysia has emerged. More than 100 companies have invested since 1986 (Table 1). In 1988 the number of Japanese companies in Malaysia increased drastically: in the year's first half the number of investors was 33 with a total value of more than 231 million ringgits.

Table 1. Japanese Enterprises in Malaysia, 1959–1988.

Year	No. of Enterprises
1959	2
1960 – 1969	26
1970 – 1972	30
1973 – 1976	80
1977 – 1979	24
1980	19
1981	13
1982	21
1983	34
1984	19
1985	14
1986	34
1987	31
1988 (Jan. – March)	20
Total	370

Sources: Kokusai Keizai (International Economics), August 1988, 164.

The Position of Japanese Companies in the Malaysian Economy

We will now examine the nature of Japanese investment in Malaysia during its most recent phase. Japanese investment is placed in a greater variety of industries compared with its European and American counterparts (Table 2). In terms of investment balance, Japanese investment

Table 2. Japanese Enterprises' Investments in Malaysia, by Industry, and
Their Ratio to Total Investment, 1987.

Industry	Japanese Investment (a)	Total Investment (b)	(b)/(a)
Food manufacturing	36,887	761,304	4.8 %
Beverages and tobacco	0	429,575	0
Textiles and textile products	195,734	376,086	52.0
Leather products	0	18,595	0
Wood and wood products	18,597	75,739	24.6
Furniture and fixtures	0	8,808	0
Paper, printing, and publishing	382	100,025	0.4
Chemicals and chemical products	20,596	547,692	3.8
Petroleum and coal	439,840	1,160,433	37.9
Rubber products	8,006	196,000	4.1
Plastic products	20,750	45,686	45.4
Non-metallic products	150,860	717,688	21.0
Basic metal products	262,402	417,779	62.8
Fabricated metal products	31,135	195,907	15.9
Machinery manufacturing	55,891	115,542	48.4
Electrical and electronic products	314,346	1,331,316	23.6
Transport equipment	183,207	233,868	78.3
Scientific and measuring equipment	3,227	48,643	6.6
Miscellaneous	17,228	64,695	26.6
Total	1,759,088	6,845,381	25.7

Sources: Malaysia Industrial Development Authority, *Statistics on Manufacturing Sectors*, 1988.

accounts for 25.7% of the total foreign investment in Malaysia. The
share of Japanese investment is particularly high in the transportation
equipment (78.3%), primary metal (62.8%), textile and textile product
(57.0%), machinery production (48.4%), and plastic products (45.4%)
industries.

Investment in petroleum and coal is the greatest in terms of absolute
assets, accounting for 37.9% of the total assets. This is followed by
investment in electric and electronic products, with a share of 23.6%.
Because European and American companies have a large investment in

Table 3.   Number of Japanese Enterprises, by Industry, 1987.

Industry	No. of Enterprises
Agriculture, forestry, fishing	7 (1)
Construction, plant engineering	90 (1)
Manufacturing	205 (6)
Transport and warehousing	19
Services (includes restaurants & hotels)	21
Commerce (includes trading companies & retailers)	54
Finance, insurance, real estate	35
Others	11
Total	442 (11)

Sources: JETRO and Japanese Embassy of Malaysia, *Survey on Japanese Enterprises*, 1989.

Note: Figures in parentheses are numbers of enterprises which seemed to be (but could not be confirmed as) Japanese enterprises.

these industries, the Japanese share is relatively small. Japanese investment is very small in the soft drink, tobacco, leather products, paper, printing and publishing, chemical and chemical products, rubber products, and scientific instruments industries.

According to a survey conducted by the Japanese Embassy and the JETRO KL Center in Malaysia in April 1987, 453 Japanese-affiliated companies were in Malaysia at that time (Japanese Embassy and JETRO 1989) (see Table 3).[1] The largest number of companies are in manufacturing, accounting for 46.6% of the total. Construction and plant engineering; commerce; and finance, insurance, and real estate follow, accounting for 20.6%, 11.9%, and 7.7% respectively.

Japanese investment has increased since the date of the survey, and it is probable that the total number of Japanese companies in Malaysia has increased. In 1987, 54 new Japanese investments (including investment for the expansion of existing companies) had been made, and in the first half of 1988 another 30 were made.

After the yen appreciation, Japanese manufacturers that had lost export competitiveness aggressively began investing in Malaysia. The following are characteristic of the recent investments by Japanese

---

1. According to Linda Golley, the first Japanese investment in Malaysia was a joint-venture textile manufacturing firm established in 1957 (Golley 1985: 263).

companies in Malaysia: (1) investments concentrated in the electric and electronics, and transportation equipment industries, (2) few investments in resource-based industries, (3) transfer of the production base from Japan and NIEs, (4) production of export products, (5) increase of small- and medium-sized companies, and (6) concentration of locations in Penang, Johore, and Selangor.[2]

The division of product and labor types among the ASEAN countries is a new development in Japanese investment, particularly in the electric and electronics industries. This can so far be best be seen in Matsushita's air conditioner factory, but it can also be seen in other companies. For example, Sharp produces audio equipment and color television sets mainly in Malaysia and such electric home appliances as electric fans, microwave ranges, and refrigerators in Thailand. Hitachi produces audio equipment in Singapore, semiconductor devices in Malaysia, and electric home appliances in Thailand.

In the automobile industry, such existing companies as Proton Saga try to diversify operations into the procurement of materials, and parts and components.

Since Japanese export-oriented companies began reducing production in Japan and increasing production in Malaysia, where the product in cost is low, investment by small- and medium-sized companies as well as large companies in the production of export goods has been increasing. There are two types of small- and medium-sized companies that invest in Malaysia. One is subcontracting companies that follow the parent companies. For example, Mitsuoka Electric Company, a manufacturer of condensers with headquarters in Osaka, has started operations in the Penang area. Because such electric and electronics companies as Matsushita, Sanyo, Sharp, and Sony had been buying components from Mitsuoka and had to pay rather expensive prices from Japan after the yen appreciation, these big corporations asked Mitsuoka to start production in Malaysia because Malaysia has not fully developed its supporting industries. Kozato Kizai in Tokyo, a producer of rubber components for the electric and electronics industry, recently decided to start production in Malaysia in early summer 1990 for the same reason.

The second type is established manufacturers of final products, for example, Sato, a hand labeler maker. Such companies already had competitive advantages in certain product lines due to their technology, marketing, and other managerial resources. Sato, for instance, controls

---

2. Interview with Yujiro Shindo, Director of JETRO's Kuala Lumpur Center.

more than 60% of the Japanese hand labeler market and more than 30% of the world market.

Regarding the concentration of investment in certain areas, investment in Johore seems to be a spillover from that in Singapore. Since Singapore began suffering from labor and land shortages it became difficult to establish a large-scale factory that would hire a large number of employees. Many companies consequently began establishing factories in Johore, where there are plenty of low-cost human resources, rather than in Singapore. As a result of such spillover and of the division of product and labor types in the ASEAN countries, Singapore began to play the host to many regional headquarters.[3] Sony, a typical case, established its operational headquarters in Singapore as well as a production base in Malaysia for providing its products to the neighboring countries.

Government Policies

Most developing countries have strict policies toward foreign investment and Malaysia is no exception. In fact, due to its plural society, Malaysia's policies are more complicated than those of other countries, and these policies naturally influence the operations and management of Japanese companies. Particularly important is the New Economic Policy (NEP) which was proposed after a confrontation between Malays and Chinese on May 13, 1969, and which has been enforced since the Second Five-year Economic Plan (1971–1975). It aims to attain economic equality by "Malaysianizing" capital and employment in the secondary and tertiary sectors.

The content of the NEP was shown concretely in the midterm report of the Second Five-year Economic Plan in 1973. The NEP aimed to increase the Bumiputera's portion of the total capital in Malaysia to 30.7% (it had been 1.9% in 1970), and the ratio of Malay employees in the secondary industries to 51.9% (30.7% in 1970). Such requirements were further defined under the Industrial Adjustment Law of 1975.

The development during the 1980s of big projects such as iron and steel works and problems such as world recession and the decline of market prices for primary materials, including oil, rubber, and tin,

---

3. Singapore introduced operational headquarters status to foreign companies that want to locate regional headquarters there. As for recent trends in Japanese investment in Malaysia and Singapore, see Takao Taniura, ed., *Ajia no Kogyoka to Chokusetu Toshi* (Industrialization of Asia and Direct Investment) (Tokyo: Institute of Developing Economies, 1989), Chap 6.

created financial problems for the Malaysian government. To solve these problems the government borrowed funds from foreign countries, increasing Malaysia's external debt to 21.3 billion ringgits (27.8% of GNP) in 1985.

Under such circumstances the use of private capital, particularly foreign private capital that does not bring financial burden to the country, became very important. The government therefore, on July 8, 1985, relaxed policies on foreign investment in order to attract foreign capital. The measure allows foreign companies to have 100% equity capital if they export more than 80% of their products and 51% of equity capital even if they export just 20% of their products.

Malaysia experienced a further blow to its economy in 1985 when it had a minus growth figure for the first time since independence. The introduction of foreign capital became necessary in order to stimulate the Malaysian economy, and Prime Minister Mahathir, who was visiting New York at the time, announced a new incentive policy on September 30, 1986. The aim was relaxation of control on foreign capital ratios and on expatriate postings.

One hundred percent foreign capital is now allowed on the condition that a company not produce products competitive with local manufacturers. The government allows 100% foreign ownership to those companies that export more than 50% of their products, employ constantly more than 350 people, and reflect the ethnic population ratios in Malaysia. Regarding expatriate postings, with each new foreign investment of more than U.S.$2 million, five ten-year expatriate postings, including one key posting, are automatically allowed. Additional expatriates may be allowed with sufficient reason. Such deregulations presently play a role in attracting Japanese investment (Morikawa 1988).

Prime Minister Mahathir introduced the "Look East Policy" in December 1981. The policy objective was to promote the industrialization and modernization of Malaysia through learning—particularly with regard to labor ethics, social consciousness, discipline, and managerial skills—from Japan and South Korea, which had attained high postwar economic growth. The Look East Policy also seemed to popularize Japanese-style management: for example, the government started a program to send selected middle-level engineers and employees from government organizations, local companies, and educational organizations to Japanese universities, high-level professional schools, and companies in order to study Japanese engineering and management skills.

Localization of Japanese Business

Localization may be defined as the transfer of the ownership and control of managerial resources from foreign companies to local people. Four major factors in localization include: human resources, capital, materials and parts and components, and technology and management skills.[4]

Human Resources. It has been said that Japanese nationals account for about 1% of the total employees in Japanese-affiliated businesses, which our research also shows. But the ratio of Japanese to local employees varies depending upon position. In addition, due to the Bumiputera policy, the ratio among the local Malay, Chinese, and Indian employees is also important (Kimura 1988).

The ratio of nationals in management at each level is shown in Fig. 1. Japanese account for 13.8% of the total management positions. The

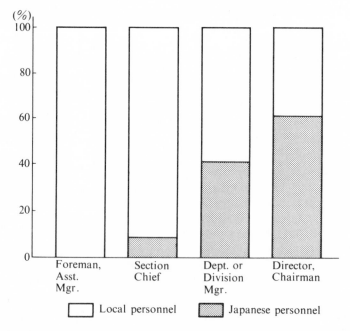

Fig. 1.   Proportions of Japanese and Local Personnel, by Job Category.

---

4. Regarding the theory of localization, see Tatsuo Kimbara, "Kokusai keiei ni okeru genchika no kansei (Possibility of localization in international management)", *Hiroshima Daigaku Keizai Ronso* (Hiroshima University Journal of Economics), Vol. 12, No. 1 (June, 1988).

Table 4.   Ethnic Group Representation in Managerial Jobs, 1987.

Position	Number of People				
	Japanese	Malay	Chinese	Indian	Total
Foreman	0	153	64	49	266
Chief	2	54	84	18	158
Assistant Mgr.	0	62	49	13	124
Manager	8	28	47	11	94
Dept. Manager	25	25	29	0	79
Factory Mgr.	18	1	4	0	23
Division Head	10	5	11	2	28
Director	38	6	4	0	58
Vice-President	0	0	0	0	0
President	14	2	6	0	22
Vice-Chairman	1	0	0	0	1
Chairman	3	5	3	0	11
Total	119	351	301	93	864

	Percentage of Total Managerial Employees			
	Japanese	Malay	Chinese	Indian
Foreman	.0	57.5	24.1	18.4
Chief	1.3	34.2	53.2	11.4
Assistant Mgr.	.0	50.0	39.5	10.5
Manager	8.5	29.8	50.0	11.7
Dept. Manager	31.5	31.6	36.7	.0
Factory Mgr.	78.3	4.3	17.4	.0
Division Head	35.7	17.9	39.3	7.1
Director	65.5	27.6	6.9	.0
Vice-President	.0	.0	.0	.0
President	63.6	9.1	27.3	.0
Vice-Chairman	100.0	.0	.0	.0
Chairman	27.3	45.5	27.3	.0
Total	13.8	40.6	34.3	10.8

	Ethnic Group Representation in Local Managerial Employees		
	Malay	Chinese	Indian
Foreman	57.5	24.1	18.4
Chief	34.6	53.8	11.5
Assistant Mgr.	50.0	39.5	10.5
Manager	32.6	54.7	12.8
Dept. Manager	46.3	53.7	.0
Factory Mgr.	20.0	80.0	.0
Division Head	27.8	61.1	11.1
Director	27.6	6.9	.0
Vice-President	80.0	20.0	.0
President	25.0	75.0	.0
Vice-Chairman	.0	.0	.0
Chairman	62.5	37.5	.0
Total	47.1	40.4	12.5

ratio decreases to 0.0% and 8.5% at the level of foreman and assistant manager and section chief respectively. It goes up to 40.8% at the level of departmental manager, the central figure of daily management. The ratio of more than 60.0% at the level of directors and chairman is the highest. Compared with the other three nations, the ratio of local people is high at the level of departmental manager and particularly high at the level of director. Considering these figures it is possible to say that localization is moving ahead as a result of the government's strong localization policy.

Japanese companies generally hire local employees roughly according to the ethnic ratio of the population in Malaysia (Table 5). If, however, we look at the ratios based upon position, the ratio of Malays, who traditionally have not entered business, decreases while that of Chinese increases as the positions ascend. At the level of chairman and director the ratios of Malays are 45.5% and 27.6% respectively (Table 4). These ratios are high due to the Bumiputera policy, but the positions seem to be nominal. The ratios of Chinese at the level of section chief, factory manager, and president are 4.7%, 80.0%, and 75.3% respectively and much higher than that of the Malays. The ratio of Indians as a whole is 12.5%, roughly the same as that of the total population, but they usually occupy positions only up to section chief. A ratio of only 11.1% exists at the level of divisional manager.

Capital. Because ownership of capital is related to the control and management of companies, most countries regulate the ownership by foreigners. Malaysia is no exception. In Malaysia, moreover, ownership among races is strictly determined by the NEP, which aimed to increase the ratio of Malay capital to 30%, to limit foreign capital to 30%, and to hold the remaining 40% for Chinese and other Malaysians. The NEP ratios were, however, altered by the Fifth Economic Plan of 1986, by which the ratio of Malay capital was decreased to 22.2%. This change

Table 5. Ethnic Group Employment by Japanese Enterprises, 1987.

Enterprise Ethnic group	Matsushita Electric	Clarion	Pioneer
Malay	49.7%	52%	75%
Chinese	30.8	40	22
Indian	18.0	8	3
Other	1.5	—	—

was made because the strict capital ownership policy reconstruction negatively influenced the Malaysian economy in spite of the fact that Japanese investment in Malaysia and other countries was distinguished by high levels of minority joint venture.[5]

The ratio of Japanese capital to total foreign capital is 60.1% on average, which is high compared with Thailand and Indonesia, but not high compared with Singapore, which is subject to fewer regulations. This situation might be attributed to the fact that recently many export-oriented companies have invested in Malaysia, and the government has relaxed ownership regulation of such companies. As mentioned earlier, the Malaysian government has tended to relax its policies because it considers foreign capital, particularly Japanese, as the locomotive driving recovery of the economy. It is said unofficially that the government will allow companies that do not export to have 100% ownership within a few years; the ratio of Japanese capital should then increase even more.

Local Procurement of Materials and Parts and Components. The governments of most developing countries want foreign companies to procure materials and parts and components locally in order to prevent a deterioration of the balance of payment and to develop local supporting industries. The trend of the ratio of local procurement by Japanese companies is shown in Fig. 2. The ratio drops from 80.0% in 1970 to 54.9% in 1975 to 51.8% in 1980. Since 1985 it has figured around 50%. The ratio declined drastically after 1975 because before 1973 most of the companies that invested in Malaysia were producing import substitution products, and it was possible for them to procure locally. After 1973, however, companies mainly in the electric and electronics industries increased investments in Malaysia—and these companies could not procure parts and components locally because the supporting industries had not been developed fully.

This becomes obvious when we look at the ratio of localization of each industry group. Only the automobile industry continuously increased the localization ratio, from 50.0% in 1985 to 60.0% in 1986 and to 65.0% in 1987. The electric and electronics industries, on the other hand, did not change the ratio, maintaining a 60% level between 1975 and 1980, and decreasing rapidly after 1980: 39.1% in 1985, 40.0% in 1986, and 37.5% in 1987. Other industries did not change the localization ratio

---

5. For the characteristics of Japanese investment in Malaysia, see Chee Peng Lim and Lee Pho Ping, *The Role of Japanese Direct Investment in Malaysia* (Singapore: Institute of Southeast Asian Studies, 1979), and Kunio Yoshihara, *Japanese Investment in Southeast Asia* (Honolulu: University Press of Hawaii, 1978).

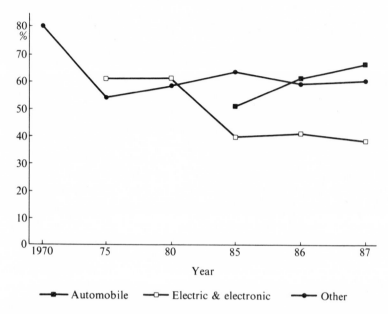

Fig. 2.   Localization Ratios, by Industry.

much between 1970 and 1987 (see Fig. 2).

A second survey by the Japanese Embassy and the JETRO KL Center in Malaysia shows the lower ratios of local procurement by Japanese businesses. In 1986 Japanese companies procured materials, parts and components from Japan, 28% from local companies, and 18% from third countries. When procuring from Japan, the Japanese subsidiaries rely upon their parent companies for 90% of their procurement. Even in the case of local procurement, more than 20% is from other Japanese companies in Malaysia. Thus true local procurement by Japanese companies may be less than 25%.

The reasons for the low rate of local procurement include lack of technological precision, delay of delivery, high cost, and the quality of management in local companies. Many Japanese companies therefore provide technological assistance and sometimes even production equipment and facilities to local companies under subcontract in order to secure satisfactory products.[6]

Transfer of Technology and Management Skills. Transfer of technology

6. Unpublished Joint Research on Japanese Affiliated Companies in Malaysia by Embassy in Malaysia and JETRO KL Centers (1987).

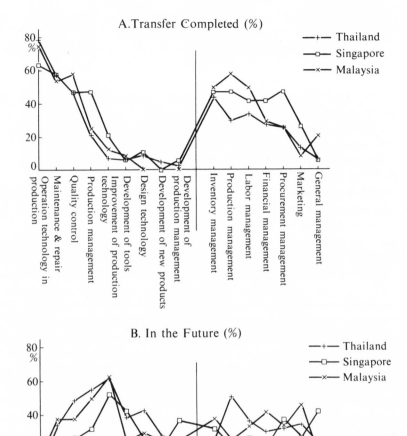

Fig. 3. Transfer of Technology and Management in Thailand, Singapore, and Malaysia.

and management skill is the central localization problem for Japanese business. Local people sometimes complain that Japanese companies are hesitant to transfer technology and management skills when compared to their Western counterparts. We will now examine the real situation of the transfer of technology and management.

We classified technology into nine types: (1) operational, (2) maintenance, (3) quality control, (4) technology improvement, (5) production, (6) design, (7) new product development, (8) molding development, and (9) production facilities development (Fig. 3).

Regarding operational, maintenance, and quality control technologies, the management staffs of many companies think that these have already been transferred, Seventy-five percent, 58.3%, and 54.2% of the companies have transferred production, quality control, and maintenance technologies, respectively. Most companies responded that production, technology improvement, and molding development technologies should be transferred in the near future, although some companies stated that they have already transferred these technologies. No companies answered that they have already transferred new product development, design, and production facilities development technologies. Less than 25% of the companies responded that they will transfer these technologies, and most are negative toward transferring them.

Management skills, which allocate resources and coordinate the flow of products, were classified into seven types: (1) labor, (2) production, (3) procurement, (4) inventory, (5) marketing, (6) financial, and (7) general. The majority of companies reported that they have already transferred labor, production, and inventory management skills. Regarding financial and procurement management, the companies that plan to transfer them in the future outnumber those that have already transferred them, though many companies reported that the transfer has already taken place.

Only 8.3% of the companies answered that they have transferred marketing management while 45.8% plan to transfer at a later time. The reason for the delay is that marketing as well as finance in Japanese subsidiaries in Malaysia are controlled by their headquarters (as they are in local factories in Japan) or by subsidiaries in Singapore and Hong Kong. In addition, Malaysia still pays more attention to production than to marketing.

It is notable that the answers given by respondents to this survey differed greatly as a function of the language used by respondents—that is, Japanese or English. These differences will be analyzed in detail in the next section.

Evaluation of Japanese-Style Management in Malaysia

The questionnaires were sent out in both Japanese and English; 16 managers responded in Japanese, eight in English. We can assume that Japanese managers answered in Japanese and local managers in English. It was therefore determined that differences in the content of answers in Japanese and English must indicate a gap in perception toward the effectiveness of Japanese-style management and transfer of technology and of management. Our analysis follows.

Application of Japanese-style Management

Rather than developing in the questionnaire a discussion about what Japanese-style management is, we simply listed 21 items that are usually thought of as factors in Japanese-style management. The differences in the content of answers given in Japanese and English are shown in Fig. 4. On the whole, the applicability of Japanese-style management was evaluated more highly in the English answers than in the Japanese. This difference arises from the distinction between expectation and reality. Japanese managers tend to think that the application of Japanese-style management is more difficult than they had expected, while local counterparts tend to think that the application is not as difficult as they had expected.

Regarding the possibility of the application, or adaptability, of Japanese-style management, "career development," "canteen facilities," "QC circle," "priority given to the shop floor," and "egalitarianism" were more positively evaluated in the Japanese answers than in the English. "Career development" and "priority given to the shop floor" were particularly given great value differences in the Japanese and English answers, 31.3 points for the Japanese and 25.5 points for the English. Among those factors more positively evaluated in English than in Japanese were "recreation," "company uniform," "job rotation," "lifetime employment," and "informal relations." Except for lifetime employment, these practices are adaptable because they fit traditional Malay customs.

If, on the other hand, the impossibility (that is, the ineffectiveness) of adaptability of Japanese-style management is examined, 43.8% of the Japanese answers and 50% of the English indicate the inadaptability of "lifetime employment," and 31.3% of the Japanese answers and 25% of English indicate the inadaptability of "seniority system." It is very interesting that two of the most distinguished characteristics of Japanese-style management are negatively evaluated

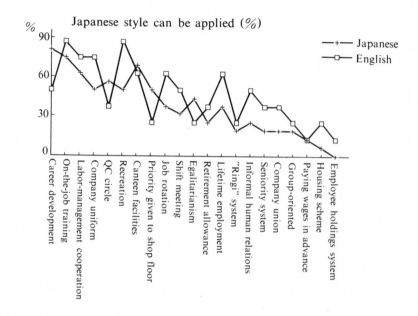

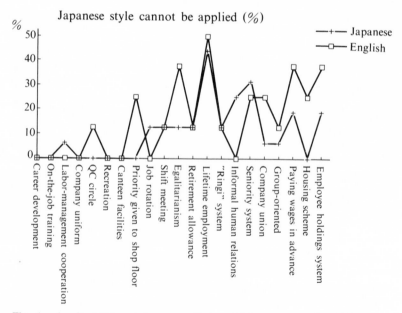

Fig. 4. Applicability of Japanese Style of Management in Malaysia:
Answers Based on Language Used.

in the process of adaptation in Malaysia.

The English answers are generally more negative about the adaptation of Japanese-style management. "Egalitarianism," "priority given to the shop floor," "in-house union," "housing scheme," "paying wages in advance," and "employees' holding system" are given quite negative adaptability values. It can thus be understood that local managers are very skeptical about the applicability of welfare schemes.

In the case of "informal relations," there is a big difference between the Japanese and English answers: many Japanese answers indicated inadaptability while all the English answers indicate adaptability. Japanese managers probably think that local employees are not sociable in Japanese terms, while local managers think that they have good informal relations because of the difference in customs.

It is also very interesting that while many English answers evaluate adaptability positively, many negative answers were also given. It may be concluded that the opinion of local managers regarding the adaptability of Japanese-style management in Malaysia is polarized.

Transfer of Technology

There are some differences between the Japanese and English evaluations of technology transfer. On the whole, English answers indicate the completion of technology transfer more than Japanese ones do, and local managers evaluated it positively. This contrasts with the criticism that Japanese companies are slow in transferring technology (Fig. 5).

As for "operational technology," "quality control," and "maintenance," 100%, 87.5%, and 75%, respectively, of the English answers say that they have completed the transfer. Among the Japanese answers, 62.5%, 43.5%, and 43.5% report the completion of transfer, while 25%, 50%, and 50% report that these technologies should be transferred in the future. "Production technology," "improvement of technology," and "development of molding" followed "operational technology," "quality control," and "maintenance" in terms of completion of transfer. Twenty-five percent of both the Japanese and English answers show completion of the transfer of production technology. Regarding "improvement of technology" and "development of molding," however, 6.3% of the Japanese answers show the completion of transfer, which is much less than the 25.0% and 12.5% given in the English answers.

There are no answers that show the completion of transfer in "production," "development of new product," and "design" technology, but English answers indicate a higher expectation of transfer in the future than do the Japanese. Local managers expect the transfer of such

A.Transfer completed

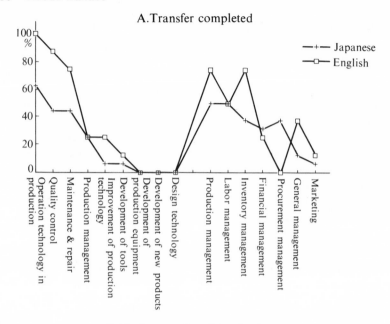

B.To be transferred in the future

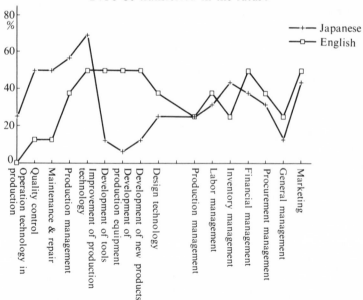

Fig. 5.   Progress of Technology and Management Transfer: Answers
          Based on Language Used.

highly dynamic technology as "production equipment," "development of new product," and "design technology," while Japanese managers think that this would be very difficult. Such discrepancy is caused by the different understanding of technology transfer held by Japanese and local managers. Japanese managers point out that Malaysian interests hold that "transfer of technology" is the same as "localization of post" and that post transfer will bring technology transfer. Japanese managers insist that post transfer also means delegation of authority, while technology transfer is one of the means for industrialization (which means how the recipient country becomes able to produce what they previously could not).

Japanese managers moreover classify the nature of technology into two types: static and dynamic. Static technology is that which is used at the beginning of operations in the host country, and its characteristics are apparent in such operation technology as assembly and operation. In this case the transfer objective is very clear and easy to carry out. In fact, local managers indicated that most static technologies have been transferred.

Dynamic technology, on the other hand, includes improvement and development technology. Japanese managers say that today's companies are always studying and developing new technologies and that the speed of technological changes is accelerating. Therefore if companies want to have competitive advantages, they have to provide the world market with higher quality products at lower prices. At the same time they have to compensate for increasing wages and other costs by higher profits created through increasing productivity and lowering costs. Companies are thus always under pressure to introduce dynamic technology, and new technologies to be transferred are continually being created. Unless the local subsidiary has a modern, large-scale institute for technological development, the transfer of dynamic technology is difficult; small scale local subsidiaries with limited local human resources and technological ability pose significant obstacles to such transfers (Japanese Chamber of Commerce and Industries 1986).

Transfer of Management

With respect to the transfer of management, no differences between Japanese and English answers are found for "production management" and "labor management." More than half of both the Japanese and English answers show the completion of transfer. There are, however, large gaps in the perception of the transfer of "inventory management" and "procurement management." Higher rates of completion for "inventory management" are found in the English answers while higher rates for "procurement management" are found in the Japanese. As for "general management," few Japanese answers show the completion of transfer, and many indicate the opinion that such transfer will be impossible in the future. Local managers, in contrast, seem to be more optimistic about the transfer of general management.

It is very interesting that few answers in either Japanese or English indicate the completion of marketing management transfer. The reason for the delay in such transfer is that marketing as well as finance in Japanese subsidiaries in Malaysia are controlled by their headquarters (as they are in local factories in Japan) or by subsidiaries in Singapore and Hong Kong. General trading companies play an important role in marketing in the case of joint ventures involving such Japanese trading companies as Mitsubishi Corporation and Mitsui Co., Ltd. Many answers do however show that marketing will be transferred in the future. Many companies also want to develop their own marketing in the future.[7]

Siea Lee Mei Ling, in her survey on Malaysian manufacturing, points out that marketing, human resource management, and information systems are management fields in which management has relatively less interest. It is a serious problem that management does not pay attention to such consumer and industrial needs, which are most important to business management (Siea Lee Mei Ling 1986).

Cultural Aspects of Japanese Business in Malaysia

The Meaning of Japanese Foreign Business Operations

As we have seen, localization of managerial resources has developed, but local people in Malaysia and other ASEAN countries are critical of Japanese businesses when compared with their Western counterparts. According to Ah Ba Sim, who conducted research on the organizational relationship between Malaysian subsidiaries and their foreign parent companies, there is less decentralization in the Japanese subsidiaries compared with their American and British counterparts. There are, for example, few (and sometimes no) expatriates in Western subsidiaries in Malaysia, while in Japanese companies Japanese nationals account for

---

7. NEC Malaysia hired a staff member for long-term planning because they want to develop their own strategies, including marketing. Interview with Eiichi Murata, M.D. of NEC Malaysia. See also Chee Peng Lim & Lee Pho Ping, "Japanese joint ventures in Malaysia," in Jomo, ed., *The Sun Also Set*, p.273.

about 1% of the total number of employees (Ah Ba Sim 1978).

Local managers also complain that Japanese companies hesitate to transfer technology and management while their Western counterparts quickly do. They make the further criticism that Japanese people in host countries do not want to socialize with them.[8] It is said that when they organize tennis games and dance parties, Japanese managers leave quickly after giving a speech and that this kind of thing is not done by Western managers.

Why is this kind of criticism raised by the local managers? What is the difference between Japanese businessmen and their Western counterparts? The culture of these countries is probably reflected in the difference. In this section the cultural aspects of Japanese business will be analyzed and the problems of localization will be considered.[9] These issues can be discussed from three points of view: the internationalization process of Japanese business; cultural differences between Japan and Malaysia; and the social characteristics of Malaysia.

When Japanese businesses start operations in foreign countries, they introduce ways of management that they have established in Japan. If indigenous business and management systems of host countries are the same as those of Japan, Japanese-style management can be adopted in the host countries smoothly and without conflicts. If, on the other hand, there are differences between the two systems, then incoming Japanese business will face conflicts that it must subsequently try to solve.

Japanese companies have had problems probably due to the timing of their entrance into Malaysia and the different cultural elements of Malaysia. Regarding some companies that have been operating in Malaysia for more than twenty years, however, the understanding of Japanese-style management developed among the local people after the Malaysian government developed the Look East Policy.

The initial problem faced by Japanese companies in Malaysia arose because Japanese companies started their foreign operations after their Western counterparts had already established operations and created a management style there. The incoming Japanese companies found in Malaysia a management system greatly influenced by British-style management. British companies have historically controlled Malaysian business, particularly the primary industries including mining and

---

8. Regarding the evaluation of Japanese business, see the Institute for the Developing Economy, *Report of Effectiveness of Economic Cooperation: Basic Data on Thailand and Malaysia* (Tokyo: Institute of Developing Economies, March 1986), pp. 308–314.

9. Regarding these questions, see the pioneering study of Hideki Imaoka, "Japanese management in Malaysia," *Southeast Asian Studies*, Vol. 22, No. 4 (March, 1985).

plantations. Indigenous businessmen have mostly been Chinese, running small retail and wholesale businesses and food and drink manufacturing businesses as well as large-scale banking corporations. In such indigenous businesses family management generally is seen, which is very different from today's modern business management.

Modern industrial businesses developed in Malaysia in the 1960s, and it was at this time, when the Malaysian labor force began to experience modern management, that Japanese companies began investing in Malaysia. Prior to Japanese investment differing management cultures had developed between high-level managers and factory laborers. Managers usually had higher educations, often British-style, and had clear ideas about management. Management of factory laborers, on the other hand, had not been established.

When Japanese companies moved production bases to Malaysia, they employed middle managers with Western ways of thinking who had to learn to understand Japanese-style management in order to develop smooth operations. But the contract system, the decision-making process, the style of communication, the evaluation of employees, the promotion system, and human relations in Japanese companies were very different from those they were used to.

Malaysia is a kind of "qualification society," much influenced by British tradition. University graduates want to be treated as such, and to be given such privileges as their own offices. In Japanese companies, however, they are treated the same as lower-educated employees. Because Malaysian university graduates have trouble with such treatment, Japanese-style management has a poor reputation, and they often leave Japanese companies. Many Japanese companies in Malaysia alternatively employ high school graduates and train them to become managers. Such high school graduates know that they cannot become managers in Western companies. In addition, for Chinese-educated Chinese, who took higher-education degrees in Nanyang University in Singapore, or in Taiwan, and whose English is comparatively less fluent, the Japanese firm presents the best-paying alternative because it is more difficult for them to get positions in European companies. They therefore tend to stay in Japanese companies longer.[10]

Malaysian workers are moreover more money oriented than Japanese. In contrast with Japanese practice, they hold QC circle activities within

---

10. Discussions of Malaysian society and Japanese businesses there are based mainly upon interviews with Japanese managers. Wendy Smith, "A Japanese factory in Malaysia: Ethnicity as a management ideology," in Jomo, ed., *The Sun Also Sets*, p.286.

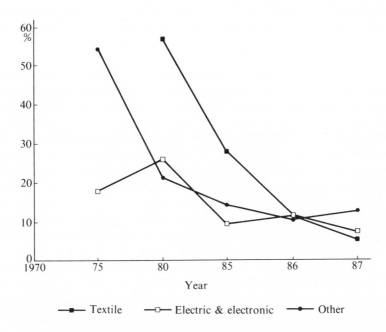

Fig. 6. Employment Turnover by Industry.

regular working hours, and they do not hesitate to job hop when they can get better wages and salaries. Job hopping differs greatly from Japanese employment customs, and most Japanese companies consider it a problem. Employee turnover in Malaysia has decreased rapidly from 39.6% in 1975 to 27.0% in 1980, 13.4% in 1985, 11.0% in 1986, and 10.6% in 1987. But turnover rates vary with the industry. Turnover in the textile industry, for example, decreased drastically from 56.9% in 1980 to 27.8% in 1985, 11.6% in 1985, and 5.2% in 1987. Certain other industries also decreased from 54.2% in 1975 to 21.4% in 1980, 14.3% in 1985, 10.4% in 1986, and 12.9% in 1987. In the electronic and electrics industries, however, the rates fluctuated (Fig. 6).

It might seem that the decline in turnover is due to a wider understanding of Japanese-style management, but most Japanese managers say that it has been caused by the severe recession in the Malaysian economy and that as the economy recovers the rate will go up.[11]

---

11. Generally speaking, local managers are satisfied with Japanese practices of management. See Imaoka, "Japanese management in Malaysia," p.23.

According to our findings, when Malaysian employees move to other companies, on average one person goes to Japanese companies in the same industry, 1.7 persons to Japanese companies in different industries, 2.5 persons to Western companies, and 2.0 persons to local companies. Compared with other countries, in Malaysia more employees move to Western companies; this indicates difference in reputation held by Western companies with long histories in Malaysia and their Japanese counterparts, which entered Malaysia relatively recently.

Roles of Middle Management

In order to adapt to Western standards and local culture, Japanese companies try to localize management. For this purpose, Japanese expatriates play an important role in creating a new management culture in which local managers give directions to local workers. In Western companies, integration between local managers and Western expatriates has been attained by Western standards.[12]

Regarding the local company's organizational structure and posts, Japanese executives and financial managers from the parent company sit on the local board of directors. In most cases the local personnel manager is a member of the board of directors. Under the president of the company generally are personnel, financial, technology, sales, and quality control departments. Many companies post locals in the position of personnel manager. Where more than one factory exists, we can sometimes find local factory managers, and a Japanese engineer is usually posted as the manager's technological assistant. When the company has just one factory, the same situation exists at the sections level. Local employees are posted at the lower levels.

Japanese companies further establish various committees in order to support the formal organization. Some committees are delegated to study such production issues as safety and health, improvement proposals, quality control, production techniques, procurement management, and office management. Other committees are related to the lives of employees, including such areas as the company newsletter, friendship clubs, and so on. Committee chairpersons are generally local employees except in the cases of important committees like quality control and procurement.

Japanese companies certainly have more employees sent from the parent company than do their Western counterparts, which seems to be

---

12. Regarding the theory of hybrid culture, see the excellent study by Kichiro Hayashi, *Cross Cultural Interface Management* (Tokyo: Yuhikaku, 1985).

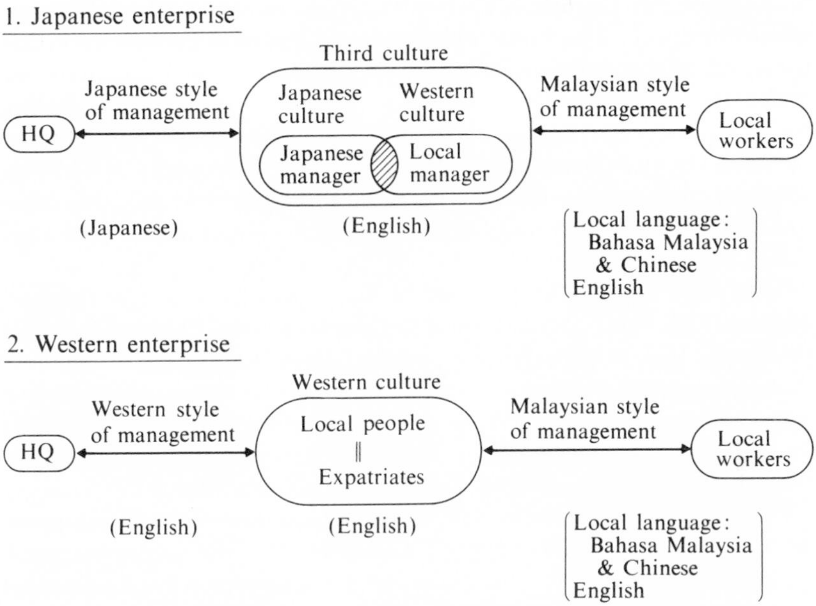

1. Japanese enterprise

2. Western enterprise

Fig. 7.   Communication Channels in Japanese and Western Enterprises.

due to the problems in communication. The differences between Japanese and Western companies regarding communication between parent company and local subsidiary, from the point of view of management and culture, are illustrated in Fig. 7.

Communication between headquarters and the local subsidiary's high-level managers is based upon Japanese-style management and the Japanese language. Local middle managers, on the other hand, hold Western standards because they were educated in Malaysia or Western countries, and usually they can speak English fluently. The ratio of English usage in Malaysia is 79.2%, which is very high compared with the 30–40% found in such other countries as Thailand, Indonesia, and even Singapore. The ratio of Japanese-only usage in Malaysia is very low, 4.2% compared with more than 10% in other countries, and the combination of Japanese and English is 16.7%, which is very high compared with other countries. The situation in Malaysia contrasts highly with that of Thailand and Indonesia, where local languages are used more often.

In Malaysia, communication between Japanese and local managers may go smoothly (Imaoka 1985), but even if Japanese and local managers speak English to each other, their cultural backgrounds are very different. Few Japanese managers are educated in Western countries, and on the other side, few local managers can speak Japanese and understand Japanese culture. In addition, as few Japanese managers can speak Bahasa Malaysia, there are some problems in communication between Japanese managers and local workers.

When conflicts arise between Japanese and local managers, they have to be solved through compromise. This results in the creation of a so-called hybrid culture, that is, a third cultural body.

Differing attitudes and values between managers and workers in Malaysia arise not only because of the society's racial plurality, but also because of its language plurality. Bahasa Malaysia and English are used in communication between local middle mangers and workers. In the textile industry, where many Chinese are employed, Chinese is added. In addition, as a result of the Bahasa Malaysia Policy, young Malay people are becoming poor in English as the use of Bahasa Malaysia is becoming popular. It is possible in the future that the same situation as now exists in Thailand and Indonesia—the prevalence of local language use—may occur in Malaysia, although that will take time.

As one means of communication, manuals in the local language are often used at the worker level because such jobs are relatively simple. In addition, the role of the local middle management is important because at the worker level the ratio of in-house lectures, quality control, and (local) OJT is high.

As most of the Japanese are not good at the local language and cannot communicate directly with the workers, there are reports of workers complaining that Japanese managers treat them with contempt. Local managers sometimes bear the brunt of such criticism. At the level of foreman, section chief, and assistant manager, however, the use of English-language manuals, OJT, and the chance of working with Japanese staff increases, resulting in more contact with Japanese managers.

The reason for the increasing use of manuals in the local language at the level of departmental manager appears to be that Malay managers are given such positions due to the Bumiputera policy. This is an additional reason for the increased number of Malay managers at that level, and for the low rate of in-Japan training for departmental and factory managers in comparison with other countries' analogous figures.

Relationship between Headquarters and Subsidiaries

Difficult problems exist in the communications between the headquarters in Japan and the subsidiary companies in Malaysia. Despite this, needless to say, as Japanese headquarters do not want to change their systems, Japanese managers in the subsidiaries play an important communications role. In any case, it is not difficult for local managers and workers to understand the systems put forth by headquarters because many Japanese are sent to the subsidiaries. As mentioned earlier, the ratio of Japanese at the section chief level is 44.0%, which is higher than that of any other middle-management level. In Japanese companies, which emphasize production management and quality control, the section chief management level is most important in creating good relations with the local managers and workers.

In order to solve the problems in communication between headquarters and subsidiaries, Japanese subsidiaries recently began hiring Malaysian students who studied in Japan through the auspices of two programs that started under the Look East Policy. One program is the dispatchment of Eastern Technical Trainees. The first group of 132 trainees, who were selected from government organizations, business companies, and educational and training organizations, went to Japan in September 1982. After studying Japanese language for half a year, they receive training based upon OJT for half a year in a Japanese organization similar to the Malaysian one they were sent from. About 230 students are annually sent to Japan, and 1,600 trainees have completed the program to date.

The second program sends Malaysian students to Japanese universities. Excellent high school graduates are selected first to study Japanese for one year and then to study Japanese high school subjects in Japanese for a second year at the University of Malaya. After these two years, they are sent to Japanese universities through the Japanese Ministry of Education. They enter as freshman students and are usually enrolled in such practical subjects as engineering, management, and economics. They are educated no differently from the Japanese students. Alternatively, some students in the program are sent to higher vocational schools after studying Japanese for one year.

The first batch of graduates from higher vocational schools returned to Malaysia in March 1986, and the first batch of university graduates in March of the following year. These students were employed by Japanese subsidiaries in Malaysia. They had mastered Japanese and understood the culture because they had studied with Japanese students. The problems caused by the dual structure of Japanese companies in the process of globalization may possibly be solved by the employment of such students because the role of Japanese expatriates in translating Japanese systems into local ones may be more readily accepted by the students. The creation of a hybrid culture in the subsidiary companies might therefore be easier (Takano 1988).

Conclusion

We now summarize the findings of our study of the characteristics and problems of Japanese businesses in Malaysia.

First, Japanese businesses have problems in the process of globalization because they started later than their European and American counterparts. When Japanese companies enter foreign countries they encounter the established Western business culture as well as the local culture.

Second, it takes time to create a hybrid culture in a company. We see that the longer the Japanese companies operate in Malaysia the more highly they evaluate local employees and the more they localize.

Third, Japanese expatriates in the subsidiaries play a very important role in the process of creating a hybrid culture. There is, however, a possibility that this role can be taken over by the local employees who studied in Japan.

Fourth, the Look East Policy of the Malaysian government plays an important role in the transfer of Japanese-style management. Under this policy students are sent to Japan to aquire Japanese production and management skills thereby publicizing the good points and potential of Japanese style management.

Finally, the management of workers has not been established in Malaysian companies as it has been in European and American companies. Japanese-type management and Western can now coexist in Malaysia. In the long run, the strong possibility of the creation of a Malaysian-style management exists. Malaysia is similar to Japan in that both countries have experienced the development of industrial and business society prior to the transformation of the traditional social system, and therefore the values of the traditional systems may be applied in management. In Malaysia, for example, the traditional idea of mutual aid called *Gotong Royong* and the decision-making process called *Musya Warat* may be applied in an adapted form to business systems, resulting in the creation of a Malaysian style of management.

Part **III**

DISCUSSION

Beyond Japanese-Style Management in ASEAN: Assessments and Adaptations*

The Role of Japanese-Affliated Companies in ASEAN Countries

YAMASHITA: It is important to discuss the role of Japanese direct investment and evaluate the management practices of Japanese-affiliated companies in the ASEAN countries. Japanese foreign investment has sharply increased in recent years, and the yen appreciation after the Plaza Agreement in September 1985 increased its influence on each host country.

Japan was a latecomer to foreign investment practices. However, it has already become one of the biggest foreign investors in the world. Its influence cannot be underestimated. Japanese capital seems to have been welcomed by the host countries in the first stage, mainly because it created new jobs. Japanese-affiliated companies at present employ about one million local people in Asia. But attitudes toward Japanese economic power have been changing as its influence has grown. Some in the host countries, including many Americans, seem to consider Japanese foreign investment formidable.

It became necessary to study carefully the role of Japanese direct investment in the host countries, and the problems it posed. A research group based at Hiroshima University has worked together with ASEAN scholars in studying Japanese investment and the practices of Japanese joint ventures in the ASEAN countries during the past four to five years. We tried to evaluate Japanese-style management and to identify the new directions of management in Japanese-affiliated companies abroad in the future.

In the first session of the Hiroshima Conference, we discussed the presence of Japanese-affiliated companies in Southeast Asian countries from the macroeconomic point of view. We looked at the various

---

* This is a condensation of the discussion at the Conference "Beyond Japanese-Style Management in ASEAN: Assessment and Adaptation," which was held in Hiroshima City, October 12–13, 1989.

269

contributions of Japanese direct investment in this region, such as job creation, technology transfer, the foreign exchange earnings of exports, and the development of related industries. We also referred to the effects—problematic and otherwise—which Japanese investment caused (see Chapters 1–4).

We would like to start the discussion by asking why Japanese direct investment has suddenly increased in this region, what its features are, and reasons why ASEAN countries have encouraged it.

PASUK: Japanese direct investment since 1985 is significantly more export-oriented. In Thailand, the Board of Investment approved 260 Japanese investment projects between January 1986 and May 1988. Of these 79% were classified as export-oriented firms which planned to export 80% of their products. The exports of Japanese firms included electronics components, electrical machinery, processed food, and auto parts. The same trend is observed in the rest of the ASEAN countries.

This trend cannot be explained only by a desire for markets or for cheap labor as a motive for foreign investment. We should pay attention to the structural changes in the Japanese economy, i.e., increased maturity and the structural shift towards high-tech industries and the trend toward globalization of Japanese firms. As a result, Japanese firms have begun production in the ASEAN countries for export. These changes have been accelerated by the yen appreciation and Japan's trade friction with the U.S. and the European countries.

The demand for foreign investment in host countries is also an important factor in the invitation to Japanese firms. Local governments provided incentives to attract the foreign capital which was expected to promote industrialization and exports. Local entrepreneurs utilized Japanese investment for profit-making. Both government and private or state capitalists recognized that foreign capital could contribute benefits, particularly in the form of new technology, additional employment, and increased efficiency levels of domestic firms.

In the 1980s, ASEAN member countries faced a fiscal and debt crisis, led mainly by the decline of oil prices. Government policies toward foreign direct investment changed to promote more deregulation and privatization which benefited private domestic and foreign capital. Thus, fiscal and debt problems had a direct impact on the attitude of ASEAN governments to the inflow of foreign capital, and the accompanying recession also influenced the attitude of domestic capital. During this period, particularly the period after 1985, Japanese firms looked for production sites which would serve as the export bases for world markets.

ABO: I think Prof. Pasuk has succeeded in explaining the causes of the sharp increase of Japanese foreign direct investment in the ASEAN countries in 1980s, by focusing on the demand from the host countries. Their demand for Japanese investment has been centered on export-oriented industries or firms, with one of the aims being to improve the balance of payments. However, the response of Japanese companies is to establish sophisticated factories equipped with high-tech machines which require qualified technicians and managers. As a result, the host country needs to import more capital goods, key components, and high-quality materials from Japan. The trade imbalance will not be improved, though it will not worsen either.

The second question is related. The greater the demand for Japanese investment, the more the host country requires Japanese coordinators. In order to maintain the quality of products and the efficiency of operation, local joint ventures need to increase the number of Japanese managers and technical experts. Although the Japanese-affiliated companies may transfer high technology to the host country, human factors are also involved in the process of technology transfer.

PASUK: We have to import more capital goods from Japan in the beginning, but I think there is a difference here between the type of importing which took place from Japan in the 1980s and that of the 1970s. If capital imports enhance the productive capacity of the industrial sector and help to deepen industrialization in the host country, then at a later date we can begin export manufacturing, and that could solve some of the problems. Of course there is variation from country to country in the rate at which each ASEAN member country can absorb these capital goods.

So I am not very pessimistic about that. In the case of Malaysia, this policy turned out to be rather a white elephant, and probably was wrong policy to start with. It involved a great deal of importing of capital goods which did not raise the productive capacity of the export sector of Malaysia, so it became a burden.

Regarding the question of whether increased Japanese investment will also increase the number of Japanese coordinators, in Thailand we need these expatriates because we have a shortage of skilled manpower, and in fact the government is even thinking of recruiting in the U.S. and other countries. So for the time being, like in the case of Thailand, there is a confluence of interest occurring, and I don't think Japanese personnel are going to be a problem. My personal view is that we cannot have technology transfer without having the expatriates there teaching the local people what to do. So the question is whether we are ready to learn from these expatriates who are working in Thailand, in Malaysia, or in Indonesia.

HIRANO: Japanese enterprises are less concerned with the socio-political situation in ASEAN countries than are European or American companies. Don't we need to awaken the Japanese manager's consciousness of socio-political circumstances in host countries?

SUTHY: I agree that Japanese companies are less concerned with socio-cultural issues in the host country, and in this respect I feel that Japanese companies lag behind U.S. and European firms. But during the last few years the situation has been changing. Recently, Keidanren has also paid a great deal of attention to the cultural aspects. Especially, the big corporations have improved their understanding of environmental and ecological problems. They are refraining from using certain chemicals which will destroy the global ecology and tend to increase the "greenhouse effect." In this sense, the Japanese firms are less aggressive than Euro-American companies.

HIRANO: There is a serious problem when we operate a business in the form of a joint venture in Southeast Asia. When the Japanese side of the joint venture wants to expand its business in the host country, local partners often refuse because they cannot afford the additional capital. As a result the joint venture is not able to expand its business.

SUTHY: Often in joint ventures the local investors are trying to earn quick profits. It depends on the scale of the enterprise. In Thailand big firms also have a vision of longer-term cooperation, but smaller local firms may have the problem of raising additional funds when their Japanese counterpart wants to increase the capital fund. Also, many of the Japanese firms are part of *keiretsu* groups of enterprises. Their major aim is to increase their share of the market, and they sometimes do not care about losses. If the local partner is asked to increase the amount of capital in such a situation, he may not be able to afford it, but the Japanese company can, because it will be financed by the member bank or other member firms of the group, as in the case of Mitsubishi, Mitsui, and so on.

PRIJONO: It is true that local entrepreneurs want a quick result. This is sometimes related to licensing and control by the government. The terms for the granting of licenses can be—and are—easily changed in Indonesia. Such changes have been made in the past. Companies with these licenses and government support are able to grow rapidly. When they engage in a joint venture, they want to see quick results. They cannot wait 25 or 30 years. They can count on just five years, because every five years there is an election. Business people are afraid of political reform, especially changes in economic policies, law, and systems.

OKADA: The international division of labor also has a strong impact on the direction of economic development in developing countries. Under the influence of foreign investment from advanced countries, one country can accelerate its industrialization through the transfer of higher technology and can export manufactured products, but others do not. So investment seems to generate economic inequality among developing countries, and especially in the ASEAN countries. We should recognize that the international division of labor has a tendency to widen the inequality among ASEAN countries.

SUTHY: Before the adjustment of exchange rates in September 1985, the new international division of labor had been eroded because of automation and robot use in the advanced countries: several production processes that had been relocated in developing countries in the 1960s and 1970s were returned to the advanced countries. After 1985, however, the global adjustment of exchange rates brought about a rapid outflow of foreign direct investment, so the "new internationalization" has been revived again. I feel that this is the actual logic of the capital accumulation process. The tendency basically is toward differentiation and also toward technical absorption by the host country. So I agree that in this aspect of technological absorptive capacity, various host countries are different. The investors will choose the particular levels of products they will relocate. So this particular selection and investment strategy then will result in unequal development in terms of technology and other aspects.

Features of Japanese-Style Management: Is Japanese Style Unique?

YAMASHITA: Foreign scholars and managers have paid a great deal of attention to Japanese companies and their ways of management, because they believed that the economic development of Japan was led by private enterprises and that its secret lay in their management style. Both Japanese and foreign observers have tended to emphasize that the management style of Japanese companies was different from those of Euro-American companies, and focused on the uniqueness of the Japanese management practices. We would like to examine here what the features of the Japanese-style management are, and compare them with Western ways of management.

TOMITA: What had been gradually formulated in Japan by the 1970s can be called a "logic of human talent" as against the "logic of capital" of Western management. This is a "logic" which aims at achieving long-run optimization supported by internally nurtured talented human resources which are optimally combined with capital and other management resources to pursue a reasonable profit. Unlike machinery and equipment, which can be depreciated year after year, the value of each individual's talent must be "appreciated" through time in line with corporate objectives, or at least the rate of its "depreciation" must be minimized. And the ability of each individual should be utilized as optimally as possible through vertical and across-the-board coordination and through integration of individual activities within an organizational hierarchy. Otherwise, some of the major practices of Japanese enterprises such as lifetime employment and length-of-service-based reward schemes (popularly known as "seniority rewards") have no advantages. Therefore, the company tries to make each individual acquire corporate-specific skills, and at the same time encourages a range of views concerning corporate management. The company at the same time tries to reduce employees' adaptability to or compatibility with the external labor market. These two conditions enabled the firm in the long run to maximize the utilization of its labor's talents in an internal market. The so-called Japanese management system can be defined as an organic combination of management practices which as a whole make it possible to provide such conditions to a significant extent.

KAWABE: The emphasis on human resources management is regarded as one of the most striking features in Japanese organization. Historically, this feature was already seen in commercial houses in the mid-18th century. Under environmental conditions in that period, it developed as a principle of managing organization. Several other principles have been formed in this process: lifelong service, total commitment to the group or organization, rank order based on seniority, harmony and cooperation among all members, participative management, and authoritarianism and paternalism. Labor management practices of the modern corporation were formed in later years, based on these principles. Here, we do not find the notion of functional contract which is commonly seen in Western employment; rather, the individual makes a total commitment. In such an organization, human resources are not simple parts which can be easily exchanged or jettisoned under unfavorable circumstances. They are fixed members who stay for life and share interests. Therefore, it is necessary for a company to devise systems to keep these members in the organization and to train employees and improve the skills they have; if they do not, the company will lose out in the changing market and technology requirements to which it must adapt. Lifetime employment and the seniority system are among the devices used to attain this goal. Consequently, investment in human resources was strengthened as a necessary part of the Japanese organization.

KIMBARA: Even though the emphasis on human resources is stressed by Japanese management, we need to ask to what extent it is carried out in a Japanese company in terms of the benefits employees get and the forms in which they are realized. It is often said by top management that a company pays a great deal of attention to the management of human resources as a most important factor in the organization. But this does not necessarily mean that the employees benefit more from the company than do other interested groups, though the company may adopt various human resource measures. Generally speaking, profit goes first to the company for future investment, second to the employees, and third to shareholders in a Japanese company. Emphasis on human resources is seen in aspects which are not related to payment—for example, security of employment until retirement age, heavy investment in training, and participation in decisions or consultation with sharing of goals and information.

TAKEUCHI: Human resource management can be realized in various forms and practices, depending on the surrounding conditions. Lifetime employment and the seniority system, which were once considered the pillars of Japanese management, are two such practices which can be changed, though the values and norms which underlie these practices are quite slow to change. I believe these practices, especially the seniority system, became possible historically when two fundamental conditions existed. One is population increase in a pyramid-like shape; the other is high growth of economy.

To avoid misunderstanding about these Japanese management practices which are often pointed to as the essence of a Japanese company, I would like to comment on the extent to which they are actually seen in Japanese companies. The lifetime employment system is basically applicable only to male permanent employees in large enterprises. Female workers, temporary workers, and those who work in small businesses do not receive much benefit from this system. In a declining industry, lifetime employment is hard to maintain. It should be noted that the proportion of those under lifetime employment is less than 30% of the total work force in Japan. It must also be pointed out that "cooperative labor-management relations" were established only in the past three decades. Before that, there were severe conflicts between labor and management. We can hardly say that cooperation is inherent to the Japanese company. These practices are strongly related to the development stage of the economy as well as to socio-cultural conditions. **KIMBARA**: Characteristic features of Japanese management depend on the internal and external conditions of the organization. And the cultural factor is just one of them. However, the most controversial point about Japanese management so far argued has been whether it is unique to Japan or not. In the sense that every social system is formed in specific socio-cultural conditions, no management system in a given country is culture-free. So it may not be useful to ask whether it is unique or not in the cultural sense. Rather, I would like to inquire to what extent culture is related to management practices and day-to-day behavior. Analysis traditionally tended to focus on cultural characteristics and employment practices. However, when we think about management problems functionally, there are other features as well. Growth strategy in the market, indirect financing supported by mutual shareholding and a bank system (though this is changing now), emphasis on production operations which encourage workplace decisions and creativity are features other than human resources management which are characteristically seen in Japanese corporations. These as a whole make up the important features of the management system.

TOMITA: There is no doubt that Japanese management has been developed and reshaped through time to take advantage of what Japanese economic institutions offer and to effectively cope with the ever-changing business environment. To my understanding, the uniqueness of Japanese management, if any, is found not in the seemingly idiosyncratic management practices themselves, but in the organic functioning of these practices. The practices when implemented as a bundle form the basis of Japanese management, and no individual practice need be considered overly unique, although to foreign concerns they may appear as idiosyncrasies of Japanese management.

Applicability of Japanese Management in the ASEAN Countries

NAKAUCHI: It is yet not very clear in my mind what is precisely meant by Japanese-style management, even after hearing the above discussion. Is there a standard type which can be applied? It may not be easy after all to spell out a standard form of management which could be readily applicable to all the developing ASEAN member countries. Substantial modification and adjustment are required of any policy if it is to be effectively applied in circumstances which contain different cultural, historical and ethical backgrounds. Perhaps it would be closer to the truth to say that there are simply two kinds of management—good management and bad management. To develop the ability to distinguish the good from the bad, it is indispensable to observe examples in many countries.

KIMBARA: Let me explain some of the examples from our joint research. While practices such as internal manpower development, on-the-job training, and quality control circles are highly applicable, others like the seniority system, lifetime employment, groupism, and the *ringi* system are low in applicability (see Chapter 1). This was the opinion of the Japanese managers we surveyed who worked for Japanese joint ventures in ASEAN countries. It indicates that operative practices are to some degree transferable to overseas Japanese-affiliated companies, but practices related to the value system and norms and way of life are less applicable. Some practices can be transferred and learned.

ABO: The question is, however, how and to what extent we can go beyond Japanese management while retaining its comparative advantages. The separation of specific elements of Japanese management and their selective transplanting to foreign countries may be a practical and useful idea. However, I want to emphasize the limitations of such a measure. In Figure 5 in Chapter 1 in this volume, for example, the applicability scores for OJT and job rotation are far higher (50–80%) than those for lifetime employment and the seniority system (less than 30%). In my understanding, however, the latter scores are essential prerequisites supporting the former. While OJT together with job rotation for flexible, multi-functional workers is a core element of the workplace-oriented Japanese management and production system, it would be difficult for the OJT system to work effectively without the Japanese-style seniority system (the promotion system based on length of service in a company) and the practice of life-time, or longer-time, employment. In short, I believe that we should take into consideration the extent to which each aspect of the Japanese system can be successfully separated from the whole.

YAMASHITA: As Professor Abo points out, we need to study the features and real strengths of Japanese management as a whole. However, our research paid more attention to the applicability or transferability of some aspects of Japanese management practices under different managerial conditions. We do not consider that the total system of Japanese companies can be transferred to the ASEAN countries. We would like to hear the opinions of those from the ASEAN countries on this point.

LIM: Japanese managerial practices, by and large, cannot be applied in Singapore for three reasons. First, Singaporeans are individualistic and economically pragmatic, and they at all times tend to job-hop. Second, Singapore is a heterogeneous society. Singapore Chinese, though very much influenced by Confucianism, are also much influenced by Western values. Japan, in contrast, is a nation of one race and one culture which is very much influenced by Confucianism. This homogeneity and cultural background makes lifetime employment and a seniority wage system practicable. Besides, Singapore employs a substantial number of "guest employees" who are expected to leave the country when their contracts expire. This adds to the impracticability of the lifetime employment and seniority wage systems in Singapore. Third, Singapore has many multinational enterprises with head offices in different countries. Even if the Japanese managerial system has been implanted in the Japanese enterprises in Singapore, other multinationals may not want to follow suit. The Japanese enterprises may provide on-the-job training, but the trained employees may be absorbed by the Western enterprises at a later stage. Japanese managerial systems cannot, therefore, be practiced without modifications and rectifications in Singapore.

MORI: I think you are correct that individualism is an important factor that may oppose the introduction of a Japanese-style managerial system in Singapore. Actually, since independence, it has been the government that promoted the individualistic ethos, for the sake of Singapore's survival. However, I am not convinced that the multi-racial and multi-cultural background of Singapore is the reason why a lifetime employment system cannot be implanted in Singapore. I do not agree that Confucianism is one of the major elements in the Japanese-style managerial system. But even if it were, with the 75% of Chinese in Singapore who are followers of Confucianism, the Japanese-style managerial system could be acceptable. Of course, job-hopping may be a problem, but it is not that serious. As Singapore is a very small country, it is very difficult to find employees anyway. This problem is confronted not only by Japanese enterprises but also by the other multinationals and local enterprises as well.

THONG: The mono-racial and mono-cultural nature of Japanese society and the geographic environment of Japan have contributed to the emergence of the distinctive characteristics of the Japanese Human Resource Management (HRM) practices that we know of today. But studies have shown that these practices can be applied, with modifications, in other environments where the workers possess different cultural values, like those in Malaysia, a multi-racial and multi-cultural country. The transference of Japanese HRM practices must be undertaken with patience and understanding, and in line with the mainstream of the basic cultural values of the local community.

MARTIRES: We identified some of the adaptable Japanese practices in a study conducted in 1985–1989. They are: discipline in the areas of honesty, diligence, punctuality, efficiency and loyalty; training of workers; job knowledge; professionalism and objectivity; and teamwork.

KIMBARA: The Japanese management system has the following strengths: stability of employment; attention to human resources as the most important factor in the organization; cooperation between labor and management; cooperation between the various levels of suppliers based on reliable long-term relationship; training and re-educating of employees; flexibility of the work force through job rotation; and strong internal identification. Through these practices, Japanese companies have developed new products and improved workers' skills and technology. Even robots were introduced successfully without causing unemployment.

On the contrary, there are also weaknesses, as follows: lack of labor mobility which limits the professionalization and value of individual skills; inefficiency of the labor force because of its rigidity and increased age of workers; promotion and payment regardless of the ability of employees; time consumed in adapting drastic changes; and lack of clearly defined responsibility criteria and job specifications.

MARTIRES: We find several weaknesses in the Japanese style of management: nurturance by Japanese management of lower staff instead of middle and top management; problems in communication; very strict and rigid policies and schedules; lack of understanding of strong Filipino family orientation (a very personal factor to the Filipino worker, who would rather be absent from work than miss a family function); and protracted decision-making. It takes the Japanese "a long time to make decisions."

PRIJONO: Concerning trade unions and labor relations, it has been said that the Indonesians are imitating the Japanese. But I think that it is the other way around. This is because labor relations in Indonesia are derived from the teachings of Mangku Negara I in the 13th century. We call it "Panca Sila industrial relations," which is based on three aspects: sense of responsibility, sense of belonging, and sense of improvement. I believe these three aspects are also found in Japanese industrial relations. On the social aspect, the Indonesians do complain that the Japanese do not want to socialize with the local people. The closeness of Japanese expatriates is also an obstacle to the transfer of technology.

I think the Japanese management system is based on an idea of family responsibility, whereby the welfare of the workers is given much attention. The Indonesian management style is closer to the Chinese management style, whereby immediate family members and relatives will become directors or president of a company regardless of their capability.

YAMASHITA: Thank you for your useful comments on the transferability of Japanese-style management. Now we would like to turn our attention to the problems of technology transfer. It seems that there are several views about this. Mr. Yasuda, may I ask you to briefly summarize the points that have been raised concerning technology transfer?

Technology Transfer

YASUDA: One of the important points is that we found a sharp difference in the definition of the concept "technology transfer" (TT). For most Japanese, TT is a matter of fostering a technology-oriented mind, because they tend to regard TT as related to human factors, as Mr. Ohno of Toyota Corporation has stressed frequently. Managerial personnel of developing countries, in contrast, sometimes regard modern technology as a kind of package of principles and formulations.

We also had some discussions about the background of technology transfer and the conditions of recipient countries. It is noteworthy that social stratification in developing countries is more severe than in developed countries (see the comments in Chapter 9). I think a national willingness to solve the problem of social partiality will be one of the decisive factors in further technology transfer by Japanese joint ventures, because their TT is definitely related to understanding and cooperation between managers and employees insofar as they concentrate on the manufacturing sectors like electric appliances and the automobile industry. These are the industrial sectors where the optimal combination of capital-intensive factors and labor-intensive ones is needed.

TAKEHANA: I once made it clear that Japanese joint ventures do not intend to promote technology transfer at higher levels like "management" and "R&D" (Takehana 1988), even if they intend to transfer at the lower levels like "operations" and "maintenance." I found that the understanding of technological development by Japanese companies is far more sophisticated than we can imagine, and it is easy for us to understand that their transfer is limited to the very lowest levels of their whole system of technological development strategy if only we can see the total system.

PRAYOON: According to our joint survey, Japanese joint ventures shifted to ASEAN countries in the 1960s were more optimistic and eager in considering the transfer of their ways of management than those shifted in the latter half of the 1980s. However, so far as I know, newly shifted companies seem to be much more aggressive in transferring their technology, including R&D capital-intensive sections, while those which came to ASEAN earlier are not always interested in transferring their modern technology and seem to concentrate on the adaptation of traditional technology. Most of those companies transferred second-hand production systems and supplied old-fashioned products.

SATO: I don't think that the newly established companies are more positive than old ones about technology transfer. In the automobile industry in Thailand, we have always paid attention to the training of employees for the production of better products, and now hundreds of engineers and managers are working at our factory. But there are still many limitations on further promotion of technology transfer. Even in the first half of the 1980s, we could not find enough parts manufacturers in the ASEAN countries, and we had to produce parts in our own factories under the severe restriction of local content and small domestic markets. For the automobile industry, it is not easy to increase production because of the high cost of equipment. I have heard various opinions criticizing Japanese companies for not being eager to transfer R&D sections to developing countries, but I do think it is quite hard for them to do so where they have neither enough market share nor sufficient supporting industries.

YAMASHITA: I would like to comment on Professor Prayoon's opinion that newly shifted companies should be much more aggressive in transferring their technology. His understanding seems to be related to the technological level of the industry involved. Those companies which came to ASEAN earlier had begun business with low-tech and labor-intensive technologies that were just adequate to produce goods for the local market. However, recent Japanese investment in ASEAN is more export-oriented, and it is necessary to produce more high-quality and internationally competitive goods. So the investing companies are installing the latest automatic production lines and training employees to operate them. They need to teach local workers about high technology, about the importance of quality control, and so on.

I think Professor Prayoon observed this aspect of technical training by new investors, and saw their eagerness; probably he saw the practices in the electronics industry in Thailand. We of course must admire their efforts to introduce high-technology factories and train workers to operate the latest machines. However, the methods of training and nurturing employees at established companies are different from those at new companies. Newly established enterprises, like Western-affiliated companies, train only in operational technology. The companies which have longer experience in Southeast Asia, however, have been trying to transfer technology in a more complete manner—not only for current production operations, but also repair and maintenance, quality control, factory management, and so on (see Chapter 1). We should appreciate these companies' efforts to promote technology transfer and nurture personnel. They have invested more time and resources in human resource development.

TAKEUCHI: When we examine the business activities of Japanese joint ventures in the ASEAN countries, we must take into account the differences in their global market structures and technological accumulation. In the 1960s, Japanese automobile manufacturers did not have sufficient market competitiveness in the advanced countries but had to depend upon the small local market of developing countries. By the 1980s, they already had enough market share in the advanced countries, and some of them needed to shift to the developing countries to supply low-priced products for the world market. Owing to this change in economic conditions, many parts manufacturers shifted operations to foreign countries, including the ASEAN countries. We can see the rapid development of supporting industries in ASEAN recently, especially at the end of the 1980s. Thus, I think that changing economic and market conditions have changed the business strategies of Japanese joint ventures.

IMAOKA: In Taiwan and Hong Kong, small and medium-scale enterprises began to develop rapidly during the 1970s and 1980s, and this became one of the factors in promoting their industrialization more effectively (Imaoka et al. 1985). However, it seems that the development of small businesses began only in the latter half of the 1980s in Thailand. I think that the formation of indigenous entrepreneurship will be the main driving force for small and medium-scale firms, among which we will see some typical growth of technology, as Prof. Takeuchi explained in his paper. Even at this point, we can say that the economic background of technology transfer in Thailand changed radically in the latter half of the 1980s, after the revaluation of the Japanese currency.

TAKEUCHI: In most of the developing countries, there frequently seems to be an idea that the economic promoters for technology transfer are the leading private enterprises of the developed country. This is also one of the points made by Mr. Takehana. In contrast, business people in advanced countries have usually considered that the transfer of new technology should be carried out by themselves. They would not be satisfied with technology that was purchased directly from abroad but further adapted and innovated at their own expense. However, most of the government officials and elites of the ASEAN countries regard it as the responsibility of multi-national corporations (MNCs). Sometimes they stress that local economies have been exploited or utilized by MNCs for extra profit. In this sense, they subscribe to the so-called "dependency theory." It is well known that Japanese public agencies, including MITI, spent huge amounts of money to catch up with the advanced countries. We can see similar behavior in Korea and Singapore nowadays, but most of the ASEAN governments do not seem to be aware of the importance of this point. Government organizations should play the active role in technological improvement, when the private sector is not yet so powerful.

SATO: Japanese businessmen in charge of local joint ventures in ASEAN countries consider that they should also take some responsibilities for the accomplishment of technology transfer. However, they have to behave within the boundary of commercial considerations, as their private companies are not social welfare organizations. It is certain that the range of TT and R&D has became more complicated, as Mr. Takehana explained. Before the 1970s oil shocks, we could concentrate just on manufacturing products, but now we are required to reduce exhaust gas and engine noise, improve security at the time of traffic accidents, and so on. We also need to adopt various microelectronic parts, which we could not have imagined in the 1970s. These kinds of social needs and market demands obliged us to improve our total system of research and development more and more, but it should be noted that there still are numerous R&D needs and possibilities even at the stage of daily operation and maintenance of the factory. Mr. Takehana regards factory operation and maintenance as lower level stages of business activity. Most high government officials in ASEAN countries also think like that, but I think they are *essential stages* through which we start to catch up with the developed countries. Without the fundamental accomplishments at the primary stages, how can we proceed to more sophisticated stages? If you look down on the fundamentals of manufacturing, why not concentrate on the commercial sector or the service sector instead of troublesome manufacturing? As Prof. Takeuchi emphasized, we all interpret "technology transfer" quite differently, but I am rather optimistic because many local employees have begun to take responsibility for their own technological development.

TAKEHANA: I myself conducted some interviews with local employees in some ASEAN countries, and found that they are confident of their ability to utilize new technology and are sorry to be unable to have a chance to do so. Compared to Japanese joint ventures (JJVs), European and American companies seem more positive about giving local employees a chance to access new technology. It is well known that Japanese parent companies do not allow independent decision-making by the top executives of local joint ventures; this is another reason that local people regard that JJVs do not have a positive attitude toward technology transfer.

SATO: I know that local people are excellent individually. However, please remember that what one can do as an individual is quite different from what one can do as a businessman. We can't transfer what we can do easily in Japan at no any extra cost. I don't think European companies give better opportunities than JJVs, if we compare companies in the same line of business. I'm sure that JJV products' local content ratios are higher than that of European companies in the automobile industry in ASEAN. Most JJVs are characterized by some degree of collective decision-making, family-like managerial systems, and so on, which might give the impression that they are not autonomous as regards technology transfer, even if these factors oblige JJVs to take a great deal of time for their decision-making.

YASUDA: We can consider technology transfer one of the dimensions of human resource development. Professor Takeuchi's report introduced some examples of "spin-off," "fade-out" and so on. He called them a kind of technology transfer. Euro-American companies are good at developing large-scale process industries and material industries which do not need to develop various supporting industries with their spin-offs and fade-outs. If we consider that technology transfer is definitely related to human resource development, JJVs seem to be good at developing human resources in supporting industries and downstream industries. I think that highly developed human interrelations have been one of the characteristics of Japanese technological development and gave a distinctive flavor to their technology transfer, but such human relations have loosened little by little in the course of recent rapid economic development, and we today find the old-style personal relationships only in exceptionally progressive branch factories in the countryside of Japan or in successful joint ventures in developing countries. However, human relations can only be based on an understanding of local value systems and cultural backgrounds, and this means that Japanese firms are now at the point of being able to accumulate their own human resources, with people who are specialized in each technological area. This will be another factor giving them a further chance of development. Last, I would like to stress that surveys of Japanese joint ventures in developing countries can give important suggestions to Japanese parent companies for revising their ways of management.

Problems and Future Prospects for Japanese Management

YAMASHITA: We have discussed various aspects of the Japanese style of management in ASEAN countries. Now we would like to summarize the characteristics of this style of management and to discuss its future prospects. I think Japanese managers, both in the ASEAN countries and in Tokyo, need to reconsider what are suitable ways of managing abroad, and should develop a new direction of management that fits local conditions.

SUTHY: Having participated in this series of presentations, I feel that most people would agree to a certain extent that a particular system of management style or operation process cannot wholly or totally be transferred to different environmental conditions. The problem is compounded when people with different cultural backgrounds are involved. In looking for a management style that can be appropriate for a particular system, I think we need to take into account the nature of the people concerned, whether Japanese, local or Western people.

KAWABE: I think one of the strongest aspects of Japanese-style management is production management and the related training and education of human resources. Japanese management pays more attention to people than its U.S. and European counterparts. Japanese companies promote this aspect in ASEAN countries.

PRIJONO: Japanese-style management is viewed more as an art than as a scientific approach. It is closely related to the Japanese way of life. Hence, Japanese-style management needs adaptation in order to apply to host countries which are different culturally. In this respect, an understanding of the cultures, habits, and situations of the host countries is essential. The source of strength of Japanese companies lies in their treatment of human resources as a valuable asset; this is an area of potential which should continue to be stressed and developed further.

SATO: I think we should divide Japanese-style management into two categories so that we can understand it clearly. One is production management together with labor management. The other is business management together with personnel management. It is my opinion that Japanese-style management refers to the former—production management with Japanese-style labor management. The main objective of Japanese manufacturers overseas is to produce high-quality products at lowest production cost and to improve productivity. To achieve this target, Japanese manufacturers introduced Japanese-style production management—for example, on-the-job training, quality control circles, dialogue between workers and middle management, idea contests, and many other methods together with very good employee welfare measures based on the philosophy of humanity, equality, and group orientation.

However, Japanese-style business management is often not well accepted by white-collar workers in the offices because of the seniority system, the vague decision-making process, and unclear job descriptions. Contrasted with production management, which easily shows results numerically, the performance of business management is not clearly visible, and it is influenced by such cultural factors as the values and attitudes of the society.

TOMITA: Through bitter experiences in situations resembling the Prisoner's Dilemma, both managers and managed have learned that a certain amount of compromise is indispensable for materializing their respective objectives. They gradually realized that mutual trust between management and labor is the prerequisite for a balanced compromise between them, and also for an equitable sharing of the fruits of their work. Hence both parties have endeavored to establish trust for their mutual benefit. In my understanding, trust between managers and managed—though sometimes they only pretend to trust each other for their respective benefit—constitutes the creed supporting Japanese management, in comparison with the mutual distrust so often observed in Western management. The challenge for us researchers is to seek the way in which Japanese management might flexibly adapt itself to the new environment of the host countries, and avoid mutual distrust and establish mutual trust between Japanese managers and local employees in a productive manner.

LIM: But I would like to suggest that the criticism directed toward Japanese investment is still strong. I make this comment because I've participated in various international conferences organized by academicians and politicians in this region. I've heard that most Japanese university graduates from ASEAN countries have complaints about Japanese heavy investment in the region. When they work for Japanese companies, they are not satisfied in terms of career advancement and remuneration. So, as suggested here, our team or groups of Japanese scholars may look at Japanese enterprises, compare them to the multinational corporations of the U.S. and Europe, and make suggestions about how to modify or rectify the Japanese management system and how to introduce it in the ASEAN countries. We should look into the cultural and religious backgrounds as well as the national politics of the ASEAN countries. We need to take them into consideration in making suggestions about how to practice Japanese-style management in the ASEAN countries.

PASUK: It seems to me that Prof. Kawabe's comment about Japan being a latecomer in the global multinational competition is an interesting one: Japanese firms have long been competitive in the world market, but it is only recently that Japanese multinationals have become truly multinational in the sense that American and some British firms have been. Once you become multinational, you have to compete with the multinational culture which has gone on before. And some of this multinational culture has established itself in these developing countries. In the ASEAN countries this is much more so than in the case of the newly industrialized countries, because the ASEAN nations had very strong links with both Great Britain and America in the past. So it seems to me also that the discussion of what Prof. Yamashita calls "a new corporate culture" for Japanese-affiliated firms suggests that Japanese firms have been feeling a certain sense of crisis about how to cope in a global multinational situation.

When we consider the applicability of Japanese-style management, we should take into account the changing situations in the ASEAN countries. I would like to note that the ASEAN countries themselves also have their own dynamics, aside from their interactions with Japanese firms and Japanese management. I would like to touch on three things which have happened in the last 15–20 years in the ASEAN countries. First, we have seen these countries coming of age in various ways. One manifestation is their having been able to get rid of all economic nationalism which was a holdover from the 19th century and early 20th century history of relations with the Western powers. By this, I mean the change in ideology among governments, business, and the public toward capitalism, or to an increased appreciation of the capitalist way of doing things.

The second thing I'd like to talk about is the changing role of the governments of these countries, which are becoming more capitalist themselves. They used to compete with the private sector, and now they accept the fact that they are not doing the job as well as the private sector. Now, they are encouraging privatization.

The third thing I'd like to touch on is that, together with changes in the dynamics of the ASEAN countries, you also see political changes.

There is political consciousness as well as economic consciousness among the populations of ASEAN countries. When I say "political consciousness" I'm talking about the increases in terms of both absolute number and ratio of the middle-class people who want more say in the government and who, perhaps, would like to accelerate the democratization process.

YASUDA: I have something to add to the discussion of the role of governments. In Thailand, for example, it is said that foreign investors did not invest in export-oriented industries, and that they were rather reluctant to transfer their technology. It is true that many Japanese firms invested a great deal in the so-called import-substitute industries, especially in the 1960s and 1970s. Why? One of the reasons is, I understand, an enforcement of the criteria of the Board of Investment of Thailand, which made it a rule to ask investors how many employees would be employed after the establishment of the firms. With this incentive, investors would often like to reduce the scale of investment, in order to employ as many workers as possible. A second reason is the business tax. In Thailand, the business tax rate has been similar to that of import taxes, and levied on the basis of production. A firm has to pay tax at the firm gate when it ships goods, and a second company which, after getting intermediate materials from the first company, modifies them and adds some value has to pay another tax. This accumulation of business taxes makes products very expensive. Therefore, foreign companies did not want to depend on local subcontractors, from the viewpoints of both cost and quality. Thus, the business directions of foreign companies are mainly decided by the policy of local governments.

NAKAUCHI: There remains, however, the important question of where the Thai economy is heading in the future. In what direction is Thailand likely to find the most fruitful economic activities in the rapidly changing world economic milieu? It is an interesting policy question whether the market-oriented economic system of Thailand can prove in the future to be an efficient system in the choice of industries that have a comparative advantage.

TAKEUCHI: The ASEAN countries have begun reforming their socio-economic structures to adapt to economic development. In the process of industrialization, it is necessary to develop values, attitudes, and disciplines in order for local work forces to adjust to the working conditions of modern industrial corporations. For this purpose, the local governments have to play an important role. For example, it was necessary for the Malaysian government to launch the "Look East Policy" to develop industrial values among workers who have grown up in the agrarian, rural villages.

The Possibility of a Hybrid Corporate Culture

YAMASHITA: Finally, we would like to discuss how the Japanese style of management should be changed in the future.

SUTHY: Management tradition is an important resource as the carrier of accumulated knowledge in the production process of the firm. So this tradition should be considered an active participant in the process of organizational growth. When we look at the constituent parts of the organization, of course, we still have the controlling group—that is, the employer or the executive—on the one hand and the employees on the other. In an organization, the goals of the two groups have to be reconciled, as Prof. Tomita explained very clearly in his presentation. I appreciated this point very much. Briefly, in an organization, in order to achieve a successful style of management, the goal of the employees as well as those of the corporation have to be seriously taken into account. Both parties should minimize the conflict between them so as to seek a consensus. My personal view is that when a management style, whether Japanese or Western, is to be introduced in different social conditions, we need to have adaptation of this process to local conditions. So I feel that we need a lot of understanding from the Japanese firms of the local culture and other local conditions.

PRAYOON: It's necessary to allow local people more participation in decision making or in discussion. If you allow more of these things and give time, I think it will produce good results in developing a successful management style and achieving organizational goals. So I would feel that in any organization, and in any management system, incentive is very important. If firms clearly keep this kind of thing in mind, I think they can maintain a lot of employees within their organization.

PRIJONO: As Prof. Thong and Prof. Kawabe said, developments in the economy bring developments in the environmental aspects. Then the lifestyle of people also changes. Adapting Japanese-style management, if there is such a thing, is quite difficult because I believe that if you plant the same seed in different soil, it will grow in different ways.

KAWABE: In the ASEAN countries we can find a dual structure between upper and lower classes. The former is usually influenced by Western attitudes and values; the latter, by indigenous cultures. Therefore, Japanese-style management confronts the established attitudes and values of managers. On the other hand, management of new industrial workers from rural areas has begun just recently, and their values and attitudes are similar to those of their Japanese counterparts. Therefore, Japanese companies have to send more expatriates to work as "interpreters" between the headquarters and local management. In the case of Western companies in Malaysia, there are many local managers who can communicate with their headquarters, but in Japanese companies there are few. Japanese expatriates cannot adapt their management style to local management without changes in attitudes and values as well as in the management systems at headquarters in Japan.

PASUK: I don't think Japan can afford to keep sending expatriates from Japan to control its firms all over the world. That happened to U.S. firms too. You don't have enough people who are willing to leave Japan. Even if there are, however, the real economic question is: "Why do you need to keep control when you can use local people who are as capable?" This is happening in U.S. firms. Many managing directors of 100% U.S. firms actually employ local people to manage; they get the shares and dividends, and they seem to be doing quite well. This process promotes greater cooperation, and management style becomes much more hybrid. It seems to me that there is an economic necessity for Japan to change.

MORI: The fundamentally important thing has to do with the transparency of decision-making. The main office in Tokyo is a closely knit society whereby historical evolution and face-saving are very important considerations. As such, very heated discussions may occur at the informal level, but seldom at the official level. Most of the difficult issues had been resolved before a question is presented to a Board of Director meeting. In the opposite direction, the contents of top-level meetings are not related to the subsidiary level. This makes it difficult for the branch office to explain to the employees why a decision was made. Transparency of decision-making is essential to achieve a better image in the host country's society.

SATO: So we agree that Japanese firms should make due efforts to modify some of their business management practices to suit the local situation in order to create higher motivation for white-collar employees. However, it is not easy. Today Prof. Mori suggested that Japanese firms should improve their decision-making process overseas. Japanese firms understand this quite well; every Japanese firm is now trying to improve and modify some parts of its management to suit local environments. In the ASEAN countries, the U.K., and the U.S.A., there are different levels of acceptability. So when we modify and improve some of our business management systems to meet the needs of local society, there are some differences, of course. To make Japanese-style management more suitable, the head offices of Japanese firms in Japan also should play an important role, such as working to understand the different cultures, histories, national characters, customs and so on. Also, they should modify some decision-making processes even in the head office, and assist and support Japanese staff stationed overseas. All Japanese firms are working on this, but, due to the lack of public relations, local people are not well aware of Japanese firms' contributions.

HIRANO: Since most Japanese corporations started their foreign investment programs fairly recently, they are interested mainly in the economic performance of their foreign subsidiaries compared with their Western counterparts. However, if Japanese companies want to attain high performance levels, they have to win good will from the society. For this it is necessary to pay attention to a wide variety of problems such as the emotional and political reactions of local people, environmental erosion, ecological problems, etc.

THONG: If Japanese companies want to be successful in Asian plural society, they need to develop "multicultural managers," be they expatriates or nationals. The multicultural manager of the future will be trained and sensitized to meet work in other countries with an open mind. He will not bring his cultural baggage with him but a proper attitude of mind which will help him to respect and to learn more quickly the dynamics of cultures other than his own. The multicultural manager must by nature and training have a special skill in developing relationships, especially across cultures, and in making a commitment to the society.

MARTIRES: Perhaps we can make suggestion that before the Japanese managers leave Japan to take managerial positions in various countries, they should undergo training on the cultural aspects of the country they are going to—perhaps a one- or two-day seminar on the value system and other factors. This would help them to really know the country better before they get out of Japan. Perhaps they could also talk with citizens of the country in Japan before they leave, about certain aspects and ways of living in the country they are going to. Japanese style is very efficient, but sometimes what really hurts you is that the managers lack a kind of connection and humanness.

TOMITA: If we talk about "Beyond Japanese-style Management," we have to think of how to reshape it based on the philosophy of Japanese management to cope with the situation in a local area. Japanese management is not a fixed thing. It is changeable. Over time, it can evolve when the environment changes. As we have seen, Japanese-style management today has come out of certain socioeconomic needs in Japan. One of the most important aspects of management is the ability to adapt to the changing environment.

KIMBARA: Actually, even in Japan, the so-called Japanese style of management has begun changing due to the new values and attitudes of young people, the changing age structure of the population, rapid technological changes, and other factors. Today, most Japanese companies are revising lifetime employment, the seniority system, and other aspects of the Japanese style of management. However, even if changes are made in the Japanese managerial system, they cannot be Western ones. I think the Japanese style of management changes to adjust to a changing environment gradually, maintaining the principles which Prof. Tomita has clearly shown.

PASUK: I think this kind of meeting is a wonderful place to react and to find a hybrid style of management that will make everybody feel richer and happier.

YAMASHITA: I think that the Japanese style of management has such competitive advantages as production management and its related human resources management, which have been widely appreciated. As a latecomer in globalization compared with its Western counterparts and because of cultural differences, Japanese-style management has some weak aspects, such as management of white-collar workers and lack of consciousness of the local community. Therefore, everyone will agree that it is necessary for Japanese business to adjust its management style to local conditions in the ASEAN countries. For this it is also necessary to make changes inside Japan, including changes in attitudes and values of the headquarters toward overseas subsidiaries. It is necessary for Japanese companies to create a hybrid corporate culture, neither Western nor Japanese, which adapts to local cultural, socio-economic, and political conditions.

SUMMARY

The Conference came to the conclusion that Japanese-style management, which so far has been quite workable in Japan, cannot be totally applied to the ASEAN countries, as the environmental factors in ASEAN countries do differ from those in Japan in various ways:

1. People in ASEAN countries are different from Japanese with respect to race, culture, and religion, which makes them differ also with respect to ways of life, characteristics, and value systems.

2. People in the ASEAN countries have been influenced, to some extent, by Western culture as well. This places Japanese enterprises, who are latecomers in multinational competition, in conflict with Western standards which have established themselves in the ASEAN countries for a number of years.

The meeting then suggested that Japanese-style management needs to be modified and adapted to local conditions. In the process, all parties, whether Japanese managers or local employees, should cooperate to create a more desirable style of management which is not only efficient in the economic sense but is also accepted by all people concerned. Proposed recommendations from the conference are as follows:

1. Japanese enterprises must try to attain a deep understanding of the local environment in the country in which they are investing so that they can adapt Japanese-style management to local conditions and create the most efficient and suitable style of management. It was suggested that before taking positions abroad, Japanese managers should undergo training on the cultural aspects and way of living of the country they are going to.

2. The headquarters in Japan must become more internationalized. Like their subsidiaries, they need to understand local conditions, modify and clarify their decision-making process, and support Japanese or multicultural staff stationed overseas.

3. The long-run organizational goals as well as the distribution of gain from management to all parties concerned should be seriously taken into consideration in order to reduce conflicts within the organization.

4. Academic institutions such as universities should also have a role in developing a managerial system which goes beyond the present Japanese-style management and becomes more international.

5. Efforts should be made to cultivate more resource people who understand the culture and value system of both Japan and the host countries, and who can act as the conversants between Japanese and local people.

It was pointed out that there were some aspects that were not discussed in detail during the conference and probably require further investigation and discussion. They are:

1. The role of local government in the process of industrialization and technology transfer.

2. Comparison of Western and Japanese companies in ASEAN countries with respect to their managerial practices.

3. Comparison of managerial practices of Japanese firms in the same industry.
4. Applicability and inapplicability of Japanese-style management in certain countries.

Most of all, it is suggested that attempts should be made to give more detailed suggestions for practical ways for Japanese firms to modify their managerial practices.

References

Abegglen, J. C. 1958. *The Japanese Factory: Aspects of Its Social Organization.* Glencoe, Ill.: The Free Press.

Abo, T., ed. 1988. *Nihon Kigyo no America Genchi Seisan* (Production in the United States by Japanese Companies). Tokyo: Toyo Keizai Shinposha.

Adachi, F. 1980. Tonan Azia jidoshakogyo ni okeru shuhenkigyo no hatten (Development of ancillary industries in the automobile industry of Asia) *Academia* 67 (Tokyo: Hitotsubashi University).

Akamatsu, K. 1956. Wagakuni sangyo hatten no ganko keitai: Kikai kigu kogyo ni tsuite (A wild-geese flying pattern of Japanese industrial development: Machine and tool industries). *Hitotsubashi Ronso* (Hitotsubashi Review), vol. 6 no. 5.

———. 1961. A theory of unbalanced growth in the world economy. *Weltwirtschaftliches Archive* 2.

Al-Aali, Abdul Rahman Y. 1987. A performance model for American manufacturing and service joint ventures in Saudi Arabia. Ph.D. diss., Georgia State University.

Alavi, H. and T. Shanin, eds. 1982. *Introduction to the Sociology of Developing Societies.* London: Macmillan.

Allen, T. W. 1973a. Direct investment of Japanese enterprises in Southeast Asia, Study no. 1. Bangkok: The Economic Cooperation Centre for Asian and Pacific Region.

———. 1973b. Direct investment of United States enterprises in Southeast Asia, Study no. 2. Bangkok: The Economic Cooperation Centre for Asian and Pacific Region.

———. 1973c. Investment of European enterprises in Southeast Asia, Study no. 3. Bangkok: The Economic Cooperation Centre for Asian and Pacific Region.

———. 1979. The ASEAN Report: Hong Kong, *Asian Wall Street Journal* vol.1.

Amin, S. 1974. *Accumulation on a World Scale: A Critique of Underdevelopment.* Translated by B. Pearce. New York: Monthly Review Press.

———. 1975. *Unequal Development.* New York: Monthly Review Press.

Aoki, M., ed. 1984. *The Economic Analysis of the Japanese Firm.* Amsterdam: North-

Holland.

Aoto, Y. et al. 1984. *Nippon: The Land and Its People*, Tokyo: Nippon Steel Company, Personnel Development Division, 2nd ed.

Ariff, M. and H. Hill 1985. *Export Oriented Industrialization: The ASEAN Experience*, Sydney: Allen and Unwin.

Arndt, H. W. 1974. Professor Kojima on macroeconomics of foreign direct investment. *Hitotsubashi Journal of Economics* vol. 15 no. 1.

Azumi, K. 1979. Nihon no soshiki kozo (Japanese organizational structure), *Soshiki kagaku* (Organizational Science), 12–4: 2–12.

Bangkok Japanese Chamber of Commerce and Industry (BJC), 1985. *Tai no Sangyo.* (Industries in Thailand) Bangkok: BJC.

——. 1987. *Nihonkigyo no Taijin Jugyoin ni taisuru Ankeito* (A Survey on Thai Employees in Japanese Joint Ventures). Bangkok: BJC.

Baran, P. 1957. *Political Economy of Growth.* New York: Monthly Review Press.

Beamish, Paul W. 1984. Joint venture performance in developing countries. Ph.D. diss., University of Western Ontario.

Bell, P. 1978. 'Cycles' of class struggle in Thailand. In *Thailand, Roots of Conflict*, ed. by A. Turton, J. Fast, and M. Caldwell. Nottingham: Spokesman.

Bellah, R. N. 1957. *Tokugawa Religion: The Values of Pre-industrial Japan.* Glencoe, Ill: The Free Press.

Bergesen, A., ed. 1980. *Studies of the Modern World-system.* New York: Acadaemic Press.

Buckley, P. J. and M. C. Casson. 1976. *The Future of the Multinational Enterprise.* London: Macmillian.

Cardoso, F. H. 1972. Dependency and development in Latin America. In Alavi and Shanin (1982).

Chee Peng Lim and Lee Poh Ping, 1979. The role of Japanese direct investment in Malaysia, Occasional Paper No. 60. Singapore: Institute of Southeast Asian Studies.

Chinwanno, C. and S. Tambunlertchai. 1983. Japanese investment in Thailand and its prospects in the 1980s. In Segikuchi, ed., *ASEAN-Japan relations: Investment.* Singapore: Institute of Southeast Asian Studies.

Chng, M. K., L. T. B. Nga, and A. Tyabji. 1986. *Technology and Skills In Singapore.* Singapore: Institute of Southeast Asian Studies.

Clark, R. 1979. *The Japanese Company.* New Haven, Conn: Yale University Press.

Cohen, R., N. Felton, M. Nkosi and J. van Liere, eds. 1979. *The Multinational Corporation: A Radical Approach (Papers by Stephen Herbert Hymer).* Cambridge: Cambridge University Press.

Cole, R. 1971. *Japanese Blue Collar: The Changing Tradition*, Berkeley: University of California Press.

Dang, Trah Tranh. 1987. Ownership, control and performance of multinational corporations: A study of U.S. wholly owned subsidiary and joint ventures in the Philippines and Taiwan. Ph. D. diss., University of California, Los Angeles.

Dore, R. 1974. *British Factory — Japanese Factory.* Berkeley: University of California Press.

Dos Santos, T. D. 1969. The structure of dependence. In Fann and Hodges (1971).

Export-Import Bank of Japan. 1989. 1988 nendo no Nihon no kaigai chokusetsu toshi (Japan's direct investment in 1988), *Monthly Report of Research Institute of Overseas Investment* (July).

——. 1989. Ajia NIEs to ASEAN no seizogyo ni taisuru Nihon no chokusetu toshi (Japan's direct investment to manufacturing sectors in Asian NIEs and ASEAN), *Monthly Report of Research Institute of Overseas Investment* (May).

Fann, K. T. and D. C. Hodges, eds. 1971. *Readings in U.S. Imperialism.* Boston: An Extending Horizon Book.

Frank, A. G. 1967. *Capitalism and Underdevelopment in Latin America: Historical Studies of Chile and Brazil.* New York: Monthly Review Press.

——. 1969. *Latin America:* Underdevelopment or revolution; essays on the development of underdevelopment and the immediate enemy. New York: Monthly Review Press.

Franko, Lawrence G. 1971. *Joint Venture Survival in Multinational Corporations.* New York: Praeger Publishers.

Friedmann, Wolfgang G. and George Kalamanoff, eds. 1961. *Joint International Business Ventures.* New York: Columbia University Press.

Frobel, F., J. Heirichs, O. Krege. 1978. *Export-oriented Industrialization of Underdeveloped Countries.* Monthly Review.

——. 1980. *The New International Division of Labour.* Cambridge: Cambridge University Press.

Goldsbrough M.. 1987. Foreign direct investment in ASEAN : Its sources and structure. *Asian Economics,* 61 (June).

Golley, L. 1985. Investment paradise: Japanese capital in Malaysia. In Jomo Kuame Sundaraw, ed., *The Sun Also Sets: Lessons in 'Looking East',* 2nd edition. Kuala Lumpur: Insan.

Hamaguchi, E. and S. Kumon, eds. 1982. *Nihonteki shudanshugi* (Japanese Collectivism). Tokyo: Yuhikaku.

Hamzah, S., Madsen, J. and Thong, G. T. S. 1989. *Managing in a Plural Society.* Singapore: Longman

Hayashi, K. 1985. *Ibunka Intafeisu Kanri* (Cross-Cultural Interface Management), Tokyo: Yuhikaku.

Hayashi, S. 1988. *Culture and Management in Japan.* Tokyo: University of Tokyo Press.

Hazama, H. 1963. *Nihonteki Keiei no Keifu* (Essence of Japanese management). Tokyo: Nihon Noritsu Kyokai.

——. 1971. *Nihonteki Keiei* (Japanese Management). Tokyo: Nihon Keizai Shinbunsha.

Hill, H. 1988. *Foreign Investment and Industrialisation in Indonesia.* Singapore: Oxford University Press.

Hiroshima University, Faculty of Economics, 1990. Nihongata keiei wa tsuyo suruka: ASEAN shokoku tono kakawari o motomete (Is Japanese-style management applicable in ASEAN?). Record of International Symposium. Hiroshima: Hiroshima University.

Hirschmeier, J. and T. Yui. 1975. *The Development of Japanese Business, 1600–1973.* London: George Allen & Unwin.

Hymer, S. 1972. The internationalization of capital. In Cohen et al. (1979).

Ichimura, S. ed. 1980. *Nihon Kigyo in Ajia* (Japanese Enterprises in Asia). Tokyo: Toyo Keizai Shinposha.

——. ed. 1988a. *Asia ni Nezuku Nihonteki Keiei* (Japanese Management in Asia). Tokyo: Toyo Keizai Shinposha.

——. ed. 1988b. *Challenges of Asian developing countries, issues, and analyses.*

Imaoka, H. 1985. Japanese management in Malaysia. *Southeast Asian Studies,* Tokyo: Asian Productivity Organization.

—— et al. (eds.). 1985. *Chushinkoku no Kogyo Hatten* (Industrial Development in NIEs), Tokyo: IDE.

Institute of Developing Economies (IDE). 1985. *The study on technology and trade frictions between Japan and developing nations.* Tokyo: IDE.

—— 1986. *Hattentojokoku Chushokigyo Kenkyu Hokokusho.*(Report of Small and Medium-scale Industries in Developing Countries) Tokyo: IDE.

Ishii, S. 1988. Wagakuni denshi-denki sangyo no Azia ni okeru kokusai bungyo no tenkai (The development of international division of labor in Japanese electronics and electrical machines industry in Asia), *Nihon Yushutsunyu Ginko, Kaigai Toshi Kenkyu shoho* (Monthly Report of Research Institute of Overseas Investment), Export-Import Bank of Japan (Feb.).

Ishikawa, K. 1981. *Nihonteki Hinshitsu Kanri* (Japanese Quality Control). Tokyo: Nikka Giren.

Ishikawa, S. 1978. *Labour Absorption in Asian Agriculture.* Singapore: ILO-ARTEP.

Itami, H. 1982. *Nihonteki Keiei o Koete* (Beyond Japanese-Style Management), Tokyo: Toyo Keizai Shinposha.

Iwata, R. 1977. *Nihonteki Keiei no Hensei Genri* (Organizing Principles of Japanese Management). Tokyo: Bunshindo.

Jamornmarn, W. 1987. *Trends in small and medium firms in Japan after the oil crisis and impact on business opportunities of small and medium firms in Thailand.*

Bangkok: Management Studies Fund.

Japanese Chamber of Commerce and Industry, Malaysia. 1986. Japanese affiliated companies and problems of technology transfer, unpublished report, Kuala Lumpur (April).

Japan, Government of. 1986. *Japan 1986: An International Comparison.* Tokyo: Keizai Koho Center (September).

—— Ministry of International Trade and Industry. 1984. *Wagakuni Kigyo no Kaigaijigyo Katsudo* (Overseas Activities of Japanese Enterprises). Tokyo.

—— Economic Planning Agency 1988. *Economic Survey of Japan 1986–87,* Tokyo.

—— Ministry of Foreign Affairs. 1988. Japan-Thailand relations. Mimeograph. Tokyo (July).

Japan, Embassy of in Malaysia and the JETRO KL Centers, 1989. Joint research report on Japanese affiliated companies in Malaysia.

JETRO. 1988. *ASEAN ni okeru nikkei kigyo katsudo ni kansuru chosa hokoku* (Report of a survey on conditions of Japanese affiliates in ASEAN). Tokyo.

Kagono, T., I. Nonaka, K. Sakakibara, and A. Okumura. 1985. *Strategic vs. Evolutionary Management: A U.S.–Japan Comparison of Strategy and Organization.* Amsterdam: North-Holland. (Japanese edition, 1983.)

Kawabe, Y. 1982. *Sogoshosha no Kenkyu* (A Study on Japanese General Trading Companies). Tokyo: Jikkyo Shuppan.

——. 1987. Application of management concepts to Malaysia: A review. Star College, *Journal of School of Business Studies,* vol. 10. Kuala Lumpur.

Killing, Peter J. 1983. *Strategies for Joint Venture Success.* New York: Praeger Publishers.

Kim, L. S. 1980. Stages of development of industrial technology in a developing country: A model. *Research Policy* no. 9.

Kimbara, T. 1988. Kokusaikeiei ni okeru genchika no kanosei (Possibility of localization in international management). *The Hiroshima Economic Review* vol. 12 no. 1.

Kimura, M. 1988. Bumiputora seisaku to keizai kozo no henyo (The Bumiputera policy and the transformation of economic structure), Horii, K. and Hagiwara, Y. eds., *Gendai Malaysia no Shakai Keizai Henyo* (Socio-Economic Transformation in Modern Malaylsia), Tokyo: Institute of Developing Economy.

Kobayashi, N. 1980. *Nihon no Takokusekikigyo* (Japanese Multinational Enterprises). Tokyo: Chuo Keizaisha.

Koike, K. 1977. *Shokuba no Rodo Kumiai to Sanka* (Labor Unions and Worker Participation at the Workplace). Tokyo: Toyo Keizai Shinposha.

——. 1981. *Nihon no Jukuren* (Japan's Skilled Labor), Tokyo: Yuhikaku.

——. and T. Inoki. 1987. *Jinzai Keisei no Kokusai Hikaku* (International Comparison of Manpower Development). Tokyo: Toyo Keizai Shinposha.

Kojima, K. 1978. *Direct Foreign Investment: A Japanese Model of Multinational Business Operations.* London: Croom Helm.

Kokusai Keizai, 1988. Nippon kigyo in Malaysia (Japanese Business in Malaysia), *Kokusai Keizai*: Special Issue on Malaysia (August).

Kono, T. 1984. *Strategy and Structure of Japanese Enterprises.* London: MacMillan.

Krause, L. B. et al., 1987. *The Singapore Economy Reconsidered.* Singapore: Institute of Southeast Asian Studies.

Kyoto University, Center for Southeast Asian Studies, 1985. Japanese management in Southeast Asia, *Tonan Ajia Kenkyu* (Southeast Asian Studies) vol. 22 no. 4 and vol. 23 no. 1.

Levine, S. B. 1958. *Industrial Relations in Postwar Japan.* Urbana, Ill.: University of Illinois Press.

Lim Hua Sing, 1983. Singapore and Japan: promises and problems in growing trade," *Marubeni Business Bulletin* no. 123, Tokyo (September).

Lim, Y.C. and P. E. Fong. 1988. Foreign investment, industrial restructuring and changing comparative advantage: The experiences of Malaysia, Thailand, Singapore and Taiwan. A report prepared for OECD. Paris: OECD.

Lo, S. Y. 1985. Industrial technology development in the Republic of Korea, Asian Development Bank, Economic Staff Paper no. 27, Manila.

Low, L. 1984. Public enterprises in Singapore, in You Poh Seng I and Lim Chong Yah, eds., *Singapore: Twenty-five Years of Development*, Singapore: Nan Yang Xing Zhou Lianhe Zaubao.

MaClintock, B. 1988. Recent theories of direct foreign investment: An institutionalist perspective. *Journal of Economic Issues* vol. 22 no. 2.

Magota, R. 1978. *Nenko Chingin no Shuen* (The End of Seniority Wages), Tokyo: Nihon Keizai Shinbunsha.

Manasian, D. 1986. Where Japan's biggest are better. *Productivity Digest* vol. 4 no. 11 (Reprinted from *Management Today*, July 1985).

Marsch, R. M. and H. Mannari. 1977. *Modernization and the Japanese Factory.* Princeton: Princeton University Press.

Mikami, T. 1982. *Management and Productivity Improvement in Japan.* Tokyo: JMA Consultants Inc., in cooperation with Japan Management Association.

Monden, Y. 1983. *Toyota Production System*, Georgia: Industrial Engineering and Management Press.

Mori, T. 1984. Nishi-taiheiyo keizaiken ni okeru nihon no toshi (Japanese investment in the western Pacific basin countries), In Iwasaki T. ed., *Nishi-taiheiyo Keizaiken no Tenbo: Chugoku no Keizai Kaihoka Seisaku o Megutte* (Economic Interdependence in the Western Pacific Basin in Perspective) Tokyo: IDE.

——. 1989. Joint venture. In Vashishtha, P. ed., *Commonalities, Complimentalities, and Cooperations : Asia–Pacific Region*, New Delhi: National Council of

Applied Economic Research.

Morikawa, S. 1988. Shizukana fujyo burio miseru toshi kankyo (Gradual improvement of investment environment); and (with Teranishi, T.) Chumoku sareru toshi kankyo to saikin no keiko (Attractive investment environment and recent trend), *Kokusai Keizai: Special Issue on Malaysia* (August).

Mroczkowski, T. and Hanaoka, M. 1989. Continuity and change in Japanese management. *California Management Review* (Winter).

Murrey, R. 1971. The Internationalization of capital and the nation state. *New Left Review* no. 67 (May–June).

Nakakita, T. 1988. The globalisation of Japanese firms and its influence on Japan's trade and developing countries. *The Developing Economies* (December). Tokyo: IDE.

Nakane, C. 1970. *Japanese Society.* Berkeley: University of California Press.

Nakano, H. 1985. A commentary on Hideki Imaoka, "Japanese management in Malaysia." *Southeast Asian Studies* vol. 23 no. 1.

Nawadhinsukh, S. 1983. Ancillary Firm Development in the Automobile Industry of Thailand. In K. Odaka, ed., *The Motor-Vehicle Industry in Asia*, Singapore: Singapore University Press.

Nomura Research Institute (NRI), 1987. *Nomura Ajia Joho* (Nomura's Information on Asia), Tokyo: NRI, (May).

Odaka, K. 1965. *Nihon no Keiei* (Management in Japan). Tokyo: Chuo Koronsha.

——. 1984. *Nihonteki Keiei* (Japanese-Style Management). Tokyo: Chuo Koronsha.

OECD. 1972. *Reviews of Manpower and Social Policies: Manpower Policy in Japan.* Paris: OECD.

——. 1988. *OECD Economic Surveys (Japan).* Paris: OECD.

Okochi, K. 1952. *Shakai Seisaku no Keizai Riron* (Economic Theory of Social Policy). Tokyo: Nihon Hyoronsha.

Okubayashi, K. 1989. The Japanese industrial relations system. *Journal of General Management* vol. 14 no. 3.

Ono, T. 1978. *Toyota Seisan Hoshiki* (Toyota Production System). Tokyo: Daiamondo-sha.

Ouchi, W. 1981. *Theory Z: How American Business can Meet the Japanese Challenge.* Reading, Massachusetts: Addison-Wesley Publishing Co.

Ozawa, T. 1979. *Multinationalism, Japanese Style: The Political Economy of Outward Dependency.* Princeton: Princeton University Press.

Palloix, C. 1975. The internationalization of capital and the circuit of social capital. In Radice (1975).

——. 1977. The self-expansion of capital on a world scale. *Review of Radical Political Economics* vol. 9 no. 2.

Parsons, T. and E. A. Shils, eds. 1951. *Toward a General Theory of Action.* Cambridge, Mass: Harvard University Press.

Pascale, R. T. and Athos, A. G. 1981. *The Art of Japanese Management: Applications for American Executives.* New York: Simon and Schuster.

Petras, J. 1979. Neo-fascism: Capital accumulation and class struggle in the Third World. In McFarlane, B. ed., *A Political Economy of Southeast Asia in the 1980s.* Adelaide: Veriken Press.

Phongpaichit, P. 1980. Economic and social transformation of Thailand, 1957–1976. Bangkok:Chulalongkorn University Social Research Institute.

———. 1987. Decision-making on overseas direct investment by Japanese small and medium industries in the late 80's. Bangkok: Institute of Asian Studies, Chulalongkorn University.

Polk, J. 1973. The new international production. *World Development* no. 5 (May).

Pornavalai, S. 1989. Japanese enterprises and the strategy of Thailand to be NIC. (in Thai). Bangkok: Faculty of Economics, Thammasat University.

Prasartset, S. 1985. The crisis of the transnationalized model of accumulation: The Thai case. United Nations University Southeast Asian Perspectives Project Meeting, Penang, Malaysia.

Putti, J. M. 1984. Matsushita culture : Beyond the boundaries of Japanese society. *Productivity Digest* (June).

Radice, H., ed. 1975. *International Firms and Modern Imperialism.* Penguin Modern Economic Readings.

Robison, R. 1986. *The Rise of Capital.* London: Allen and Unwin.

Saito, M. 1979. *Gijutsu Iten Ron* (Technology Transfer). Tokyo: Bunshindo.

Sakuma, M. 1983. *Nihonteki Keiei no Kokusaisei* (Internationalism of Japanese Management). Tokyo: Yuhikaku.

Salih, K. and Z. A. Yusof. 1989. Overview of the new economical policy and framework for the post-1990 economic policy. Kuala Lumpur: Malaysian Institute of Economic Research.

Satikarn, M. 1981. *Technology Transfer.* Singapore: Singapore University Press.

Schumpeter, J. 1930. *History of Economic Analysis.* Boston: Harvard University Press.

Sekiguchi, S. ed. *ASEAN–Japan Relations, Investment.* Singapore: Institute of Southeast Asian Studies.

Servan-Schreiber, J–J. 1967. *Le défi américain.* Paris: Denoël.

Shimada, H. 1974. The structure of earnings and investments in human resources: A comparison between the United States and Japan. Ph.D. diss., University of Wisconsin.

———. 1980. *The Japanese Employment System.* Japanese Industrial Relations Series, no. 6. Tokyo: Japan Institute of Labor.

———. 1987. *Hyumanuea no Keizaigaku* (Economics of Humanwares). Tokyo: Iwanami Shoten.

Shinohara, M. 1982. *Industrial Growth, Trade, and Dynamic Patterns in the Japanese Economy.* Tokyo: University of Tokyo Press.

———. and Fu-chen Lo. 1989. *Global Adjustment and the Future of Asian–Pacific Economy.* Tokyo: Institute of Developing Economies and Asian Productivity Development Council.

Shiowattana, P. et. al. 1987. The study on status of electronics industry in Thailand. Board of Investment and the ASEAN Promotion Center on Trade, Investment and Tourism. Bangkok: Chulalongkorn University.

———. 1990. Japanese technology transfer in Thailand. In Yoshihara, K. ed., *Japan in Thailand.* Kuala Lumpur: Falcon Press.

Shishido, Y. 1981. *Enjotaikoku Nihon no Sentaku.* (Options of Japanese Economic Aids) Tokyo: Toyo Keizai Shinposha.

Siea, L. M. L. 1986. *Malaysia manufacturing future survey report,* vols. 1 and 2. Kuala Lumpur: University of Malaya.

Sim, A. B. 1978. Decentralisation and performance: A comparative study of Malaysian subsidiaries of different national origins. Kuala Lumpur: University of Malaya.

Singapore Government, Ministry of Trade and Indsutry, 1986. Economic Committee of the Singapore Economy, *New Directions Singapore,* Singapore.

———. Economic Development Board, 1986. *Annual Report 1985/86.*

Snow, Charles C., ed. 1989. *Strategy, Organization Design, and Human Resource Management.* Greenwich, Connecticut: JAI Press.

Steven, R. 1988. Japanese foreign direct investment in Southeast Asia: From ASEAN to JASEAN. *Bulletin of Concerned Asian Scholars* vol. 20 no. 4.

Stopford, John M. and Louis T. Wells, Jr. 1972. *Managing the Multinational Enterprise.* New York: Basic Books.

Suehiro, A. 1989a. Bangkok Bank: Management reforms of Thai commercial bank, *East Asian Cultural Studies.* no. 1–4. Tokyo: UNESCO The Centre for East Asian Cultural Studies.

———. 1989b. Tai: 1987 nen iko no gaikokujin toshi rasshu (Thailand: Foreign investment rush after 1987). In Taniura, T. ed., *Azia no Kogyoka to Chokusetsutoshi* (Industrialization and Foreign Direct Investment), Tokyo: IDE.

———. 1989c. *Capital Accumulation in Thailand.* Tokyo: The Centre for East Asian Cultural Studies.

———. 1990. Tai ni okeru sangyo konguromaritto no keieikaikaku (The Managerial Reformation by an Industrial Conglomerate in Thailand) in *Quarterly Economic Survey* vol. 11 no. 4. Osaka: Osaka City University.

———. and Yasuda, O. eds. 1987. *Tai no Kogyoka: NAIC eno Chosen* (Industrialization of Thailand: Challange to NAIC), Tokyo: IDE.

Sumiya, M. 1964. *Nihon no Rodo Mondai* (Labor Problems in Japan). Tokyo:

304   References

University of Tokyo Press.

Sunkel, O. and E. E. Fuenzalida. 1979. Transnationalization and its national consequences. In Villamil (1979).

Takano, T. 1988. Shinshutsu suru Nippon kigyo eno messeji (Message to Japanese companies which want to invest in Malaysia), *Kokusai Keizai: Special Issue on Malaysia* (August).

Takehana, S. 1988. The concept of "Technology" in the theory of technology transfer: With special reference to the case of an electric appliance manufacturer in Indonesia. Hiroshima University Institute for Pease Science, *Hiroshima Peace Science*, no.11.

Takeuchi, J. 1982. *Agro-Industrialization of Urban-based Small Industries*. Tokyo: United Nations University.

——. 1989a. The role of small and medium scale firms and Japanse industrialization. Mimeograph. Zurich.

——. 1989b. Some aspects of technology transfer by Japanese management in Thailand. Mimeograph. Hiroshima.

Tambunlertchai, S. 1987. Trade and investment between Thailand and Japan. Institute of East Asian Studies, Thammasat University (August).

Thong, G. T. S. and Jain, H. C. 1988. Human resource management practices of Japanese and Malaysian companies: A comparative study. *Malaysian Management Review* vol. 23 no. 2.

Thurow, L.C., ed. 1985. *The Management Challenge: Japanese Views*. Cambridge, Mass.: MIT Press.

Tominomori, K. 1981–1982. Mechanism of Japanese management and its foundation. *Hokudai Economic Papers* vol. X.

Tomita, T. 1985. Japanese management as applied in the Philippines. *The Philippine Review of Economics and Business* vol. 22 nos. 1 and 2.

——. 1987. Transferability of Japanese-style management to Britain, in Blumenthal, T. ed., *Japanese Management at Home and Abroad*. Israel: Ben-Gurion University of the Nagev Press.

——. 1988. Azia ni okeru Nihonkigyo no romukanri (Personnel management of Japanese corporation in Asia), in *Nihon Romugakkai Nenpo* (Annual Report of Japan Society for Personnel and Labor Research). Tokyo.

Tsuda, M. 1977. *Nihonteki Keiei no Ronri* (The Logic of Japanese Management). Tokyo: Chuo Keizaisha.

United Nations. 1973. *Multinational Corporation in World Development*. New York: United Nations.

——. United Nations Commission on Transnational Corporations. 1978. *Transnational Corporations in World Development: A Reexamination*. New York: United Nations.

Urabe, K. 1977. *Keiei Sanka to Nihonteki Roshi Kankei* (Management Participation and Japanese Industrial Relations). Tokyo: Hakuto Shobo.

Vernon, R. 1966. International investment and international trade in the product cycle. *The Quarterly Journal of Economics* no. 80.

———. 1971. *Sovereignty at Bay: The Multinational Spread of U.S. Enterprise.* New York: Basic Books.

Villamil, J. J. ed. 1979. *Transnational Capital and National Development, New Perspectives on Dependence.* London: The Harvester Press.

Vogel, E. F. ed. 1975. *Modern Japanese Organization and Decision Making.* Berkeley: University of California Press.

———. 1979. *Japan as Number One: Lessons for America.* Cambridge, Mass: Harvard University Press.

Wallerstein, I. 1974. *The Modern World-system I: Capitalist Agriculture and the Origins of the European World-economy in the Sixteen Century.* New York: Academic Press.

———. 1980. *The Modern World-system, II. Mercantilism and the Consolidation of European World-economy, 1600–1750.* New York: Academic Press.

Weinstein, F. B. 1976. Multinational corporation and the Third World: Case of Japan and Southeast Asia. *International Organization* no. 30 (Summer).

Westphal, L. E. 1987. Managing technological development: Lessons from the newly industrializing countries. *World Development* no. 15.

White, M. and M. Trevor. 1983. *Under Japanese Management.* London: Policy Studies Institute.

Williamson, O. 1973. Market and hierachies: Some considerations. *American Economic Review* no. 63 (May).

Yamashita, S. ed. 1988. *ASEAN shokoku no kaihatsu katei to nihon no kakawarikata ni kansuru kenkyu* (A study on the Japanese involvement in the development process of ASEAN countries) Hiroshima University, unpublished.

———. 1989. Nihon no kaigai chokusetsu toshi to Ajia no keizai hatten (Japanese direct investment and economic development in Asia), In Taniura T., ed., *Azia no Kogyoka to Chokusetsu toshi* (Industrialization in Asia and Direct Investment), Tokyo: IDE.

———, J. Takeuchi, N. Kawabe, and S. Takehana. 1989. ASEAN shokoku ni okeru nihonteki keiei to gijytsuiten ni kansuru keieisha no ishiki chosa (Japanese manager's consciousness on the Japanese type management and technology transfer in ASEAN countries), *The Hiroshima Economic Studies* no. 10 (March).

Yamazawa, I. and T. Watanabe. 1988. Industrial restructuring and technology transfer. In Ichimura (1988a).

Yamklinfung, P. 1972. Social development in peri-urban areas: A study of the needs and problems of children and youth in four slums in Bangkok. Bangkok: Chulalongkorn University.

Yoshihara, H., K. Hayashi, and K. Yasumuro 1983. *Nihonkigyo no Global Keiei* (Global Management by Japanese Enterprises). Tokyo: Toyo Keizai Shinposha.

Yoshihara, K. 1976. *Foreign Investment and Domestic Response*, Singapore: Institute of Southeast Asia Studies.

——, K. Sakuma, H. Itami, and T. Kagono. 1981. *Nihonkigyo no Takakuka Senryaku* (Diversification Strategy of Japanese Enterprises). Tokyo: Nihon Keizai Shinbunsha.

Yoshino, M. Y. 1968. *Japan's Managerial Systems.* Cambridge, Mass: MIT Press.

List of Contributors

Tetsuo Abo, University of Tokyo, Tokyo, Japan
Atsumu Hirano, Bank of Tokyo, Tokyo, Japan
Hideki Imaoka, Tsukuba University, Tsukuba, Japan (Mie University, Tsu, Japan)
Nobuo Kawabe, Waseda University, Tokyo, Japan (Hiroshima University, Hiroshima, Japan)
Tatsuo Kimbara, Hiroshima University, Hiroshima, Japan
Lim Hua Sing, Chukyo University, Nagoya, Japan (Singapore National University, Singapore)
Concepcion Martires, University of the Philippines, Manila, Philippines
Takeshi Mori, Institute of Developing Economies, Tokyo, Japan
Tsuneo Nakauchi, International Christian University, Tokyo, Japan
Yoshitaka Okada, International University of Japan, Niigata, Japan
Pasuk Phongpaichit, Chulalongkorn University, Bangkok, Thailand (Institute of Southeast Asian Studies, Singapore)
Suthy Prasartset, Chulalongkorn University, Bangkok, Thailand
Ichiro Sato, Toyota Tokyo Kyoiku Center, Tokyo, Japan (Toyota Motor Thailand Co., Bangkok, Thailand)
Prayoon Shiowattana, Technological Promotion Association (Thai-Japan), Bangkok, Thailand (Chulalongkorn University, Bangkok, Thailand)
Akira Suehiro, Osaka City University, Osaka, Japan
Seiji Takehana, O.T.G. Thai Co., Ltd., Bangkok, Thailand (Hiroshima University, Hiroshima, Japan)
Johzen Takeuchi, Hiroshima University, Hiroshima, Japan
Gregory Thong Tin Sin, Nanyang Technological Institute, Singapore (University of Malaya, Kuala Lumpur, Malaysia)
Prijono Tjiptoherijanto, University of Indonesia, Jakarta, Indonesia
Teruhiko Tomita, Shiga University, Hikone, Japan
Shoichi Yamashita, Hiroshima University, Hiroshima, Japan
Osamu Yasuda, Economic Planning Agency, Tokyo, Japan

Institutions in parentheses are affiliations at the time of the 1989 Hiroshima conference.

Index

accumulation, of capital, 55–56, 57, 59–60, 80, 162, 273
Akamatsu Kaname, 3–4, 62
Asahi Glass, 41, 43
ASEAN Complementary Scheme, 214, 216
Association for Overseas Technical Scholarship (AOTS), 226
Astra Corporation, 41
automation technology, 46
automobile industry, 203–4, 207, 209, 214–16, 281

banking, 36, 39
"boomerang effect," 62–63
Bumiputera policy, 31, 32, 33, 39–40, 44, 145, 148, 244, 248, 264

capital. *See* domestic capital; state capital
career development, 14, 20, 151
Charoen Pokphand, 36, 43, 84
chemical industry, 95, 96, 99
Chinese capital, domestic, 14, 29, 30, 31, 32, 33, 36, 41,43, 53
comparative advantage, 24, 25, 52
conglomerates, 36
credit leverage, 70

Daihatsu, 41
Daikin, 43
Data General, 170
Development Bank of Singapore, 34
dollar, depreciation of the, 10
domestic capital, 26, 27, 29–30, 34–35, 36, 40, 41–45, 47, 48, 270
domestic market, Japanese, 232

electronics industry, 7, 82–83; in

Singapore, 93, 96, 106–10; in Thailand, 169–74, 178–93, 207–9, 213–14, 218–20, 281
employment, creation of, 72, 105–110
enterprise unions, 111, 113, 128, 136, 139, 140, 148, 150
entrepreneurs, 26, 218–31, 272
Europe: investment in Singapore, 85, 112; investment in Thailand, 202; Japanese investment in, 8, 9, 46, 147; and trade friction, 4, 8, 9, 11, 270
exports, 4, 5–6, 10–11, 13, 17, 23, 39, 42, 52, 64, 65, 84

family businesses, 220, 228
Ford, 73
foreign direct investment: demand for, 25–37, 41–45, 46–48, 153–54, 270, 271; characteristics of Japanese, 4–5, 7–14, 23–25, 45–46, 50, 60–66, 68–69, 86–92, 173–74, 178–79, 201–3, 204–6, 213–14, 239–44, 258–59, 269; policies towards, 10–11, 17, 26, 27–28, 30–31, 33–34, 39–40, 48–49, 83, 153, 159–60, 162, 169–70, 212, 244–45, 266, 270, 271, 272, 288
Fuji Xerox, 41

General Agreement on Tariffs and Trade (GATT), 56, 58
General Schedule of Preference (GSP), 90–91
Gobel group, 41
governments, role in promoting foreign investment, 26–28, 48, 50, 270; Japanese, 25, 62; in Malaysia, 244–45; in Singapore, 100; in Thailand,